17.50

ATLANTA 1864

GREAT CAMPAIGNS OF THE CIVIL WAR

SERIES EDITORS

Anne J. Bailey
Georgia College &
State University

Brooks D. Simpson
Arizona State University

RICHARD M. MCMURRY

Atlanta 1864

Last Chance for the Confederacy

University of Nebraska Press
Lincoln and London

© 2000 by the University of Nebraska Press
All rights reserved
Manufactured in the United States of America
⊗
Library of Congress Cataloging-in-Publication Data
McMurry, Richard M.
Atlanta 1864 : last chance for the Confederacy / Richard M. McMurry.
p.   cm. — (Great campaigns of the Civil War)
Includes bibliographical references (p.) and index.
ISBN 0-8032-3212-8 (cl. : alk. paper)
1. Atlanta Campaign, 1864.   I. Title.   II. Series.
E476.7.M268 2000
973.7'37—dc21   99-087560

To my parents

Contents

Illustrations

Maps

Series Editors' Introduction

Americans remain fascinated by the Civil War. Movies, television, and video—even computer software—have augmented the ever-expanding list of books on the war. Although it stands to reason that a large portion of recent work concentrates on military aspects of the conflict, historians have expanded our scope of inquiry to include civilians, especially women; the destruction of slavery and the evolving understanding of what freedom meant to millions of former slaves; and an even greater emphasis on the experiences of the common soldier on both sides. Other studies have demonstrated the interrelationships of war, politics, and policy and how civilians' concerns back home influenced both soldiers and politicians. Although one cannot fully comprehend this central event in American history without understanding that military operations were fundamental in determining the course and outcome of the war, it is time for students of battles and campaigns to incorporate nonmilitary themes in their accounts. The most pressing challenge facing Civil War scholarship today is the integration of various perspectives and emphases into a new narrative that explains not only what happened, why, and how, but also why it mattered.

The series Great Campaigns of the Civil War offers readers concise syntheses of the major campaigns of the war, reflecting the findings of recent scholarship. The series points to new ways of viewing military campaigns by looking beyond the battlefield and the headquarters tent to the wider political and social context within which these campaigns unfolded; it also shows how campaigns and battles left their imprint on many Americans, from presidents and generals down to privates and civilians. The ends and means of waging war reflect larger political objectives and priorities as well as social values. Historians may continue to debate among themselves as to which of these campaigns constituted true turning points, but each of the campaigns treated in this series contributed to shaping the course of the conflict, opening opportunities, and eliminating alternatives.

The Atlanta campaign was one of the most significant in the western theater during the Civil War. The fighting through the North Georgia mountains in mid-1864 was the result of policy initiated in Washington by Ulysses S. Grant soon after his promotion to general in chief. When the spring campaigns opened, Grant planned to move the Union armies simultaneously to prevent the Confederates from shifting reinforcements between theaters. From May until September, Union and Confederate armies engaged in continuous military operations from the Tennessee border to the outskirts of Atlanta. The combat tested the endurance of the men and the skill of their commanders, Union general William Tecumseh Sherman and Confederate general Joseph E. Johnston. When the Confederate president decided that Johnston had failed to stop the Union armies, he replaced him with the more aggressive John Bell Hood. The decisions Sherman, Johnston, and Hood made, as well as those of the two presidents, Abraham Lincoln and Jefferson Davis, determined the events that led to the fall of Atlanta in September. The loss of the Georgia citadel had far-reaching consequences, militarily, politically, and socially. This was the first time that Federal armies had occupied soil in the interior of the state and the first time that large numbers of the state's noncombatants had been displaced by the fighting. Moreover, it occurred on the eve of the critical presidential election. Lincoln needed a victory somewhere to retain the White House in November, for Grant was unable to defeat the Confederate army in Virginia. Sherman's victory came at a crucial time for the Northern president. In this volume Richard McMurry shows the enormous importance of the western theater to the outcome of the Civil War and the pivotal consequences of the loss of Atlanta to the Confederate cause.

Preface

Four great campaigns determined the military outcome of the American Civil War. The first of those epic struggles was the Fort Henry–Fort Donelson–Shiloh campaign (and its ancillary operations) in the late winter and spring of 1862. By those victories Union forces secured control of Missouri, Kentucky, and most of West and Central Tennessee as well as of crucial slices of Alabama, Arkansas, and Mississippi. Equally important, those operations opened the Cumberland and the lower Tennessee Rivers as well as all but about three hundred miles of the Mississippi itself to vessels of the Federal navy. Memphis, Nashville, New Orleans, and Pensacola, along with the key railroad town of Corinth, Mississippi, fell to the Yankees. Finally, as my graduate school mentor Bell Wiley was fond of pointing out, those operations touched off a spate of recrimination and debilitating and divisive quarrels in Secessionist political circles. Those sharp differences grew over the next three years, and they did much to weaken the Rebels' war effort.

The second great operation took place along the middle part of the Confederate portion of the Mississippi River in the first half of 1863. When the Rebel garrison at Port Hudson, Louisiana, surrendered on July 9, the entire length of the great river passed back under the control of the Federal government and the would-be Southern nation had been split in half. Total Secessionist losses in those operations exceeded the *combined* casualties of the Union and Confederate armies at Gettysburg. Rebel morale sagged, and the debilitating political quarrels and fault-finding among the Southerners intensified. Victory in this campaign also freed the Union's mighty Army of the Tennessee to join the national forces operating in the even more important Nashville-Chattanooga-Atlanta corridor.

In the second half of 1863 Northern armies advanced into eastern and southeastern Tennessee. This great Tullahoma-Chickamauga-Chattanooga campaign secured the Federal government's hold on the Volunteer State and set the stage for the even more crucial Atlanta campaign of the following year. Federal success in that last great operation marked the end of any rational hope that the Confederacy could establish its independence.

Albert Castel's 1992 work *Decision in the West: The Atlanta Campaign of 1864* is one of the best studies of a Civil War military operation we have. Finding something new to say about military events in North Georgia in the spring and summer of 1864 or discovering some new approach or developing a different slant on those events has not been an easy task. I hope I have been able to do so. Readers will have to judge. In trying to offer some new ideas about the campaign I have had the great advantage of being able to use Castel's work as well as that of other historians, many of whom I have been privileged to know.

I hope this book will help readers grasp the importance of what happened in North Georgia in that long-ago summer, why the campaign turned out as it did, and what those 1864 events meant both to Americans at the time and to all of us (and not just those of us in this country) who have come along since.

If this book helps to inform readers and to get them to think about the events of the last year of the war, it will have achieved its purpose, and the time and effort I put into it will have been well spent.

Acknowledgments

My mother was born in a house a short distance east of Cheatham's Hill and not far south of Kennesaw Mountain. Many of her uncles, aunts, and cousins lived in houses west of Marietta on and near the 1864 battlefield. I still have several bullets, cannonballs, bayonets, belt buckles, and other military artifacts found on the farm where she lived as a girl. My parents encouraged my early interest in the war. In a very real sense my fascination with the Atlanta campaign and this book itself both had their origins decades ago in almost weekly trips when they took my brother and me to visit my mother's brother and his wife and children, who lived in the old family place.

More recently I have been fortunate to have had the help of friends who were kind enough to plow through an earlier version of this work. Anne Bailey, Albert Castel, Larry Daniel, Steve Davis, and Gary Gallagher all gave their time to critique the manuscript, and it has benefited greatly from their efforts. Albert also generously made available the maps used in his *Decision in the West* and granted permission to reproduce them in this volume.

My son Jonathan not only read and criticized the manuscript, but he also patiently answered many questions about one of those infernal machines that have taken over the planet. Even he, however, has not been able to explain why the damn thing once took it upon itself to convert the numbers of the first five notes to chapter 1—and only those numbers—(in both text and notes) from Arabic numerals to lower case Roman numerals. ("I don't think it can do that, but if it can you're the one who could get it to do it.") For my part, I am just thankful that it did not decide to translate the entire work into medieval Swahili and print it upside down in the Cyrillic alphabet.

Over the years I have also profited greatly from talking over Civil War matters in general and the Atlanta campaign and those involved in it in particular with friends and fellow Civil Warriors. In addition to those listed above, I owe great thanks in this regard to Ed Bearss, Tom Connelly, Jack Davis, Lesley Gordon, Dennis Kelly, Grady McWhiney, Charlie Roland, Dick Sommers, and Craig Symonds. A special thanks should go to Bell Wiley, who directed my dissertation on the campaign and whose influence will always be great on anything I write about the war.

ATLANTA 1864

CHAPTER ONE

Presidents and Generals

Late in the afternoon of Tuesday, the eighth of March 1864—almost at the beginning of the fourth year of the American Civil War—Maj. Gen. Ulysses S. Grant, his fourteen-year-old son, and two of the general's staff officers arrived by train in Washington DC. At that time Grant commanded the Military Division of the Mississippi, an assignment that gave him authority over almost all Union land forces operating in the vast region between the Mississippi River and the Appalachian Mountains. In the military jargon of the day, this area was known as "the West."

Grant had come to Washington from his headquarters in Nashville, Tennessee, in response to a summons from President Abraham Lincoln. The chief executive, after three frustrating years of war, was still seeking a general who "would take the responsibility and act" to place in overall command of the Federal armies. Grant, he had concluded, was that man.

The general made his way from the railroad station to Willard's Hotel, two blocks from the White House. There he took a room and went to eat supper. At forty-two, slightly built, and with stooped shoulders, Grant was not an imposing man. When he registered at the hotel, the desk clerk snorted that he had only a small room available. Grant assured the man that the room would be satisfactory and signed the register. Not until the clerk checked the signature ("U. S. Grant & son, Galena, Ill.") did he realize who this new guest was and arrange for him to have proper quarters. Later, at supper, the other hotel guests broke into applause when they learned his identity.

After eating, Grant walked to the White House for the president's weekly reception. He reached the Executive Mansion about 9:30, and his entry created quite a stir. There, for the first time, he met the president, as well as Mrs. Lincoln, some of the cabinet members, and assorted hangers-on. All crowded around the general, anxious to see him, shake his hand, and cheer him.

The national capital's excitement over Grant was certainly understandable. During the preceding three years, he had emerged as the most successful of the Northern army commanders. While other Federal generals, especially those operating in the area around Washington, had suffered defeat after defeat, Grant's armies in the West had marched from victory to victory.

Early in 1862, troops under Grant's command had moved into West Tennessee. There, in cooperation with the Federal navy, they had captured Fort Henry on the Tennessee River and Fort Donelson on the Cumberland River. In so doing they had opened the lower and middle stretches of those streams to the gunboats of the Union navy and forced the Confederates to abandon their positions in Kentucky along with almost all of West Tennessee. Those successes marked the beginning of the slow but inexorable process of dismembering the Southern nation.

In mid-1863 Grant's forces had captured Vicksburg, Mississippi, along with its defending thirty-thousand-man garrison. By that conquest Grant had split the Confederacy in half. In the following fall Grant had directed the Yankee armies that drove the Secessionists away from Chattanooga in southeastern Tennessee and secured the national government's grip on the Volunteer State.

By the end of 1863 Grant had played the central role in all three of the great strategic successes won by Federal arms. It was logical, therefore, that early in the following year President Lincoln decided to place him in command of all Union land forces and to confer upon him the recently revived grade of lieutenant general (held earlier only by George Washington, although the aged Winfield Scott then held it by brevet).

The promotion formalities took place the day after the president's reception. Early that afternoon Grant and his entourage—the two staff officers and his son—went to the White House. There, in a brief, simple ceremony, Lincoln thanked Grant for his past successes, promised to sustain him in the coming months, and presented him with his new commission. A nervous Grant, in equally brief remarks, accepted the new assignment and soon busied himself with preparations for the 1864 campaign.[1]

Lieutenant General Grant ascended to his new post at what seemed a most favorable time. The great battles and campaigns of 1863 (Vicksburg, Chattanooga, and Gettysburg in Pennsylvania) had inflicted stunning losses on the Rebels. Vicksburg and Chattanooga had also produced major changes in the strategic situation of the opposing armies—changes that very clearly tipped the military balance toward the Federals. Gettysburg had brought no alteration in the relative strength or position of the opposing armies or in the course of the war. That engagement did, however, boost Northern morale. In conjunction with Grant's successes at Vicksburg and Chattanooga it also made it certain that the Southerners could not gain a military victory over the Union armies that would compel the Federal government to recognize Confederate independence.

Things, however, were not that simple. The war had been going on for three years. While Grant had won great successes for the Union cause in the West, the press, the politicians, and the public had focused their attention on events in Virginia. There a long and sometimes spectacular string of local victories by the Rebels had created a strong impression that the Federals had met with failure. Few people, therefore, realized how successful the national armies had been elsewhere in 1861, 1862, and 1863.

Many in the North, furthermore, had never favored the use of force to hold unwilling states in the Union. Large numbers who had initially supported the war had been sickened by the carnage that marked the conflict's first three years. (The number of deaths in the Federal army had exceeded the number in the Confederate forces by about one hundred thousand.) They and thousands of others were appalled at the sight of veterans who returned from the army missing an eye, an arm, or a leg, or with their bodies wasted by disease.

The financial cost of the war, like the human toll, had soared far beyond what anyone had anticipated in the long-ago days of 1861 when eager young volunteers had flocked to the colors, anxious to get into battle before the conflict ended in glorious and bloodless victory. Tens of thousands all across the North were deeply alarmed by the many changes the prolonged conflict was forcing onto their society. They resented the higher taxes that took an increasing part of their wealth, the draft that forced thousands of unwilling young men into military service, and the infringements on civil liberties that marked the Lincoln administration's sometimes clumsy efforts to deal with its domestic critics.

All those matters were symbolic of the increasing power and expanding reach of the Federal government that came with the war. Such developments alarmed Americans raised on the traditional nineteenth-century doctrine of a limited national government and maximum freedom for the states and for individual citizens. Hundreds of thousands who had supported the war in 1861 and 1862 bemoaned the fact that what had begun as a crusade to preserve the Union had in late 1862 become also a war against slavery.

In the winter of 1863–64 there were numerous reasons why large segments of the Northern population were, at most, lukewarm in their support of the national cause. No one could know how much it would take to convince the majority of people in the United States that continuing the struggle would cost more than any possible result would be worth. Somewhere, though, there was a point beyond which popular support for the war would not go. Success—or, at least the perception of success—by the Federal armies would push that point farther out in time. Failure or perceived failure, on the other hand, would bring it closer. Individuals, of course, would reach that point at different times. Already, in the winter of 1863–64, many citizens in the North could take no more of the war.

Several ambitious, antiadministration politicians saw in this cauldron of war-weariness, anger, fear, and resentment the opportunity to gain (or regain) political power. Important elections were, after all, scheduled for the fall of 1864. If by then a majority of Northern voters concluded that the Federal government's war effort had failed, they might well vote the Lincoln administration out of office and replace it with "peace men" willing to end the war on whatever terms they could get. Almost all those who held such views belonged to, or were sympathetic with, the Democratic Party.

Lincoln and Grant, then, were like men three-fourths of the way up a rickety ladder. If the Northern public concluded that they could not continue up the ladder to their goal, support for the war effort might dissolve. Any number of factors—a massive battlefield defeat, constantly increasing casualties, higher taxes, greater draft calls, or even the absence of significant military success—could undermine popular support for the war and destabilize the ground at the foot of the ladder.

Northern leaders, therefore, had ample reason to worry as they prepared for the renewed military operations that would come with the spring. Even though they had climbed high, a misstep on the ladder could yet send them and their cause crashing to the ground. All those factors led many to the conclusion that if the Federal government were to achieve victory, it must at least be obviously on the way to doing so before the fall elections.

In truth, the national government had always possessed more than ample resources of men and matériel to win the war. The Yankees' great problem was to find a general who had the will to apply those resources ruthlessly, the competence to do so effectively, the willingness to work with the president in a way that furthered the overall policies of the government, and the ability to get the job done before public support for the war reached its limit.

President Lincoln certainly had the will to win and the determination to use whatever force was necessary to achieve victory. In the war's first three years, however, the Federal chief executive had been unable to find a general with comparable determination, and he did not have the inclination, technical knowledge, ability, or time to exercise day-to-day command of the national armies himself. In Grant, Lincoln hoped, he had finally found the man who could bring the war to a victorious conclusion.[2]

Abraham Lincoln was not the only American commander in chief seeking a new general that winter. Some two and one-half months before Grant journeyed to Washington the Confederates also found themselves in need of a replacement commander for an important assignment.

Separated from the Federal capital by barely more than one hundred miles of Virginia countryside, President Jefferson Davis, in Richmond, faced even more daunting problems than did his Union counterpart. Whereas Lincoln had the success and momentum of the North's 1863 victories upon which to build his effort for the coming year, Davis and the Confederates faced the far more difficult task of rebuilding their armies after a series of shattering defeats.

Unlike Lincoln, Davis did not select a general to entrust with overall command of his nation's armies. The Confederate president was a man of considerable military experience—graduate of the United States Military Academy, seven years an officer in the Regular Army, wounded Mexican War hero, former United States secretary of war, and former chairman of a legislative military affairs committee. He took literally his constitutional designation as commander in chief of his nation's armed forces. He, therefore, kept in his own hands control of all important (as well as of many unimportant) military matters. His desk in the Executive Mansion in Richmond was the de facto headquarters of the Rebel armies, and he intended to play the major role in developing the grand strategy that he hoped would lead the Secessionists to independence in 1864.

As he went about preparing his country for the onslaught she would face in the spring, Davis could feel very confident about Rebel military prospects in Virginia. There Gen. Robert E. Lee and the Army of Northern Virginia would meet the invading Yankees, and Confederates had every reason to anticipate that Lee and his veteran troops would stymie future Union efforts just as they had done with those of 1861, 1862, and 1863.

Davis's chief military problem that harsh, cold winter—as it had been since the war began—was in the West. From the Appalachians westward across the Mississippi Valley his armies had known only failure in one campaign after another. Battle by battle they had been driven back, losing their toeholds in Kentucky and Missouri; the great Mississippi River itself; and all or large slices of Arkansas, Louisiana, Tennessee, Mississippi, and Alabama. When Grant shooed the Secessionists away from Chattanooga in November 1863, they fled south to Dalton in northwestern Georgia. There the dispirited Rebels huddled about their campfires while their president in far-off Richmond decided what to do.

Obviously the Confederate army at Dalton—the Army of Tennessee was its official designation—must have a new commander. Gen. Braxton Bragg, who had been at the head of that army for some eighteen months before his defeat at Chattanooga, had proved both unsuccessful and unpopular. He resigned early in December. Lt. Gen. William J. Hardee, the senior officer then with the army, assumed temporary command but made it clear that he did not want the responsibility on a permanent basis. President Davis's first major task that winter—and as it turned out, one of the two or three most important decisions he made as the Confederacy's chief executive—was to find a permanent replacement for Bragg.

Whereas Lincoln had in Grant the obvious choice for a new commander, Davis found himself with no successful general to place in such an important post. Davis's problem was complicated by the grade structure of the Rebel army, by his own predilection for placing graduates of the United States Military Academy in all important commands, by the long-standing military practice of seniority, by the sordid internal politics of the Army of Tennessee, and above all by the personal relationships among the Confederacy's top political and military figures.

The highest grade in the Secessionists' military hierarchy was that of "full general." Such officers held the most important commands and were subordinate only to higher-ranking (more senior) full generals and to the civilian authorities in Richmond. Five full generals—all Academy graduates—were in Confederate military service in December 1863. One, the aged Samuel Cooper, performed only administrative duties in the War Department in Richmond. Lee was another, and sending him to the Army of Tennessee would simply shift the problem of finding a suitable new army commander from the West to Virginia. Bragg, of course, could not be restored to the post he had just vacated.

Davis thus found himself with only two full generals who might be placed in command of the Army of Tennessee. One was Joseph E. Johnston, then heading the Department of Mississippi and East Louisiana; the other was Pierre Gustave Toutant Beauregard, then in charge of Confederate forces on the South Atlantic Coast. Unless the president elected to dip into the pool of lower-ranking general officers and elevate one of those men above his fellows, he would have to select either Johnston or Beauregard.

The chief executive found himself on the horns of a nasty dilemma. He hated, despised, and distrusted both Johnston and Beauregard. Those two officers returned the sentiments with compound interest. Davis knew that both generals cooperated more or less openly with the government's political enemies, and he had good reason to doubt the ability of either to command a field army successfully.

Promoting a subordinate general—none of whom had demonstrated much aptitude for high command—would generate enormous problems of morale and resentment among officers who had been his seniors and who had been passed over. In Davis's view such a step could be justified only under very unusual circumstances. James Longstreet, the Confederacy's ranking lieutenant general, had just proved resoundingly unsuccessful in independent command in East Tennessee. Leonidas Polk, the senior lieutenant general in the West, was a troublemaker of the first magnitude and an officer of demonstrated incompetence. He had mishandled his troops in many battles and disobeyed orders in several others. His bungling in Kentucky in 1861 and his unceasing efforts to undermine Braxton Bragg during 1862–63 had contributed much to the steady stream of failures that characterized Confederate command in the West. Only Polk's long friendship with Jefferson Davis and the great prestige he enjoyed as a bishop in the Episcopal Church kept him from facing a court-martial. As a general, Hardee was a bit more competent than Polk, but he too had labored assiduously to undermine Bragg, and he had already made it clear that he did not want the responsibility of army command.

Longstreet, Polk, and Hardee along with other lieutenant generals (E. Kirby Smith, Daniel Harvey Hill) were or had been deeply involved in the internecine squabbles in the Army of Tennessee that had revolved around Braxton Bragg. Appointment of one of them might well rekindle those destructive quarrels with the coterie of Bragg loyalists who still commanded many regiments, brigades, and divisions in the army as well as its cavalry corps.

Other lieutenant generals (Theophilus Holmes, John C. Pemberton) had proved failures in command or were in poor health (Richard S. Ewell, Ambrose Powell Hill). The senior major generals in the West (William W. Loring, Benjamin Franklin Cheatham, Samuel G. French) were even less qualified, not Military Academy alumni, members of the anti-Bragg faction, and/or too fond of alcohol. Besides, jumping a major general over all the lieutenant generals would touch off many protests, and Jefferson Davis did not need to stir up more quarrels in the Confederacy.

Davis could have faced up to those problems when they arose earlier in the war. He had chosen not to do so, and they had festered on to haunt the army and the Confederacy. Never did the South's paucity of competent military commanders loom so clearly or as so great an obstacle on the region's road to independence as it did in December 1863.

Finally, after about two weeks' deliberation, the president settled on Joseph E. Johnston as Bragg's successor. Within the parameters of Davis's dilemma the choice made sense. Johnston was the senior general available for the post. Except for Lee and Bragg, he had more experience at the head of a large army than did any other Confederate. Physically he was a brave man as his many wounds (inflicted by Indians, Mexicans, and Yankees) all testified. He possessed a fair degree of administrative ability. He had the knack of winning and holding the loyalty of most of his subordinates—a trait that, employed wisely, might prove valuable in healing some of the internal problems of the Army of Tennessee. Indeed, as an outsider, Johnston might be able to bridge the gap between the army's old pro-Bragg and anti-Bragg factions. Finally, Johnston commanded a great deal of very vocal support from the public, the press, many of his fellow officers, and his numerous and powerful political friends who had come to regard him as an outstanding general whose great talents had been wasted by Jefferson Davis. The appointment was very popular.[3]

Four potential troubles lurked in any situation that put Jefferson Davis and Joseph E. Johnston in an "official" relationship with the former the commander in chief and the latter holding what proved to be the nation's most crucial military command. First, and probably most serious, Davis and Johnston each tended to assume that every fair-minded person would see any given situation the way he did and would, therefore, agree with him about any issue. For this reason neither was willing to devote much time and energy to explaining matters. If someone else did not agree, then he was, by definition, not fair-minded. The bitter personal feelings and professional resentments that existed between the two men constituted a second potential source of trouble. Johnston's tendency to shy away from responsibility and rarely decide controversial matters or take professional risks was a third.

The final potential danger inherent in the new command arrangement stemmed from the fact that President Davis often proved very reluctant to face up to serious problems (no matter how obvious they were) or to decide great issues (no matter how pressing they became). On many occasions during his presidency he refused to act the role of a commander in chief, refused to allow anyone else to make major decisions, and occupied his time with minutiae better left to the secretary of war or even to a clerk. Meanwhile, events continued on their course with little or no effort on the part of the Rebel government to control, guide, or even influence them.

What Jefferson Davis did—the work of a minister of war—he usually did fairly well. What he sometimes left undone—the work of a commander in chief—did not get done. As a result, a partial vacuum often existed at the top of the Confederate military hierarchy. In that vacuum many important decisions often went unmade, many crucial problems unaddressed.[4]

Robert E. Lee, a man of great tact, self-confidence, and self-control, learned early in the war to work around and to adapt himself to Davis's personal peculiarities rather than trying to oppose the president. Lee patiently supplied Davis with the military and administrative details the chief executive craved, explained matters at length, adopted a respectful (some critics have unfairly said obsequious) attitude in his correspondence with the government, and made it clear that he understood and accepted the president's authority.

By keeping Davis well-informed about military matters, not talking to the press, and steering clear of political involvement, Lee won the president's trust. Lee also demonstrated an ability to win battles, a willingness to exercise command, the intelligence to weigh risks and take appropriate action, and the moral courage to accept responsibility for his decisions and acts. With a great deal of effort, Lee kept Davis's confidence and wholehearted support. As a result, the president gave Lee virtually a free hand to conduct the war in Virginia, and the Confederacy enjoyed great success there.[5]

Davis and Joseph E. Johnston, by contrast, had quarreled frequently over many issues since the late summer of 1861, when Johnston had accused the president of treating him unfairly in the matter of his rank among Confederate generals. To his dying day Johnston, a vain and petty man when it came to such matters, believed himself entitled to the highest rank in the Rebel army. Davis, however, interpreted Confederate military legislation to mean that Johnston stood fourth in rank among the army's full generals. The deep bitterness and distrust that stemmed from this matter destroyed any possibility that the two men could work well together. The spat over Johnston's rank marked the beginning of a series of wrangles over strategy, army organization, logistics, railroads, personnel, security leaks, and many other matters.

So deep did their differences run that in the spring of 1862, when Johnston commanded the principal Confederate army in Virginia, he and Davis had what an observer reported as "some heated discussion" over the strategy the Rebels should adopt to defend Richmond. A frustrated Johnston tendered his resignation, but Davis refused to accept it. By the late summer of 1863, when Johnston commanded Secessionist forces in Mississippi, he—or at least his wife and close friends—had become paranoid enough to believe that Davis was actively seeking to bring about his failure and disgrace.

Owing to his experiences with the government, Johnston often hesitated to take any major action without specific orders from Richmond, and he usually complained at length about government interference with his command when he received such instructions. His military operations were, therefore, characterized by extreme caution. He simply was reluctant to take any major risk. He might fail, and who could doubt that the chief executive would lay the blame for that failure at his doorstep? Johnston's correspondence with the government was marked by carping, evasiveness, and complaints and was filled with excuses as to why he could not act.

Johnston brought all those attitudes, beliefs, and habits to Dalton, where he arrived on December 26. Fearful of Davis's enmity, he always kept one eye on Richmond and remained constantly on guard lest the president and his sycophants launch some new hostile effort. Johnston, in summary, absolutely would not (or could not) confide in, depend on, trust, work harmoniously with, or even communicate freely and openly with any government headed by Jefferson Davis.

On the other hand, events of the war's first three years had convinced Davis that Johnston—despite the good reputation he enjoyed and the high esteem in which many held him—was an uncooperative, secretive, petty man and a timid, pessimistic commander convinced of his inability to hold any position to which he was sent and afraid to risk his great reputation in an attempt to do so. Even worse, Johnston exhibited little appreciation of the all-important political side of warfare or of the Confederacy's massive logistical problems. He often seemed blind to the impact of his military operations on public opinion and morale and on civilians' willingness to support the government and the war effort. The president was also well aware of Johnston's close cooperation with the administration's political foes in Congress and in the press in their unceasing efforts to embarrass the government.

Davis's selection of Johnston to command the Army of Tennessee represented the triumph of hope over experience. It can be explained only on the grounds that no better alternative existed. In the winter of 1863–64 Lee was the Confederacy's only general competent to command an army. The president's choice can be understood only with the assumption that Davis hoped that Johnston would be willing to put personal feelings aside and to work with the government to meet the great crisis confronting the Rebels in the third winter of the war. Davis naively believed (despite overwhelming evidence to the contrary, including his own army experience) that officers could and would cooperate effectively in their official capacities even when they despised each other.[6]

When Lincoln named Grant as his new commanding general, he could look forward to working in harmony with a capable officer whom he respected and quickly came to trust. When Davis selected Johnston to command the Army of Tennessee, he clearly did so with great foreboding.

CHAPTER TWO

Grand Strategy for 1864

Even before leaving for Washington to accept his lieutenant general's commission from the hands of President Lincoln, Grant knew that he would be elevated to higher command. Earlier, in response to a request from Maj. Gen. Henry W. Halleck, who functioned as Lincoln's chief of staff, Grant had put together some ideas about what he thought the Federal armies should attempt in 1864 and how they should go about the work. He first proposed that the Unionists undertake major operations in eastern North Carolina, south of Richmond, where they could threaten the railroads supplying the Rebel capital. Shifting large numbers of troops to that area, however, would at least have created the appearance of leaving Washington itself exposed to the Confederates. Such a campaign, furthermore, would remind many Northern voters of the Yankees' failed 1862 effort in southeastern Virginia. For those reasons, the Lincoln administration found Grant's suggestion politically unacceptable.

By the time he got to Washington in March, or soon thereafter, Grant had worked out another proposal for the spring campaign. Not long after the promotion ceremony he won Lincoln's approval for his revised plan.

Grant's basic task was simple. He had to destroy the Confederate States of America—a would-be nation that for all practical purposes had been reduced to Central and southern Virginia, the Carolinas, Georgia, Florida, Alabama south of the Tennessee River, and the eastern half of Mississippi. Two great armies defended that area, one in North Georgia, the other in East-Central Virginia. Scattered lesser forces here and there across the South added their mite to the strength of Rebeldom.

Knowing from the first that they were outnumbered, the Confederates had realized early in the conflict that their best chance was to shift their available troops about to concentrate as many of them as possible for the defense of whatever area was menaced by the Yankees. The Secessionists thus used their interior lines to shuttle troops from unthreatened regions to endangered points. By keeping their soldiers on the move, they could partially compensate for their inferior numbers and bring together their largest available force where and when it was most needed.

Several times in the war's first three years the Rebels had shifted troops to counter Federal offensives. Almost all those transfers had been over relatively short distances, but in the fall of 1863 Confederate reinforcements brought west by rail from Virginia had played a crucial role in turning back a Federal thrust into North Georgia. The telegraph, the railroads, and the faster communication and transportation they brought made this strategy feasible.

If the Southerners could continue this method of waging war and combine it with some good generalship, hard fighting, and a bit of luck, they could hold on to enough of their territory to sustain their claim to national sovereignty. Indeed, in their ability to shuttle troops rapidly from one area to another, the Confederates, in some respects, would find themselves better off in 1864. The territorial losses they had suffered in 1862 and 1863 had squeezed their armies closer together, reducing the distances they would have to travel to reinforce one another. The Union armies, by contrast, were farther apart than they had been earlier in the war because they were on exterior lines. (A Yankee army at Chattanooga was farther removed from Federal forces in Virginia—by the route it would have to travel—than it had been the year before, when it was at Nashville.)

Well aware that the Secessionists had often thwarted Union offensives by using troops from one area to help defend another, Grant reasoned that the Northerners should counter the Rebel strategy by pressing forward on several fronts simultaneously, or, as he put it in an early April letter, "to work all parts of the army together." If the Yankees could do so, the Confederates, threatened at several points, would be unable to concentrate at any.

In technical terms, Grant proposed to use "concentration in time" (all Union armies advancing simultaneously) to offset the Southerners' "concentration in space." With numerical superiority everywhere, the Yankees could reasonably count on winning somewhere—and it really did not matter where. Once the Federals broke through at some point, the Secessionists would have to weaken their forces at other places to attempt to repair the damage. The other points would then be even more vulnerable to the Northerners who threatened them.

The idea of overcoming the Confederate strategy by simultaneous offensives was an obvious ploy, and it did not originate with Grant. In fact, Union forces had made limited and partial efforts at such undertakings on several earlier occasions. Never before, however, had the Yankees had an overall commander who would assume responsibility for making such a plan for all their armies, who had the willpower as well as the legal authority to see that his subordinates carried out his plan, and who enjoyed the full support of the government.

To implement his grand strategy, Grant planned to launch five attacking columns at the embattled Confederacy. One of those threats would be directed by Maj. Gen. Benjamin F. Butler commanding the Army of the James in southeastern Virginia. Butler's objective would be the Richmond-Petersburg area. Capture of either of those cities would cut most of the railroads supplying Rebel troops in northern Virginia and inflict a severe blow on the Confederates' ability to maintain an army in the Old Dominion.

As the second part of his plan, Grant would have the main Federal force in the East, the Army of the Potomac commanded by Maj. Gen. George Gordon Meade, move forward from its camps along the Rappahannock River in East-Central Virginia. Meade would confront the Army of Northern Virginia under Robert E. Lee, the Confederacy's best and only successful large military force.

While Butler and Meade assailed the Secessionists in eastern and Central Virginia, Maj. Gen. Franz Sigel would lead Grant's third column into the western part of the state. Sigel's force would move south, up the valley of the Shenandoah River whence came much of the food supply for the Rebel troops serving in the Old Dominion. Occupation of the Shenandoah Valley by a Northern force would deal a severe blow to the Confederates' ability to feed a large army in Virginia.

The fourth part of Grant's plan called for an advance from the Chattanooga, Tennessee, area into North Georgia. This invading column would endeavor to wreck Rebel industrial and transportation facilities in the Central South. Its advance would extend the area of Federal control to the south and southwest. Grant hoped that this column, which he would command in person, would be able to establish a new line of control from Chattanooga through Atlanta, Georgia, and Montgomery, Alabama, to Mobile on the Gulf of Mexico.

While the other four campaigns were under way, Maj. Gen. Nathaniel P. Banks would move east along the Gulf Coast from occupied New Orleans (seized by the Yankees in April 1862) against Mobile, the Confederates' last important port on the Gulf. Capture of Mobile would both deprive the Secessionists of a major city and cut their last east-west rail line.

Grant envisioned the campaigns in Central Virginia and North Georgia as the major operations. Any of the thrusts, however, could have decisive results and be converted into the effort that brought final victory. Butler, for example, could occupy Richmond and swing northward to assail the right and rear of the Secessionists confronting Meade. Sigel might move up the Shenandoah Valley, turn east through the Blue Ridge Mountains, and wreak havoc in the Gordonsville-Charlottesville area or threaten the left and rear of Lee's army as it battled Meade in its front and perhaps Butler on its right and rear. If Banks pushed north from Mobile, he could take Montgomery, the Confederacy's first national capital, and the great munitions-industrial complex at Selma; cut the Rebel forces in Georgia off from their sources of supply in Alabama and Mississippi; and threaten the left and rear of the Confederates facing Grant in North Georgia.

Within the framework of Union strategic thinking, Grant's basic plan was sensible (see appendix 1). It took advantage of several Northern strengths, and it exploited many Southern weaknesses. If executed properly, it would pin down most Secessionist forces. It offered several alternate routes to final victory, and it had enough flexibility to exploit any of them. It put the Rebels in a terrible position—the Unionists could win anywhere that any one of their armies could achieve success; to win, the South had to be victorious everywhere.[1]

The new Federal commander, however, had made one crucial error of omission, and neither he nor anyone else knew the answers to two ominous questions that hovered over his strategy.

Large numbers of Confederate troops garrisoned points along the Atlantic Coast from eastern North Carolina to northern Florida. Grant had made no provisions in his plans to keep those soldiers occupied. Thus they would be free to reinforce any endangered point. This omission may have been owing to the widely held belief that the summer climate along the Southern seaboard was so unhealthful for white men—especially for Northerners—that any military operations undertaken there at that time of the year would fail. Whatever the reason, Grant's decision not to threaten the Confederacy's Atlantic Coast freed a large number of Southern troops for redeployment elsewhere.

Two serious questions clouded the plan. First, did four of the five generals entrusted with command of the invading columns possess the ability and the will to conduct successfully the type of driving, relentless campaign that the new lieutenant general envisioned? Except for Grant himself, none of the officers directing the Yankee columns had accomplished much on the battlefield. Three of them (Butler, Sigel, and Banks) were men of very limited military ability but of considerable influence with important blocs of voters in the North. This last fact explains their retention in command. It also leads to the second question.

The United States Constitution mandated that elections be held in the fall of 1864. So, too, did the constitutions of several Northern states. What impact would the year's military operations have on those elections—and vice versa? What if large numbers of antiwar politicians should be elected to national office (including, perhaps, even the presidency) or to power in such key states as Illinois, Indiana, and Ohio? Certainly in both 1862 and 1863 the outcome of elections in the North had reflected the results of recent military campaigns. In the fall elections of the former year the Democrats had scored impressive political gains, in large part because Confederate victories in Virginia the preceding summer had created the impression that the Republican government of Abraham Lincoln was not conducting a successful war. Federal battlefield triumphs in the summer of the latter year had helped produce Republican successes in the fall elections of 1863. In all likelihood the 1864 voting would follow the same pattern.

If Grant could not demonstrate significant progress toward crushing the Confederacy by the fall of 1864, would Northern voters become dissatisfied enough to deny President Lincoln a second term? Would they conclude that the Federal government could not win the war at an acceptable price and choose a new president? If so, would he be willing to abandon the effort to hold the Union together? Might he pursue some different policy to bring about reunion, perhaps by agreeing to some ironclad guarantees to protect slavery?

Abraham Lincoln—a political animal if ever there was one—undoubtedly gave a great deal of thought to the fact that he would have to face the voters only eight months after he appointed Grant commanding general. If Grant concerned himself at all with such matters in March 1864 he probably reasoned that a successful military campaign would lead to an election victory by supporters of the war.

Not long after assuming his new responsibilities, Grant made two decisions that were to make final Northern success far more costly than it otherwise would have been and actually greatly enhanced the Confederacy's chances of gaining its independence. The new lieutenant general decided to make the campaign in Virginia the Federal government's primary operation in 1864, and he determined to go to the Old Dominion to direct the operations of the Army of the Potomac himself.

Grant originally had planned to stay with the armies in the West in 1864. In Washington in March, however, he soon saw what he later termed "the situation"—by which he meant the close control politicians in the national capital often sought to exercise over Yankee military operations in nearby Virginia. This realization, Grant wrote, led him to conclude that he should personally assume control of the Army of the Potomac.

In his *Memoirs*, published in 1885, Grant commented that "it was plain" that the new commanding general should be in the Old Dominion. No other officer, he declared, would have had the status, prestige, and rank to resist the pressures that would be applied to the commander in Virginia by those who would beseech him "to desist from his own plans and pursue others." Lincoln, too, may have wanted Grant to take the field against Lee, who had become the hope of the Confederacy and the great nemesis of Unionists everywhere. If Grant could defeat Lee, or break up or destroy his army, or capture Richmond, he would deal secession a serious if not fatal blow. Certainly Grant would never have put such a decision into effect without the president's blessing.

The military's traditional practice of seniority may also have influenced Grant's decision to alter his original plan. Although Meade commanded the largest Union army in the Virginia theater, he stood only fourth in rank among Yankee generals in that area. The three officers who outranked him were all men of very limited military ability. Both Butler (date of rank May 16, 1861) and Sigel (March 21, 1862) stood ahead of Meade, whose commission as major general dated from November 29, 1862. So too did Maj. Gen. Ambrose E. Burnside (March 18, 1862), whose IX Corps was slated to cooperate with Meade's army.

Burnside privately pledged to waive seniority and to serve under Meade's command, but Grant did not know that at the time he decided to take personal control of the Union effort in Virginia. Butler and Sigel were political generals—or, more accurately, politicians who held generals' commissions—and they might well squawk if placed in the shadow of a junior officer or insist on exercising command over him. Such a brouhaha would, at the least, impair the effective conduct of military operations in an area where the Rebels could be expected to take immediate advantage of any confusion among the Federals. As lieutenant general, Grant could ride herd on all the major generals and keep them working toward a common objective.

Whatever the reasons behind the two decisions, and whoever made them, they were the greatest military blunders made by Federal authorities during the war. By 1864 two irrefutable facts about the conflict should have been clear to all who would look. For one thing, neither side was likely to win the war in Virginia. The Confederates there were too skilled to lose, at least as long as Lee lived, but not strong enough to win. The Northerners, on the other hand, were too strong to lose the war in Virginia but not skilled enough to win it there. Second, thanks to Grant and his soldiers, the Federals were well along toward achieving military victory in the West.

Grant was the best of the Union generals. By personally taking charge of the Army of the Potomac, he confined himself to the one theater of operations where the Confederates were at their strongest, where the obstacles to Northern success were greatest, and where the Rebels' best army and their one competent army commander could nullify his own abilities.

The consequences of Grant's (or Lincoln's) decision are hidden by the ultimate outcome of the war. They may be seen, however, in the 1864 political history of the United States, in the wartime casualty lists, and most poignantly in the military cemeteries that dot Virginia, Tennessee, and Georgia. Tens of thousands of Americans—North and South—paid for this misjudgment with their lives and many tens of thousands more with painful wounds. The outcome of the war remained doubtful much longer, and the United States itself came much closer to having to pay the price of national division than otherwise would have been the case.[2]

Grant's decision to take personal direction of the Federal effort in Virginia necessitated selection of another officer to assume his old position in the West. Normally in such a situation the senior general serving in the old command would replace the former chief. In this case the senior officer was Maj. Gen. George H. Thomas, commander of the Army of the Cumberland, one of the three field armies operating under the umbrella command of the Military Division of the Mississippi. Thomas was destined to finish the war as one of the very few general officers on either side who never suffered defeat on a battlefield where he was in command. On several other occasions when he was not in overall command, Thomas and his troops played the crucial role in achieving victory (Chattanooga, 1863), staving off defeat (Stones River, 1862), or preventing defeat from becoming disaster (Chickamauga, 1863). Thomas, in summary, was a man of great integrity, a very capable general, and a superb soldier. He was not, however, to be the new commander of the Military Division of the Mississippi.

Grant may have resented what he understood to have been Thomas's role in some spring 1862 army political squabbles, and he certainly did not trust him to handle the western command in the way envisioned for the grand plan of 1864. Thomas had a reputation as a solid but plodding general. More significantly, he was an officer who had spent almost all of the war in the Army of the Cumberland, whereas Grant had risen to supreme command through the Army of the Tennessee, another of the Federals' western armies. Some degree of friction and rivalry naturally existed between those two commands. Thomas, furthermore, was a Virginian who had remained loyal to the national government when the Old Dominion seceded. Because his native state had no representation in the national Congress, he had no powerful patrons to advance his career. The reverse, in fact, was the case. Thomas's predecessors as commander of the Army of the Cumberland had been Maj. Gens. Don Carlos Buell and William S. Rosecrans—both very unpopular with several powerful members of the Lincoln administration and the Republican Party. Thomas had been loyal to Buell and Rosecrans and had thereby placed himself beyond the pale of political preference.

For all those reasons, Grant bypassed Thomas. He chose instead to elevate his protégé, Maj. Gen. William Tecumseh Sherman, commander of the Army of the Tennessee.

On the basis of his record, Sherman did not merit such a promotion, certainly not ahead of Thomas. He and his brigade had been caught up in the general rout of the Yankee army at First Manassas in July 1861. Later that year, when he commanded in Kentucky, Sherman had suffered a near nervous breakdown under the pressure he then faced. Although he had performed well in the April 1862 fighting at Shiloh, he had been caught by surprise when the Confederates launched their attack on the Union camps there. In the following December he had suffered a stinging defeat at Walnut Hills (or Chickasaw Bluffs) near Vicksburg, Mississippi. His role in Grant's great campaign that reestablished Union control over the Mississippi River had been relatively limited, and he had clearly failed in the fighting at Chattanooga in November 1863 when the Confederates repulsed his attack on the northern end of their position.

Over the two years preceding the spring of 1864, however, Sherman and Grant had become very close friends. They had much in common. Both were midwesterners (born in Ohio, although Grant later moved to Illinois). Both were Military Academy graduates (Sherman Class of 1840, Grant 1843). Both had rather undistinguished careers in the antebellum United States Army. Neither had made much of a success in his postarmy civilian career in the 1850s.

Grant, however, had found his true calling in the Civil War. Sherman had been fortunate to become associated with him in the winter of 1861–62, and the two quickly became fast friends. In the imperturbable Grant, Sherman found the anchor he needed to function well in a high military position. The two men learned to trust each other absolutely. They would work well together. That was enough for Grant, and when he went east in March 1864 he tapped Sherman to succeed to chief command of the Yankee troops in the West. Lincoln, of course, ratified Grant's choice.

As a human being and as a very competent army officer, Thomas resented Grant's decision and the situation in which it placed him. As a practical man, a patriot, and a good soldier, he silently accepted the new arrangement.

Elevation of Sherman to command the Military Division of the Mississippi guaranteed that there would be close and cordial cooperation between the new Union military chief and the general who would direct the major campaign in the West. Only time would tell if it would also bring wise direction to the conduct of that campaign.[3]

In 1864 the Confederacy had no military counterpart to Grant. President Jefferson Davis, as commander in chief, therefore undertook to develop the Rebels' military as well as their geopolitical grand strategy for the year. Like Lincoln, Davis was well aware that crucial elections would take place in the North that fall.

In many ways Davis's home-front situation was better than Lincoln's even though his country had lost vast slices of its territory. Among Confederates devotion to "the Cause" remained high. Many Southerners who had despaired of success had long since gone over to the Yankees and taken the oath of allegiance. Rebel soldiers and civilians alike drew inspiration from the fact that after three years of war the Federal government had been unable to snuff out the much weaker Confederacy. Like Northerners, most Secessionists usually focused their attention on events in Virginia, and Lee's victories in the Old Dominion had inspired white Southerners from the Atlantic to the Rio Grande. The infectious confidence that Lee's men had in their general and in themselves spread to hundreds of thousands of their fellow citizens. Northerners viewing events in Virginia could not see how much their armies had accomplished elsewhere in the war's first three years; Rebels, wearing the same blinders and looking only at the same battles and campaigns, concluded that their outlook was much brighter than it really was.

Although the Confederates had lost large portions of their territory, the core areas they still held were surprisingly firm in their determination to see the war through to Southern independence. Indeed, in early 1864 a series of minor victories in Mississippi, Florida, Tennessee, and North Carolina boosted Rebel confidence and stiffened Secessionist determination. "The omens are all good for us. Thus far military events have been every where in our favor," wrote Col. Josiah Gorgas, the Rebels' chief of ordnance, on May 2. It is impossible to measure such things, but the preponderance of evidence indicates that in early 1864 the level of public support for the Rebel war effort among white Southerners in the area under Confederate control was considerably higher than was popular devotion to the Federal cause in the North.[4]

Davis was anxious to seize the initiative, throw the Yankees off balance, and disrupt whatever plans they might be making for 1864. He believed that a great opportunity to do so had presented itself in the West, and soon after ordering Johnston to Dalton he moved to take advantage of it.

The President had received an 11 December 1863, telegram from Hardee in which the Army of Tennessee's temporary commander reported that his men had recovered from the defeats they had suffered the previous fall, were in good spirits, and could soon "commence active operations against the enemy." Several other reports gave Davis similar encouraging pictures of the army's condition. The president, therefore, wanted Johnston to take the offensive as soon as possible, drive or maneuver the Federals out of Chattanooga, and restore as much of Tennessee as he could to Confederate control. (The president, who sometimes exhibited a great capacity for wishful thinking, chose to disregard the few pessimistic reports about the condition of the army that came to him—including a later letter from Hardee.) On December 23, as Johnston was making his way to the army in North Georgia, Davis wrote to express his hope that the Rebels at Dalton would soon undertake an offensive movement into Tennessee.

This letter opened a four-month, on-again, off-again comedy of confused correspondence about the condition of Johnston's army and what its objective and strategy should be. The exchange resolved nothing and only widened the already great gulf between the president in Richmond and the general in Dalton.

All through this period Davis and the Confederate authorities, citing various reports but choosing to ignore others, insisted that Johnston's army was, or could quickly be made, capable of such offensive operations as they envisioned. They also maintained, based on several intelligence reports, that the Union force in Johnston's front was relatively weak because the Yankees were concentrating their strength in Virginia, where they would make their major effort in 1864. During the winter and early spring Davis and his advisers suggested several plans to reinforce Johnston so that he could seize the initiative and move into East Tennessee.

To each of those proposals Johnston replied with general assertions that his army was heavily outnumbered by the enemy in his front and that it was poorly organized; inadequately equipped and supplied; and lacked almost all logistical, transportation, and engineering capability for a winter campaign in the wilds of East Tennessee. Besides, Johnston maintained, the enemy would undoubtedly be prepared to advance long before his own army could possibly be ready for an aggressive campaign.

Believing correctly that the Unionists had the capability to launch more than one major effort, Johnston countered the administration's proposals with a strategy of his own: "I can see no other mode of taking the offensive here than to beat the enemy when he advances and then to move forward." When the time came for the Confederates to go over to the offensive, Johnston suggested, it would be better for them to shift westward into Alabama or Mississippi and advance from that area into Central or West Tennessee rather than trying to move forward from North Georgia into the eastern part of the Volunteer State.

This early 1864 correspondence between Davis and the Richmond authorities on the one hand and Johnston on the other typified the wartime relationship between the Rebel government and the general. Neither Johnston nor Confederate officials paid much attention to the other's point of view. Neither really sought to communicate freely with the other or to understand the other's situation. Davis did not, for example, expound on the great political implications of the forthcoming military operations; Johnston did not provide much detailed information on the condition of his army or the enemy forces in his front.

On several occasions the authorities worked out proposals for an offensive campaign by Johnston's army without consulting the general. When they finally communicated the plans to Johnston, he rejected them without offering much in the way of an explanation or putting forth any alternative except his vague proposal to await the enemy's advance. He might, for example, have proposed some minor cavalry raids against the railroads in Tennessee to hamper the Yankees' buildup for the campaign that all knew would begin in the spring. As it turned out, such an effort may well have been the Rebels' best—if not their only—chance to achieve success in the West in 1864.

Perhaps nothing better illustrates the dead-end nature of this futile correspondence than the letter written on March 4 by Gen. Braxton Bragg, then in Richmond as military adviser to the president. Referring to earlier, glowing reports about the condition of the army's artillery horses and to Johnston's own gloomy assessments, Bragg wrote, "The deficiency you report . . . seems very large and is so different from the account given by General Hardee . . . that hopes are entertained there must be some error on your part."

Johnston chose not to respond to this comment although it offered him a perfect opening to present to the government a detailed report on his army's strength, condition, and logistical needs. On other occasions when Johnston did attempt to make something more than general statements that his command was not ready and could not be ready before the Federals moved forward, he gave conflicting testimony.

Confederate efforts to fathom Yankee intentions for 1864 also deepened and widened the gulf of misunderstanding between Davis and Johnston. During the winter Rebel authorities received reports from several sources that the Federal government was shifting men from its western armies to the East. Such intelligence, if confirmed, might indicate that the main Union effort would come in Virginia. Grant's presence in the Old Dominion seemed to confirm this assessment.

In truth, there was some basis for the reports. The IX Corps, which had gone west in 1863, returned to the East early in 1864, and several newspapers reported that other Union troops would soon follow. In addition, many Federal units extended their original three-year enlistments and received a "veteran furlough" for doing so. All during the winter scores of those veteran regiments left the Chattanooga area for a month-long visit to their homes. Movement of those units north through Tennessee and Kentucky gave additional credence to reports of a transfer of troops away from the army in Johnston's front. For those reasons, Confederate authorities concluded that the Yankees were shifting troops to Virginia and hoped that offensive action by Johnston might halt such movements as well as reestablish Secessionist control over much of Tennessee.

Whenever the Rebel government queried Johnston about the Yankee forces in the West, he responded with a general comment that they were not moving east. Once again, Johnston neglected an excellent opportunity to give his government detailed reports on the situation in his front, the strength of the enemy forces he faced, and what he thought they might be preparing to do.

If done politely and professionally, such reports would have gone far to remove some of the misunderstandings that so hampered the Southerners. As it was, however, this epistolary stalemate made communication and cooperation between Davis and Johnston even more difficult. Each man could easily find in the letters and telegrams additional evidence to strengthen his distrust of the other. Davis's belief that Johnston was too timid to undertake any meaningful action was confirmed. The general had no end of excuses as to why he could not act. Johnston saw in the government's unrealistic proposals yet more efforts to push him into foolish actions that most likely would result in the destruction of his army and the ruination of his reputation. Were the general's family members, his political friends in Richmond, and some of his military staff correct when they warned him that the chief executive's hatred ran so deep that he would risk destruction of the Army of Tennessee simply to bring disgrace upon a personal enemy?

Both Davis and Johnston reacted to this impasse in characteristic fashion. The president simply dropped the matter, turned to other things, and hoped for the best. If Johnston could "beat the enemy when he advances and then . . . move forward," all would be well for the Rebels. The general, on the other hand, withdrew into the world of his army where he could go about his daily activities without much interference from Richmond. The less he had to deal with the Davis government, Johnston reasoned, the better off he would be and the more likely he was to achieve success.[5]

Beyond any reasonable doubt, Johnston was correct about the impossibility of the Army of Tennessee's conducting large-scale offensive operations that winter. The point that must be understood, however, is the great—and growing—distrust that existed between Davis and Johnston and the barriers that blocked communication between them. The distance between Richmond and Dalton was much greater than that shown on the map.

CHAPTER THREE

Preparations for the Field

"The great question of the campaign," Sherman was to write a decade later, "was one of supplies." Indeed, as Sherman—a former supply officer —well knew, logistics had determined the outcome of more military operations than had any other single factor. Once he had formally assumed the position previously held by Grant, which he did on March 18, Sherman went to work to provide the men and animals of his command with the supplies they would need for the spring operations. Fortunately for the Yankees, he was able to build on the sound logistical work that Grant (another former supply officer) had begun during the earlier part of the winter. In the seven weeks between the time Sherman ascended to his new post and the opening of the campaign he managed to accumulate enough supplies to last the spring and summer. His success in that great effort went far to determine the outcome of the campaign before the first shot was fired.

As he wrestled with what he later termed "the troublesome question of transportation and supplies," Sherman found himself facing two great logistical problems. He had to provide adequate quantities of food, forage, shoes, clothing, medicine, ammunition, blankets, and all the other items that an army of one hundred thousand men and some thirty-five thousand horses and mules would need to sustain itself in the field. Sherman's second problem was to move those supplies from his great base in Nashville to his forward depots ("secondary bases," he called them) and thence on to the troops at the front.

The first problem turned out to be no problem at all. Throughout the war the Federal government almost always provided amply for its armies, and all during the winter and spring Northern railroads and steamboats poured a steady torrent of supplies of all kinds into Nashville. By early May government warehouses in the Tennessee capital and in Chattanooga bulged with more supplies than Sherman's troops would need for four months of active campaigning.

Sherman found the second problem much more complex and difficult. South of Chattanooga the Yankees would enter a region closed completely to Union naval power. With a very few exceptions, Federal armies campaigning in the West in the war's first three years had had the valuable support of the United States Navy. The great rivers of the West served as lines of transportation, communication, and supply leading into and through the Upper South. The Rebels could not wreck or close those rivers. Union gunboats, transports, supply vessels, and hospital boats moved virtually at will along the Ohio, Mississippi, Tennessee, and Cumberland Rivers, and their presence had been a crucial factor in many Federal victories.

The rivers beyond Chattanooga flowed off to the south, to the Gulf of Mexico. They offered no entrance from the Ohio, the Mississippi, or the Tennessee, and they were not navigable or their distant mouths were closed by Confederate fortifications. To get supplies to his men once they had moved into the region south of Chattanooga, Sherman would have to find some other means of transportation.

Fortunately for the Yankees, another way of moving the matériel for Sherman's force was available. From Nashville, two lines of railroad tracks climbed up across the hills to Chattanooga. One, the Alabama & Tennessee, ran directly south to Decatur, Alabama, where it connected with the Memphis & Charleston, which ran east to Stevenson, Alabama. The second rail line, the Nashville & Chattanooga, ran southeast from Nashville directly to Stevenson, where it was joined by the Memphis & Charleston before it continued on to the east.

Together those two rail lines would enable the Unionists to move supplies easily from Nashville to Chattanooga—if they had enough locomotives and freight cars to do the job and if the tracks and bridges were not damaged by floods or rockslides or torn up by Confederate raiders. The thirty-mile stretch between Stevenson and Chattanooga (which included the great bridge over the Tennessee River at Bridgeport, Alabama) was potentially a bottleneck. In addition to those railroads, the Yankees, if they were lucky, would sometimes find the Tennessee River high enough for small boats to bring supplies as far forward as Chattanooga.

The Western & Atlantic Railroad (w&a) stretched away from Chattanooga to the southeast. The state of Georgia had built that line in the antebellum decades to promote economic development in the region recently opened to white settlement between Chattanooga and Atlanta and to draw through Georgia some of the trade to and from the Mississippi Valley. In the spring and summer of 1864 the w&a would supply—from different directions—both the Union force invading Georgia and the Confederate army defending it.

In late 1863, almost immediately after his armies secured the national government's hold on Chattanooga, Grant put his troops to work repairing the rail lines connecting that city with Nashville. Under the direction of Brig. Gen. Grenville M. Dodge, later builder of the great Union Pacific Railroad, Yankee soldiers demonstrated their ability to put a badly damaged rail line back into running order. In only forty days they repaired or relaid the 102 miles of track and rebuilt 182 bridges between Nashville and Decatur, Alabama.

Late in January Grant tapped Col. Daniel C. McCallum to supervise the railroads in the Military Division of the Mississippi—a post McCallum retained when Sherman succeeded Grant. McCallum created a Department of Transportation directed by Col. Adna Anderson and a Department of Construction under Col. William W. Wright. Anderson was to be responsible for the daily operation of the railroads that would supply Sherman's force as it advanced from Chattanooga, Wright for keeping the lines repaired.

To make possible Anderson's task, Sherman closed the railroads south of Nashville to civilian traffic and terminated the policy of providing food to citizens who lived in the vicinity of his camps. When his actions drew howls from several important political figures, including President Lincoln, Sherman responded by pointing out that "the railroad cannot supply the army and the people too. One or the other must quit." On another occasion he declared, "If we feed a mouth except soldiers on active duty we are lost."

Federal veterans returning from furlough were often required to walk from Nashville to their winter camps near Chattanooga or at intermediate points. Sometimes they had to drive herds of beef cattle as they did so, thereby freeing more space on the trains that crawled along the tracks to and from Chattanooga. Sherman also secured permission from Federal authorities to seize and retain all trains arriving in Nashville from the north. Within a short time he had, thanks to this drastic hijacking measure, so increased the rolling stock on McCallum's railroads south of Nashville that some 130 or more carloads of supplies rolled into Chattanooga each day. On April 23, a gleeful Sherman boasted, a record 193 cars loaded with supplies departed Nashville for Chattanooga. Each freight car contained ten tons of supplies, and the Yankees were soon meeting the daily needs of their armies and advanced posts and even beginning to accumulate a large surplus in Chattanooga.

As supplies of all kinds piled up in Nashville and Chattanooga, Sherman took steps to ensure that Wright and his construction crews would be able to keep the rail lines open. Materials for replacing ties, bridges, and rails were stockpiled in Chattanooga and later at forward points in North Georgia. Special trains loaded with such materials and details of engineer troops stood ready to move to any point where nature or the Rebels might damage the tracks.

So important did Sherman think his railroads that he left behind in Tennessee and northern Alabama an infantry division along with detachments of other troops to guard them. His engineers built fortified blockhouses at important bridges in which he stationed garrisons to oppose any Confederate effort to interrupt the flow of supplies. To protect his rail lines in Kentucky and Tennessee, Sherman relied on thousands of troops called up in the summer for one hundred days' service. Those units, raised in Ohio, Indiana, Illinois, Iowa, and Wisconsin, freed veteran soldiers to guard the railroads closer to the front or to join the invading force itself. Later, when much of northwestern Georgia had passed under Federal control, Sherman created a separate command (the District of the Etowah, under Maj. Gen. James Steedman) to defend the railroads in northern Georgia and Alabama.

Protection of the rail line was rendered a bit less crucial as stockpiles built up in Nashville and Chattanooga during the spring. The surpluses in Sherman's warehouses meant that no disruption of rail lines north of the Tennessee capital would affect his operations during the summer and any break between Nashville and Chattanooga probably would not. Often in the former and at times in the latter case the Cumberland and Tennessee Rivers might offer alternate lines of supply.

Sherman's preparations paid handsome dividends in the spring and summer of 1864. Yankee track crews quickly repaired any damage that the rail lines suffered. As the Union force swept southward, Wright's men swarmed in its wake, repairing, rebuilding, or replacing track, ties, roadbed, and bridges. Not far behind the construction crews came the locomotives pulling cars filled with supplies. Rarely did more than a day or two elapse between the occupation of an area by Sherman's advancing troops and the arrival of trains loaded with food, ammunition, and medicine.

In the end the great story of Union logistics in the Georgia campaign was that there was no story—neither nature nor the Rebels ever seriously interrupted the flow of supplies to Sherman's railhead. During the summer Confederate soldiers came to complain that it was no use for them to destroy the railroad as their army retreated because Sherman carried with him not only new rails, spikes, and ties but also extra bridges and even duplicate tunnels.[1]

The railroad, then, would supply Sherman's troops, thereby making possible his advance into Georgia. In another way, however, dependence on the Western & Atlantic limited the Yankee commander's strategic options. Once he and his men entered the rugged area immediately south of Chattanooga, Sherman could advance only toward Atlanta because that was the only place to which the railroad ran.

Sherman further limited his ability to maneuver by ordering drastic reductions in the number of wagons that accompanied his troops. He did so believing that such action would make his force "a mobile machine, willing and able to start at a minute's notice, and to subsist on the scantiest food." In fact, however, Sherman's reduction in his wagon transportation severely limited his mobility because as the number of wagons declined, so did the Yankees' ability to operate away from the railroad.

The Federal commander seems to have expected to deal with this problem by having his men and animals live off the country. Unfortunately for Sherman, very little food was to be found in the area where his invading force would operate that spring and summer. "The northern portion of this State," wrote a Confederate commissary officer from Atlanta on New Year's Day, "has been completely exhausted. A large portion of the citizens are now compelled to look elsewhere for family supplies." This scarcity and the resulting supply problem for the Federals were exacerbated in 1864 by a crop shortage and by the Confederates' practice of stripping the sparsely populated North Georgia region as the Rebel army retreated through it ahead of Sherman's men.

Thus Sherman could not depend on North Georgia to provide much food for his troops, especially in the early weeks of the campaign before the 1864 crops ripened. Even had he been able to feed his men and animals from North Georgia's fields and farms, Sherman would still have needed wagons to gather the supplies and to haul ammunition, rations, medicine, shoes, and other necessities from his railhead to individual units in the field.

For better or worse, then, Sherman and his Yankees were tied to the railroad. They could not permit the line connecting them with their base at Chattanooga to be broken, nor could they get very far away from it or stay away from it for very long.[2]

Like Sherman, Joseph E. Johnston had had experience keeping supplies flowing to military units. He had served as quartermaster general of the United States Army in 1860–61 before following his native Virginia into the Confederacy. He too well understood the necessity of providing troops with adequate food, clothing, and ammunition. The Confederacy lacked the North's capability to produce and transport supplies and equipment, but in early 1864 several factors lessened the Rebels' disadvantages. For one thing, Johnston had only about forty-five thousand men at Dalton to feed and clothe. For another, most of his troops were camped within a few miles of his headquarters in Dalton and could, therefore, draw supplies from the railhead relatively easily. Sherman, by contrast, had to provide daily supplies for troops scattered from Knoxville to Chattanooga, to Decatur, to Nashville. Johnston managed to alleviate his logistical difficulties by sending many of his army's animals thirty or forty miles south to winter along the Coosa or Etowah Rivers or in some other area where forage for them was relatively abundant. Eventually some two-thirds of the Army of Tennessee's cavalry mounts and about one-half of its artillery horses were sent to Rome and the Etowah Valley respectively. Such action greatly reduced the army's demands on the Rebels' transportation.

Johnston, unlike his Federal counterpart, did not have to worry about protecting a railroad running through several hundred miles of nominally hostile territory. The Secessionists could rely on steamboats to bring supplies from Central Alabama up the Coosa River to the railroad at Rome and even in the case of at least one small boat on up the Oostanaula to Resaca. The great Rebel base was Atlanta. The rail network below that city connected it with such industrial centers as Macon in Central Georgia, Columbus and Montgomery to the southwest, and Augusta to the east, as well as to the great agricultural areas of eastern Mississippi and western Alabama whence came many of the foodstuffs for the Confederate troops at Dalton. Johnston's most serious logistical problem was to get his supplies from Atlanta to Dalton over the tracks of the state-owned and state-operated Western & Atlantic.

When Johnston arrived in Dalton, he found the Army of Tennessee in need of food, ammunition, blankets, shoes, and clothing. He soon determined that the difficulty stemmed chiefly from a shortage of locomotives and freight cars on the W&A. On January 12, therefore, Johnston informed both Confederate authorities and Georgia governor Joseph E. Brown that he would have to abandon Dalton and fall back toward Atlanta unless the railroad could be operated so as to bring him more supplies.

Jolted by the general's warning, the two governments acted quickly to accelerate the delivery of supplies to the army in North Georgia. The War Department managed to pry more cars and locomotives from other lines and transfer them to the W&A. State officials quickly reformed the railroad's operations to improve utilization of the rolling stock. Johnston himself instituted some helpful changes. Like Sherman, he ordered the beef cattle for his troops driven to the army and slaughtered there rather than having the animals shipped north by rail.

By late January Johnston was able to report that the railroad was then meeting the daily needs of the army. Three months later one of his soldiers begged his homefolk not to send him any more meat because he then had such a supply that he probably would have to abandon it and leave it behind if the army had to move.

So long as each commander could prevent the other from interrupting his rail line, his troops would not suffer a shortage of supplies. The tracks of the W&A adequately supplied both armies and drew them both inexorably toward Atlanta.[3]

The one-hundred-thousand-man force that Sherman labored so hard and so successfully to feed and supply lay in winter camps scattered across the area from Nashville south to northern Alabama and Georgia and eastward from the Tennessee capital to Knoxville. Its three armies, acting more or less independently, were the forces that had overrun so much of the Confederacy in the war's first three years. In the winter of 1863–64 they were united under one command and stood poised to continue their work in the coming spring. In modern military jargon the command would be called an "army group."

George Thomas's Army of the Cumberland was the largest component of Sherman's Military Division of the Mississippi. In 1861, 1862, and 1863 the Army of the Cumberland (sometimes under other names) had maneuvered and fought its way southward along the Louisville-Nashville-Chattanooga corridor. The winter of 1863–64 found it concentrated in the Chattanooga area. When the campaign opened in May 1864, the army consisted of three infantry corps—the IV, XIV, and XX—and a cavalry corps. Maj. Gen. Oliver Otis Howard commanded the IV Corps; Maj. Gen. John M. Palmer the XIV; and Maj. Gen. Joseph Hooker the XX. Brig. Gen. Washington L. Elliott commanded the Cavalry Corps. Each of the corps consisted of three divisions.

Hooker, by far the most capable of Thomas's corps commanders, simply did not fit into the command structure of the Military Division of the Mississippi. In early 1863 he had commanded the Army of the Potomac. In the fall of that year he had come west in command of what became the XX Corps when the Federals rushed reinforcements from Virginia to Tennessee. He regarded himself as a better general than Sherman, and in some respects he clearly was. He and Sherman did not get along, and Hooker found himself a victim of the Halleck-Grant-Sherman Army of the Tennessee clique that dominated the Union military establishment after early 1864. (Thomas and Meade were the clique's other most conspicuous victims, but their cases reflected almost entirely professional and style of command differences rather than a bitter clash of personalities.)[4]

On April 30 the Army of the Cumberland numbered 72,938 officers and men. Each of the infantry corps had a strength of about 21,000; the Cavalry Corps of some 9,000. The army's artillery numbered 130 guns, organized with two or three batteries (each of four or six guns) assigned to each division.

The Army of the Tennessee, which had operated under Halleck's general direction early in the war, had been Grant's and then Sherman's. Under their command it had spent 1861, 1862, and most of 1863 reestablishing Federal control of the Tennessee and Mississippi Rivers. When Sherman succeeded Grant as supreme commander in the West, his favorite subordinate, Maj. Gen. James B. McPherson, took command of the Army of the Tennessee.

Like Thomas's force, McPherson's army consisted of three infantry corps—the XV, XVI, and XVII. Maj. Gen. John A. Logan commanded the XV Corps, which was organized into three divisions for field service with Sherman. The XVI Corps had been divided. Two of its divisions had remained in the Mississippi Valley, and the other two shifted to Tennessee. The latter two, the "Left Wing, XVI Corps," were commanded by Brig. Gen. Grenville M. Dodge. Several thousand troops of the XVII Corps had also remained in the Mississippi Valley. Maj. Gen. Francis P. Blair commanded the two divisions of that corps slated to operate with Sherman. In late April, however, Blair and his two divisions had not yet reached the front. They were still in Indiana, Illinois, and Ohio, where they had gone under the veteran furlough policy. The remainder of McPherson's field army was strung out along the railroads south from Nashville to Decatur and thence eastward toward Chattanooga.

At the end of April the two corps with McPherson numbered 24,380 officers and men. The Army of the Tennessee had ninety-six pieces of artillery, with two or three batteries attached to each of its five infantry divisions. Except for a few men acting as escorts, guides, scouts, and couriers, the army included no mounted troops.

The third element in Sherman's army group, the Army of the Ohio, was based in Knoxville, which it had captured in the late summer of 1863 by moving southeast from Kentucky. This tiny force, only 12,805 officers and men on April 30, was an army only by the vagaries of law and bureaucracy. (At one time the Army of the Ohio had been larger, but many of its troops had been reassigned to other areas.) Maj. Gen. John M. Schofield commanded both the army and its principal component, the XXIII Corps. The army also included a division of cavalry. The XXIII Corps was organized into three divisions. Twenty-three cannon accompanied the army.[5]

This structure of Sherman's force was the end product of several weeks of reorganization during which the Yankee commander sought to shape his units for the spring campaign. The resulting organization had two glaring weaknesses. The more serious difficulty stemmed from the difference in the sizes of the three armies. During the coming operations this great disparity of strength would sometimes cause problems. The Army of the Cumberland proved too large for rapid movement, and the other two armies often proved too weak to accomplish their missions. Schofield, who at the time did not question the arrangement, wrote after the war that Sherman had not adopted the obvious remedy of transferring troops from the Army of the Cumberland to the other armies because Thomas did not want to give up any of his men and the men did not want to leave the army in which they had been serving. The XX Corps, however, had not come to the West until the fall of 1863 and had not been part of the Army of the Cumberland for very long. The corps itself was a new organization created during the winter by merging several units. Some of its troops could have been shifted to McPherson and Schofield to bolster their weak forces. Another problem, however, existed with the XX Corps and its commander.

To remedy difficulties caused by the sizes of his armies, Sherman often detached elements of Thomas's army and sent them to "co-operate with" or to "support" or to "operate with" McPherson or Schofield. On several occasions such ad hoc arrangements only created more problems. Hooker, an able, vain, and pompous officer who believed that he deserved a far higher position than he held, outranked McPherson and Schofield and resented being sent to serve with (or, worse yet, under) them. John Palmer of the XIV Corps was junior to McPherson but believed he out-ranked Schofield and proved as averse to serving under a lower-ranking officer as did Hooker.

In some instances, not surprisingly, Hooker or Palmer refused to obey orders from Schofield or McPherson or fell into arguments with them over whose troops should take precedence in a marching column or at a river crossing. Such petty silliness wasted time and resources and sometimes cost the lives of good troops who were sacrificed to a general's false sense of pride. (That fall, after the obstreperousness of Hooker and Palmer had hampered the Yankees' operations and led to their leaving Sherman's command, the Federal government ruled that assignment of a general to command an army or a corps gave him temporary superiority of rank over officers of the same grade who held command at lower levels even if their commissions antedated his.)

The second problem with Sherman's organization stemmed from the cavalry. The army group contained four divisions of horsemen (three with Thomas, one with Schofield), in all about twelve thousand troopers. Sherman elected to take personal control of those horsemen. He did not, however, create a single cavalry force to operate under his direct command. Rather, he treated the divisions separately. In the early weeks of the campaign he usually deployed one mounted division to guard each flank of the army group, one to protect his line of supply in the area immediately behind the front, and one as a reserve. In so using his cavalry, Sherman deprived himself of a large, fast-striking mounted force that at several times in the campaign might have inflicted great damage on the Confederates.

The Federal commander's decision effectively to confine the Union cavalry to a defensive role may have been dictated by the absence of a trustworthy general to place in command of the army group's horsemen, by a simple failure on Sherman's part to appreciate the potential of a large and aggressive mounted force, by a belief that Northern cavalry could not cope with either Rebel infantry or horsemen, or by the conviction that the Yankee supply line was so important that it had to be protected even at the expense of depriving the Unionists of an effective offensive cavalry force. Whatever the reason for its organization and employment, Sherman's cavalry was virtually impotent during the first half of the summer's campaign and ineffective in the last part.

The flaws in the organization of Sherman's army group can best be seen in retrospect. At the time the problems to which they were to lead were not so obvious. A military force, however, does not have to have perfect organization; it needs only to be good enough to defeat its opponent. The summer campaign of 1864 would tell if Sherman's awkward, unbalanced force could meet that test.[6]

Joseph E. Johnston also labored over problems of organization that winter. Upon arriving in Dalton, Johnston found the Army of Tennessee divided into two infantry corps and a cavalry corps. One of the infantry corps was commanded by Hardee, who, upon Johnston's arrival, stepped down from his temporary post at the head of the army; the other by Maj. Gen. Thomas C. Hindman. Hardee had a corps of four divisions. Hindman's Corps consisted of three divisions.[7] The four-division Cavalry Corps was under Maj. Gen. Joseph Wheeler. About half the army's horsemen, however, were then operating with Confederate forces in East Tennessee, and many others were stationed at points south of Dalton where their horses could rest and obtain forage.

From the time he took command, Johnston wanted to change this organization. He believed that the army would be more flexible and easier to handle if the infantry were organized into three corps. On December 31 he requested permission to make such a change and recommended that his longtime friend and protégé Maj. Gen. William H. C. Whiting be sent to command the new third corps. Over the following two months Johnston repeated the request, substituting the name of Maj. Gen. Mansfield Lovell when he learned that the authorities would not entrust Whiting with such an important and prestigious assignment.

Like so many matters that arose during the war, this simple request widened the divide between Johnston and the Davis government. In requesting first Whiting and then Lovell, Johnston, perhaps unknowingly for he was usually somewhat naive in such matters, had nominated two officers who had become identified as political enemies of Jefferson Davis and his administration. He had requested one officer (Whiting) who had angered Davis by his 1861 attitude toward troops from Davis's home state of Mississippi and who had done very little to deserve such an honor and another (Lovell) who was associated with the catastrophic 1862 loss of New Orleans.

To the beleaguered president it must have seemed that Johnston was seeking promotion and honor for two of the administration's political enemies. Nor did Johnston justify his request with detailed reasons for changing the army's basic structure. As was his wont, he sent only curt, general messages carrying the implication that the request should be granted simply because he wished it.

Eventually the authorities denied Johnston permission to form a third infantry corps in the Army of Tennessee because, the government maintained, the army was too small to justify such an organization. To Johnston it must have seemed that once again Jefferson Davis had chosen to slight him.

Confederate authorities, in fact, had plans of their own for the high command of the Army of Tennessee. In the fall of 1863, long before Bragg left the army, Jefferson Davis had decided (upon Bragg's recommendation) to promote John Bell Hood to lieutenant general and to assign him to command a corps in the Rebels' chief western army. Hood was one of the South's most distinguished living officers. At that time he was recovering from two serious wounds that had cost him his right leg (Chickamauga) and the use of his left arm (Gettysburg). Not until February 1864 was he able to return to the field. He reached Dalton late that month and relieved Hindman, who reverted to the command of a division. Johnston welcomed Hood, who was widely and correctly regarded as a fighting general. Hindman, who lost his chance for promotion, submitted his resignation, but Davis refused to accept it.[8]

During the winter Johnston accomplished a great deal. He dramatically transformed the army by bringing about improvements in its supply situation. That success, in turn, helped rebuild morale. So, too, did the system of furloughs he implemented. His reorganization of several parts of the army restoring the division structure that had existed before late 1863 also helped boost the troops' spirits. Under Johnston's early 1864 reorganization several brigades were returned to the divisions to which they had earlier belonged. They, therefore, found themselves reunited with commanders and comrades whom they knew and trusted. A regular program of drill, along with frequent parades, mock battles, and other exercises and ceremonies, improved the tone of the army. By late April new recruits and veterans returning from the hospitals had boosted the army's strength to fifty-five thousand officers and men. In many ways the Army of Tennessee by May 1864 was a much better force than it had been at the end of 1863. Joseph E. Johnston deserves the lion's share of the credit for that transformation.[9]

Johnston had done a fine job with his army's rank and file, but the same could not be said for the relations among his general officers and their personal and professional relationship with him. Many of the old command problems that so bedeviled the army in 1861, 1862, and 1863 lingered on into 1864. Johnston's presence in Dalton, however, gave them a new, more complex form. The arrival of John Bell Hood in late February added yet another layer of complexity to the mess.

Since at least mid-1862 the Army of Tennessee had been severely handicapped by a deep fissure between two groups of its high-ranking officers. Subordinate generals in the army who opposed Braxton Bragg had worked ceaselessly to undermine his authority and to bring about his removal from command. They clashed with a smaller group of loyalist generals who had sought to sustain the embattled Bragg. This rupture had weakened the army and had been a crucial factor in the failure of Confederate command in the West. Much of the long-standing bitterness between the two factions lingered on after Bragg left the army late in 1863.

Early in 1864 President Davis summoned Bragg to Richmond to be his chief military adviser. This new assignment put Bragg in position to continue meddling in the internal affairs of his former army, and over the next eight months he often did so. With Bragg having a powerful voice in Richmond, it would be unlikely, for instance, that any general identified with the old anti-Bragg faction in the Army of Tennessee would receive promotion no matter how capable he proved himself. Conversely, pro-Bragg generals were likely to be favorably regarded by the government even if they were demonstrably less competent than their peers.

Another development loomed even more ominously over the Rebels. With Johnston at the head of the army at Dalton and Bragg at the president's side in Richmond, the intramural squabbles in the Army of Tennessee became tied into the bitter long-standing feud between President Davis and his new commander in North Georgia.

From early 1864 Bragg was an integral part of the Davis administration. Johnston, an avowed enemy of the chief executive, had strong ties to many of the administration's political foes. The two squabbles now connected in such a way that friends of Bragg became also supporters of the president and, therefore, enemies of Johnston. Johnston's advocates were critics of Davis and now of Bragg also. Bragg's old enemies in the army itself, however, did not necessarily become supporters of Johnston.

Those confusing developments led during the winter to an odd situation. Several of Johnston's subordinate generals—Bragg loyalists—in their out-of-channels correspondence with their old chief went out of their way to contradict Johnston's official statements to the government about his army's condition and its capability for an offensive. That correspondence strengthened the impression in Richmond that only Johnston's unwillingness stood in the way of the Rebels' launching a campaign to regain Tennessee. Those letters weakened the government's preexisting frail confidence in Johnston and in so doing greatly decreased the already slight probability that there would be any significant level of cooperation between army headquarters and the administration in Richmond.

The messy situation also led to a strained relationship within the army between Johnston on the one hand and each of his chief subordinates on the other. Johnston and Hardee had had several disputes in the fall of 1863 when they served together in Mississippi. Johnston's gloomy early 1864 picture of the army's condition contrasted sharply with the optimistic reports Hardee had sent to Richmond during his temporary command in December 1863. In the early months of 1864 Johnston usually did not consult at length with Hardee. That slight irked the latter, who, except for the mid-May to mid-June period, ranked second in the army only to the commanding general. Thus Hardee, a bitter enemy of Bragg but then with no special animus toward Davis, did not gravitate into the pro-Johnston camp in early 1864.

Hood, an outsider who spent the first years of the war in Virginia, had no previous connection with either of the preexisting blocs in the army although he owed his promotion in part to Bragg, who had advocated it in the fall of 1863 while in command of the army. Johnston looked to Hood as the officer most likely to help the army. Even as he ignored Hardee, Johnston turned to the new lieutenant general as the subordinate upon whom he could most rely. Hood, meanwhile, carried on unofficial correspondence with some of the Richmond authorities. His letters often contained criticisms of Johnston and were filled with hints that the army could soon take the offensive and regain Tennessee if only its commander were willing to make the effort.

Wheeler, the army's third corps chief, had long been allied with the pro-Bragg faction and, in fact, owed his position almost exclusively to Bragg's patronage. In the first half of 1864 he too sent to Richmond several letters highly critical of Johnston's management of military affairs in North Georgia.

In summary, the high command of the Army of Tennessee was, as the historian Steven Woodworth has termed it, "a pit of vipers." Johnston inherited a command muddle when he reached Dalton—a condition that grew directly from Jefferson Davis's refusal to deal with the problem in earlier years. The situation in the army's high command did not get any better that winter and spring, although the trouble did not take the form of the open revolts that had so often flared up against Bragg. The conflicts in the army's high command were more subtle under Johnston. He may not even have been aware of the situation, but it was to prove very harmful to the Rebels in Georgia that summer. It helped to poison relations and to increase the distrust between Johnston's headquarters and the government. It hampered cooperation among the army's generals, and it opened the way for unscrupulous officers (both within and outside the army) to maneuver against one another in pursuit of personal advancement or to reward their friends and to punish their enemies.

This mess in the Army of Tennessee exacerbated the long-standing turmoil in the army's high command. It added yet one more serious handicap to the great burden carried by the Confederates in North Georgia in 1864.[10]

Quarrels such as those that did so much to weaken the Army of Tennessee seem to be characteristic of large human organizations—especially those without a strong, competent, and respected leader. Only rarely, however, do they have such great consequences for an entire nation. The circumstances that made the situation in Johnston's army so disastrous for the Rebels stemmed directly from the political-military structure of the Confederacy and from the peculiar personalities of Jefferson Davis, Joseph E. Johnston, and Braxton Bragg.

In the Union army, by contrast, the long-standing trust between Grant and Sherman and that developing between Lincoln and Grant meant that such divisions would have no real impact. If, for example, Joseph Hooker wanted to criticize Sherman—and he did—he could find no one in real authority in the Lincoln administration who would pay attention to his tirades. He was reduced to writing whining letters to men who were not really important figures in the Northern government—malcontents such as Secretary of the Treasury Salmon P. Chase, who was soon to be eased out of office before being kicked upstairs to the Supreme Court.[11]

Johnston's critics, on the other hand, would always find President Davis and General Bragg receptive to unfavorable comments about the commander in North Georgia. All the Rebels would pay a very high price for Jefferson Davis's long-standing evasion of the command personnel problems in the West.

CHAPTER FOUR

The Best Laid Plans

Johnston's decision to wait passively in his defensive works at Dalton meant that the Rebel commander had yielded the initiative completely to his opponent. Sherman, therefore, enjoyed the great advantage of selecting the time, place, and manner of opening the campaign. Johnston anticipated that once the advancing Union armies had been defeated, he would be able to assume the offensive. Until Sherman began his operations, however, Johnston and the Confederates would do little other than fortify their position, drill, rest, and wait.

Several high, parallel ridges—some of the last, southernmost dribbles of the great Appalachian Mountains—cut diagonally across the north-western corner of Georgia and extend into northeastern Alabama. These ridges give the whole area the appearance of an old-fashioned washboard. Dalton is situated just to the east of one of these heights. This steep, towering elevation, Rocky Face Ridge, so named because of the sheer rock wall (or palisade) that scars its western side, rises about four miles northwest of Dalton and stretches south for some twenty-three miles almost to the Oostanaula River. Near its southern end this ridge fans out to such an extent (some two and one-half miles east to west) that it is, in fact, three ridges. The westernmost of these heights is Horn Mountain, the center Mill Creek Mountain. At their highest points Rocky Face Ridge and Mill Creek Mountain tower about eight hundred feet above the surrounding valleys, Horn Mountain about six hundred feet.

Three passes offered routes through this mountain barrier. Mill Creek Gap, known locally as Buzzard's Roost, sliced through the ridge imme-diately northwest of Dalton. The Western & Atlantic Railroad and a wagon road passed through this opening in the Rocky Face to link Dalton and Chattanooga. Dug Gap (sometimes called Mill Gap, especially by Sherman's Yankees), a man-made crossing, literally notched the top of the ridge about three miles south of Mill Creek Gap. Some thirteen miles southwest of Dalton, Snake Creek Gap pierced the ridge. A long, narrow passage, Snake Creek Gap ran from north to south between Horn and Mill Creek Mountains. It led into a more open area near Sugar Valley along the right bank of the Oostanaula River a short distance west of the little village of Resaca, where the W&A Railroad crossed the Oostanaula. Only at these three gaps could an army get through the Rocky Face.

The ridge shielded Johnston and the Confederates at Dalton against any direct attack from the west. Rocky Face Ridge, however, was only a small part of the strategic position Johnston would have to hold to keep Sherman's Yankees out of Georgia. The ridge, in fact, constituted no more than the right center of the long line the Rebels had to defend. The right end of the line lay in Crow Valley directly north of Dalton, the left at Rome, some forty miles southwest of Dalton.

The Oostanaula River flows past the southern end of Rocky Face Ridge and then runs off to the southwest. At Rome, some twenty-five miles from the ridge's southern tip (more as the river flows), the Oostanaula joins the Etowah (or Hightower) River, which comes out of the southeast. The two streams unite to form the Coosa, which flows west into Alabama and then turns to the south, eventually reaching the Gulf of Mexico at Mobile.

Johnston's true line of defense began in Crow Valley, ran south along Rocky Face Ridge, and thence continued down the Oostanaula to Rome. It stretched for a few more miles on down the Coosa. Rome was also important because of its industrial capacity, as a river port, and as the western terminus of the Rome Railroad, a branch line that ran east from the city some fifteen miles to join the W&A at Kingston. Although there was no rail line west of Rome, loss of the town would sever Johnston's shortest and most direct line of communication with Rebel forces in Alabama. (A railroad did reach Blue Mountain [now Anniston], Alabama, fifty-five miles southwest of Rome. The Rome–Blue Mountain rail gap was one of the Rebels' great strategic weaknesses.)

The Yankees could reach Rome by marching directly south from Chattanooga through the valleys that paralleled Rocky Face Ridge on the west or by moving southeast from the line of the Tennessee River in North Alabama across several of the ridges that run through the area. Once at Rome, the Northerners would find no significant natural barrier between themselves and Johnston's railroad supply line at Kingston. If the Federals

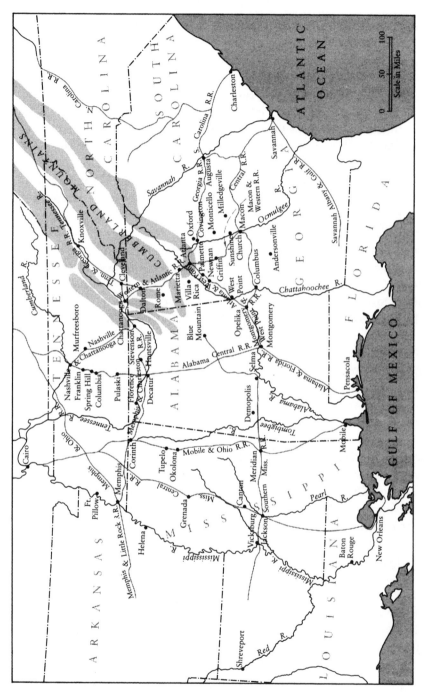

The Western Theater, 1864

chose, they could move southeast from Rome up the Etowah to cut the w&a where it crossed that stream.

A strong Union force poised at Rome would make it impossible for Johnston and the Confederates to remain at Dalton. Johnston would have to attack the Yankees at Rome in an effort to drive them away, flee into the mountain wilderness east of Dalton, or retreat southward as rapidly as possible in an effort to keep a rail link with Atlanta and the rest of Rebeldom. He could not halt such a retreat north of the Etowah, and the point where the w&a crosses that river is some forty-five miles south of Dalton—just about halfway from Dalton to Atlanta.

Johnston realized that he could not remain at Dalton if the Federals occupied Rome, but he seems to have given no serious thought to dealing with the problem. He made only a few references to the matter in his wartime correspondence and none at all in his postwar writings. In four months, from late December 1863 through April 1864, he is not known to have visited Rome or any point south of Dalton except for a brief trip to Atlanta in mid-March. He made but little effort to prepare either Rome or the line of the Oostanaula to block a possible Union advance. He did not try to work out a plan to defend northwestern Georgia in coordination with Lt. Gen. Leonidas Polk, who commanded Secessionist forces in Alabama and Mississippi, although he was advised to do so by Secretary of War James A. Seddon. Nor did Johnston make any effort to work with state authorities to muster whatever help they could provide. In mid-February, when the governor sent two regiments of State Line troops to North Georgia, Johnston posted them at Resaca to guard the bridges there.

Johnston obviously let himself get drawn too deeply into the problem of defending Dalton. He forgot that he was charged with the protection of Georgia and became instead merely the chief of an outpost who focused almost exclusively on matters in his immediate vicinity. "The near danger appears much greater than the distant one," he had written in May 1863. Eight months later he, too, fell into that all-too-common trap.[1]

To be sure, Johnston faced problems aplenty at Dalton. Although the Confederate position there was invulnerable against an attack from the west, it was open to the north in Crow Valley. There no natural barriers would help the Southerners block a Yankee advance. Sherman could move into Crow Valley by coming directly south from East Tennessee or simply by swinging around the northern end of Rocky Face Ridge. If the Federals could thus reach Dalton, they would flank or envelop the Confederate line on the ridge to the west.

The ridge paralleled the Rebels' line of supply, further complicating Johnston's problems and weakening his position. (Ideally, an army's line of supply should run perpendicular to its defensive line.) South of Dalton, all the way to the Oostanaula, the W&A Railroad lay but a short distance east of the base of the ridge. Any Union force that got through Dug Gap, or Snake Creek Gap, or around the southern end of the ridge, or across the Oostanaula downstream from Resaca (where for several miles the tracks paralleled the river) would be positioned to break the railroad and cut off the Secessionists at Dalton from their base in Atlanta. Such a thrust would constitute the same sort of threat to Johnston—although a more immediate one—as would an enemy force at Rome. Should such a force reach and hold the railroad at any point north of the Oostanaula, it might well trap the Confederates in their Dalton fortifications.

If Johnston wanted to remain at Dalton, he would have to seal the entire Crow Valley–Rocky Face Ridge–Oostanaula–Rome line and, perhaps, several miles of the Coosa below Rome as well. It would be a tough job, and it would take complete, accurate, and timely information about Sherman's dispositions as well as great skill, alertness, boldness, and flexibility on Johnston's part.

Like almost all terrain, however, the Confederate position at Dalton had strengths as well as weaknesses. A bold, energetic, alert commander could find several ways to use the Rocky Face to baffle an enemy to the west. The sections of the line along the ridge itself were so strong that no sane general would make a serious attack on them. The ridge also served as a fortress from behind which the Rebels might sally out against isolated parts of any Union force to the west. The Southerners might, for example, launch quick strikes out from Mill Creek Gap or down from Dug Gap into the valley west of the Rocky Face to slow the approach of an enemy or to punish his columns. Good roads and the railroad in the valley east of the ridge gave Johnston the capability of shifting troops quickly between Crow Valley and Resaca to reinforce one or the other end of the ridge.

The railroad, in fact, gave Johnston the means of moving men and supplies from Dalton and the Rocky Face Ridge area all the way to Rome. Troops posted at Resaca, for example, were about midpoint on the long Rebel front and had rail connections to both Crow Valley and Rome. Although the line Johnston had to hold was convex (usually a bad position because it put an army on an exterior line), the W&A in effect gave Johnston an interior line linking Dalton, Resaca, Calhoun (just south of the Oostanaula), and Rome. Rebel troops could move from point to point along that line by rail much more rapidly than Sherman's Unionists could make the corresponding overland marches. The Confederates could also supply themselves by rail while their enemies would have to rely on wagons to haul supplies over rugged terrain and bad roads. In early 1864 at least one small steamboat plied the Oostanaula as far up as Resaca. Johnston could have used it for transportation and as a scouting and patrol vessel along the river part of his front.

Rome itself offered the Confederate commander a point at which to base troops who would threaten the right flank and rear of any enemy force operating against Rebel positions near the southern end of Rocky Face Ridge. If a Yankee presence at Rome would compel Johnston to give up Dalton, a Secessionist force there would, at the least, slow and embarrass any Union operations directed against the Resaca area. Johnston might, for example, have organized his dismounted cavalry temporarily as an infantry division and posted it at Rome, where it would enjoy rail communication with both Dalton and Atlanta. Any Yankees trying to take the town would have to haul their supplies over rough roads from Chattanooga or from the Tennessee River in northern Alabama. Such a ploy would have given Sherman something more to worry about as he planned for the spring.

At Dalton, then, Johnston had both problems and opportunities. Owing to his essentially pessimistic nature, his very limited view of his situation, his reluctance to run a risk lest he fail and open himself to criticism from President Davis, his strong preference for concentrating his troops under his own immediate command, and his general lack of initiative, Johnston saw only the problems that might arise from his situation. Another commander, of a different personality, outlook, temperament, and enjoying a better relationship with his government and subordinates, would have been far more alert to whatever opportunities might come his way and far more likely to have tried to take advantage of them.

A decade after the war Johnston wrote that the position his army occupied at Dalton "had little to recommend it as a defensive one." He then asserted that he would have abandoned it during the winter had not the civilian authorities hoped to launch an offensive from Dalton into Tennessee and stressed "the bad effect of a retrograde movement [from Dalton] upon the spirit of the Southern people." Davis wrote Johnston on January 12, "The falling back of the army would be so detrimental both from military and political considerations."

The Confederate commander thus felt constrained to occupy a position he regarded as weak, which he believed he could not hold because his government hoped to launch an offensive that he thought impracticable and out of a fear that he would damage popular support for the war effort if he retreated. It was a terrible situation for which Jefferson Davis was responsible and a frustrating dilemma for Johnston—exactly the sort of condition in which he could not function very well. Except for objecting to the specifics of various proposals for offensive movements by his army, Johnston explained none of those matters to the Davis administration. He did nothing to prepare either the government or the public for the probability that he would have to abandon Dalton, nor did he give any thought to where he would take his army when he did. Instead, he busied himself in the minutiae of his immediate command.[2]

In the first four months of 1864 Johnston kept his men at work constructing fortifications in the Dalton area to enhance his already strong positions on the ridge and to block the opening through Crow Valley. The Rebels built heavy trenches and artillery emplacements. They dammed Mill Creek to create a water barrier in Buzzard's Roost, and they positioned huge rocks to roll down from the heights onto attacking Yankees. What they did not do was fortify Snake Creek Gap. Indeed, it is not certain that their commander even knew it existed.

By late April the Army of Tennessee occupied a strongly fortified line that resembled a fishhook. The extreme right of the line, the point and barb of the hook, rested in Crow Valley where it bent back to the south and actually faced to the east. The curve of the hook ran from east to west across Crow Valley to Rocky Face Ridge, and the shank stretched off southward along the top of the ridge to Dug Gap, the eye of the hook. (Those familiar with the Battle of Gettysburg will note the similarity of Johnston's line to the position occupied by the Union army on that occasion.) South of Dug Gap Johnston left the ridge completely unoccupied.

Johnston's dispositions and preparations at Dalton adumbrated the general strategy he would employ that spring and summer. He would concentrate his army, deploy it in a naturally strong position, strengthen its front with massive earthworks and other man-made obstacles—and wait in the hope that Sherman would order his men forward in direct frontal assaults on the Rebel fortifications. If the Northern commander did so, Johnston could reasonably expect to inflict heavy losses on the attackers. If Sherman did not. . . .[3]

While Johnston sought some way to thwart the coming Union advance into Georgia, his Yankee counterpart had to decide how to execute his role in the Federal grand strategy for 1864. Sherman's mission was to defeat the Confederate army in North Georgia or at least to keep the Rebel commander in his front so busy that he could not detach troops to reinforce Secessionist armies in other areas.

Grant's instructions to Sherman came in a letter penned on April 4 and were simple enough: "You I propose to move against Johnston's army, to break it up, and to get into the interior of the enemy's country as far as you can, inflicting all the damage you can against their war resources." Grant left the details of carrying out this mission to his trusted lieutenant. Because Grant gave him a free hand, Sherman would have the opportunity in 1864 to put into practice some ideas about warfare he had developed over the past three years.

William T. Sherman had never been, was not in 1864, and probably never would have become a very good battlefield general. He simply did not (or could not) handle very well all the tactical details involved in commanding an army in battle. Nor did he have the "killer instinct"— the driving compulsion to inflict maximum casualties on his opponent.

Sherman's concept of how the Federal government should go about waging its war against the seceded states may have stemmed in part from his own long association with the South and Southerners. He was fighting men whose families he knew and admired. Some of the enemies his forces met in battle were the very boys who had been students in the school in Louisiana (now Louisiana State University) that he had superintended before the war. Sherman, moreover, agreed with the Confederates about almost every public issue except secession. In part, also, his attitude may have been the result of a, perhaps subconscious, realization that battles were uncertain affairs at best. Often they did not turn out as those who initiated them envisioned.

At some level Sherman may also have sensed what students of military history now realize to have been one of the key developments of the mid-nineteenth century: technological changes in weaponry, especially the development of rifled shoulder arms with their greatly enhanced accuracy and increased killing range, had so augmented the defensive power of

an army that it was almost impossible for any military force to win a
"decisive" battlefield victory.

The only exceptions to this tactical reality came when a general managed to maneuver to catch his enemy completely by surprise, or to bring
overwhelming numbers to bear on the opposing army or a part of it, or
when faulty deployment or some other command error made it impossible
for an enemy force to hold its position. Even when an army was beaten
in battle, it could usually get away to fight again another day. In many
cases the victorious army suffered such heavy casualties that it was in no
condition to follow up on its battlefield success.

For those reasons it was most unlikely that any large force handled by a
general of even mediocre ability could be "destroyed" in battle. If beaten
at all, it would more likely lose through long-term attrition (which, in all
probability, would also force the victor to pay a heavy price), or because
it had lost the will to fight, or because the society for which it fought had
been cut out from under it.

We shall never know how much of this Sherman consciously understood in April 1864, how much he only sensed, or why. We do know that he
stood apart from virtually all his contemporaries who doggedly plodded
along trying to win the great, decisive battle that would settle everything.
He believed in the winter of 1863–64, or would soon come to believe, that
it was more effective to wage war against an enemy society—its morale,
economy, transportation system—than against its armies. "Whenever a
result can be achieved without battle," Sherman wrote in January 1864,
"I prefer it."

In effect, Sherman eventually came to envision a war of raids aimed at
the enemy's society rather than a war of battles against its armies. Raids, of
course, had long been a feature of warfare. Almost always, however, they
had been conducted by relatively small, quick-striking, usually mounted
forces and had been intended only to penetrate behind the opposing army,
wreck or damage some objective, and hasten back to friendly lines.

In 1864, by contrast, the North was to adopt the practice of making
raids with entire armies—massive forces (infantry and artillery as well
as cavalry) strong enough to fight their way to an objective and able
to wreck it thoroughly when they got there. Since they did not seek to
occupy an area but only to destroy its usefulness to the enemy, they could
then march on to another goal. Eventually, of course, they would have
to return to friendly territory. In 1864 two factors made such a strategy
especially appealing to the Federals. The Confederacy had been reduced

to such a small area (thanks to Grant's 1862–63 victories) that, once a raiding force broke into the interior, it could quickly pass entirely across Rebeldom, and the presence of the Union navy along the coast meant that the raiding column would find friendly territory at any point where it could reach salt water.

Sherman would eventually come to practice this form of warfare even as almost all other generals fought great, bloody, inconclusive battles in futile attempts to destroy the enemy. In 1864, ironically, Sherman was to be presented with two opportunities (almost unmatched in the war) when—in all probability—he could, with relative ease, have destroyed the army that opposed him. He rejected both.[4]

Although Sherman may not have handled an army on the battlefield very well, he did have a grasp of grand strategy and the larger military issues of the war that few of his contemporaries could match. He knew the defensive strength of Johnston's position at Dalton, and he knew from his first moment as commander of the Military Division of the Mississippi that he was not going to shatter his armies in futile assaults against it. Sherman, in fact, knew northwestern Georgia better than did his Confederate counterpart. He had ridden over much of the region in the 1840s when his duties as an army officer took him there. Johnston, in contrast, had viewed the area only while traveling along the railroad five or six times before 1864.

Studying his maps, the Yankee commander quickly grasped the importance of Rome. Within a week after assuming command of the Military Division of the Mississippi, Sherman was making inquiries about possible routes across northeastern Alabama from the Decatur area to the Coosa River valley.

Soon Sherman's plan had taken shape. He would send McPherson and the Army of the Tennessee from their bases in northern Alabama and South Central Tennessee to the Rome area. Banks's campaign from New Orleans against Mobile would draw Rebel forces in Alabama toward the Gulf Coast, opening the way for McPherson. Meanwhile, Thomas and Schofield would move against the northern end of Johnston's position at Dalton. They would endeavor to distract the Confederates there from events going on off to the southwest and to fix them in their Dalton fortifications, but they would not make a major attack.

Once McPherson entered the Coosa River valley near Rome, the Rebels could not remain at Dalton and, Sherman thought, probably would not make another stand north of the Etowah River. Sherman, in fact, anticipated that the Confederate commander would abandon not only Dalton but also the remainder of North Georgia and retreat all the way to Atlanta.

Years later several historians would seek to make much of the allegation that in adopting this plan to open the campaign Sherman violated both the letter and the spirit of Grant's instructions. Sherman, they charge, chose to neglect the first part of his orders (to "break up" Johnston's army) in favor of the second (to "get into the interior" of the Confederacy to wreck its resources). Grant's instructions to Sherman must be understood as general guidelines, not as a specific timetable. Grant did not direct his subordinate to defeat the Army of Tennessee, *then* get into the interior. His instructions read *and* get into the interior. Perhaps Grant chose to list the two goals alphabetically or, more likely, to put the shorter one first for the sake of style (Grant was a fine writer). At any rate the criticism—like so much historical writing—is much ado about nothing. Grant knew what Sherman intended and could have overruled him had he thought it necessary. When Sherman explained in a letter of April 10 that he expected to maneuver Johnston as far as Atlanta without a major battle, Grant raised no objection.

McPherson's army—and be it not forgotten that it had been Sherman's and even earlier Grant's—thus became the key element in the Federal plan. Four divisions that were slated to be part of McPherson's force, however, were absent when Sherman devised the opening moves of the campaign (two from the XVI Corps in the Lower Mississippi Valley; two from the XVII Corps in Illinois). By late April, when those absent units rejoined the army in North Alabama, McPherson would have nine divisions totaling some forty thousand to forty-five thousand men. His army would then be strong enough to venture far out into Alabama and Georgia on a campaign such as Sherman anticipated.[5]

Originally Grant had hoped to have the Yankee armies begin their spring offensive on April 27. Bad weather in Virginia hampered his preparations there and forced him to postpone the opening date of the campaign until the thirtieth. Then, at Sherman's request, he agreed to a further delay, first until May 2 and then until the fifth.

At noon on April 28 Sherman left Nashville, transferring his headquarters to Chattanooga, and "prepared for taking the field in person." Some thirty-five miles southeast of Chattanooga Joseph E. Johnston and the Confederates also realized that the time for opening the campaign was at hand.

The great struggle for North Georgia would be waged by one general who did not want to fight except in very limited circumstances and under conditions that seemed never to exist and by another who preferred not to fight at all.[6]

CHAPTER FIVE

To the Oostanaula

By the time Sherman moved his headquarters from Nashville to Chattanooga, Grant's grand strategy for the Union's 1864 military operations had begun to fall apart. It had, in fact, started to unravel even before Grant conceived it.

In January 1864 high officials in the Lincoln administration had decided to send a military expedition up the Red River into western Louisiana. They also hoped to occupy a portion of East Texas. The campaign evolved out of a complex mixture of diplomatic, economic, military, and political motives. American military forces in the area might help dissuade the French government from its efforts to establish control over Mexico. The scheme might also result in acquisition of large quantities of cotton that would enrich powerful men in the North. Whatever the motives behind it, the Red River Expedition took on a life of its own. It was to have a profound effect on the struggle for North Georgia.

Federal authorities selected Maj. Gen. Nathaniel P. Banks, then in charge of occupied New Orleans, as commander of the Red River force. The troops assigned to the expedition included two veteran divisions of the XVI Corps and a detachment from the XVII Corps. Northern planners assumed that Banks could quickly reestablish a strong Federal presence in western Louisiana, return the borrowed Army of the Tennessee troops to McPherson in northern Alabama, and then launch his own campaign against Mobile in accordance with Grant's 1864 concept.

Unfortunately for the Unionists, Banks did not get his expedition under way on time. He then ran into a strong Rebel force at Mansfield, Louisiana, where he suffered a defeat on April 8. Over the following weeks, Banks came close to losing the fleet accompaning his column because the falling water level in the river almost stranded the vessels. The campaign turned into a fiasco.

By the time Banks extracted his army and got the expedition and the fleet to safety, it was too late to return the borrowed troops to McPherson for the campaign in Georgia. Banks's losses and the general chaos that failure of the expedition created in his own command compelled him to abandon the projected effort against Mobile. The Rebels had won the first round of the 1864 campaign.

As April wore along, Sherman became increasingly concerned about his absent troops. On the twentieth, while still in Nashville, he heard "a rumor" that Banks had been checked along the Red River. Additional reports received the next afternoon confirmed the rumor and also brought the unwelcome news that Banks refused "for obvious reasons" to release the troops he had borrowed from the Army of the Tennessee. On the twenty-second Grant formally notified Sherman that those men would not be joining him in Georgia. "Do not let this delay or embarrass," admonished Grant.

Loss of the Army of the Tennessee veterans forced Sherman to alter his plans. With only seven, rather than the anticipated nine, divisions, McPherson's army would be reduced to about thirty-five thousand men and, Sherman feared, would be too weak to operate at a great distance from the main Federal column. The potential danger to McPherson increased when Banks canceled the campaign against Mobile, thereby freeing Confederate forces in Mississippi and Alabama from the need to defend the Gulf Coast and releasing them to move north to oppose the Army of the Tennessee.

On April 23, therefore, Sherman abandoned the planned march on Rome and changed the Army of the Tennessee's objective. He ordered McPherson to cross the Tennessee River and move directly east to Lebanon, Alabama, and thence on to Summerville, Georgia. At Summerville, McPherson would be about twenty miles northwest of Rome. Depending on the circumstances, he could then turn toward Rome or go north to LaFayette and then east through Ship's (now Maddox) Gap in Taylor's Ridge to the small crossroads hamlet of Villanow. From Villanow the Yankees could turn south and march about thirty miles to Rome or continue east some three miles into the northern end of Snake Creek Gap.

If he took the latter route, McPherson would remain much closer to Thomas and the Army of the Cumberland, thereby greatly diminishing

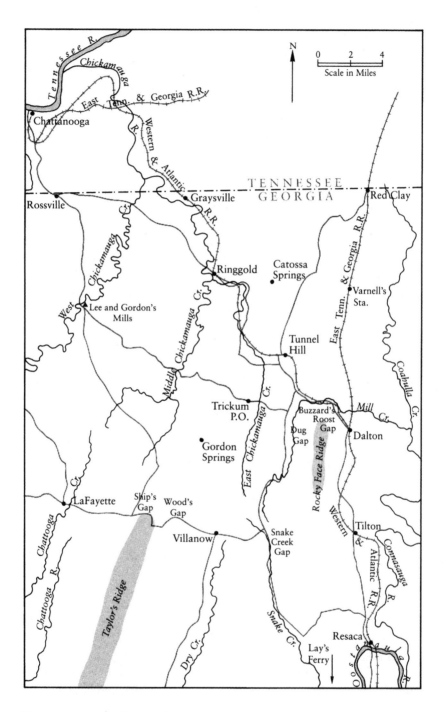

Chattanooga to the Oostanaula

the likelihood that the Confederates would pounce on his isolated force. Still thinking only of prying Johnston out of his strong Dalton fortifications, Sherman believed that McPherson's presence in the LaFayette-Villanow-Rome area would compel the Rebels to abandon northwestern Georgia and retreat southward along the railroad.

More bad news soon reached the Federal commander. For several days he had suspected that he would have to begin the campaign without the two XVII Corps divisions then in Illinois as well as without the troops who were stuck in Louisiana with Banks. The XVII Corps units had run into administrative problems that delayed them, and they had not yet even reached their rendezvous at Cairo, Illinois. By April 27 it became obvious that the XVII Corps units would not arrive in time and that McPherson would have only five divisions totaling some twenty-four thousand men. With the opening of the campaign only days away, Sherman had to make yet another alteration in his plans.

The Federal commander decided to abandon the projected move on Rome. He would have McPherson march from the Decatur-Huntsville, Alabama, area up the north side of the Tennessee River into Chattanooga. From Chattanooga the Army of the Tennessee would go south toward LaFayette, marching through the valley west of Taylor's Ridge. Sherman instructed McPherson to turn east and proceed through Villanow and Snake Creek Gap to cut Johnston's railroad near Resaca.

Part of Thomas's army would be in the valley east of Taylor's Ridge, confronting the Rebels on Rocky Face Ridge. Taylor's Ridge would screen McPherson's column from Confederate observers on the Rocky Face. At the same time, the several gaps in Taylor's Ridge would permit fairly easy communication between McPherson and Thomas. Under this new scheme McPherson's force would simply operate as the right element of Sherman's army group, not as an independent column many miles removed from the main body.

In making this third plan, Sherman adopted a suggestion put forth several weeks earlier by Thomas. During some late February skirmishing in the Dalton area the Thirty-ninth Indiana Mounted Infantry of the XIV Corps had surprised the Rebels at Dug Gap, seized that pass, and held it for several hours until chased away by Confederate reinforcements. Although in itself unimportant, this episode drew Thomas's attention to the part of Rocky Face Ridge south of Mill Creek Gap. Soon some of his scouts discovered Snake Creek Gap and brought word that Johnston had done nothing to obstruct or fortify it.

This discovery led Thomas in March to propose that his great Army of the Cumberland swing through Snake Creek Gap and seize Johnston's railroad in the Resaca area just east of the southern end of the gap. Sherman rejected the idea in favor of his planned move on Rome.

In the changed circumstances of late April Sherman resurrected Thomas's suggestion with two major changes. Because, Sherman said, he wanted to use the large Army of the Cumberland as a stable base around which to maneuver the smaller, more nimble armies of McPherson and Schofield, he would send the Army of the Tennessee through Snake Creek Gap. Once east of the Rocky Face, McPherson would simply cut the railroad and then fall back to the west. When Johnston abandoned Dalton and retreated, as Sherman believed he then would have to do, McPherson would attack his flank. Meanwhile, Thomas and Schofield, following hard on the heels of the Rebels, would assail Johnston from the north.

With the Oostanaula on the south and a stronger Yankee force attacking from the north and west, thought Sherman, Johnston's army should be trapped and destroyed or dispersed into the mountains to the east. It might, therefore, turn out that Sherman—a general who preferred maneuver to battle—would destroy his enemy in a great battle at the very beginning of a campaign that he had hoped to wage by maneuver.[1]

While Sherman in Nashville made and altered his plans, Johnston sat at his headquarters desk in Dalton, puzzled over his maps, and studied the various reports he received. He was trying to determine what move his enemy would attempt. Once he had done that, he then had to work out the best way to thwart the coming onslaught. Since he was outnumbered (and believed himself more outnumbered than he, in fact, was), Johnston knew that his best hope was to ascertain where Sherman would strike and then to concentrate enough Rebel troops at that point in time to mount a successful defense. If he discerned Sherman's objective soon enough and acted quickly, the Confederates would have a chance. If he failed to penetrate Sherman's designs, they would not. Information ("intelligence" in military jargon) thus became the key to Johnston's hope of keeping Sherman out of Georgia.

During the winter and spring Johnston's scouts and patrols brought back intelligence about the Yankee forces in southeastern Tennessee. An intelligent and experienced general, Johnston also organized (or may have inherited from Bragg) a system of spies in Chattanooga, Nashville, and other points behind Sherman's lines. From those sources the Confederate commander had derived enough information to develop by mid- to late April a surprisingly accurate picture of Sherman's intentions.

Johnston knew the general positions of Sherman's major units, especially those units in the Army of the Cumberland that, from their base in Chattanooga, most directly threatened the Secessionists at Dalton. The Southern commander also knew or guessed that the Yankees in Chattanooga would move directly against his positions around Mill Creek Gap and on the Crow Valley line. He believed they would strike at the northern end of Rocky Face Ridge and menace Dalton from the north. The Crow Valley area, he thought, was the weakest part of the Rebel position at Dalton and, therefore, would be the most logical objective for the Federals.

It is also clear, both from the correspondence of the Southern generals and from their subsequent actions, that Johnston was convinced that, simultaneously with Sherman's movement on Dalton, McPherson would cross the Tennessee River and march either southeast directly for Rome or south into the interior of Alabama toward the Selma-Montgomery area. If McPherson's column moved on the latter objective, it would be operating entirely in Central Alabama and—under Confederate military policy—would be of no immediate concern to Johnston. If, however, McPherson's goal was Rome, his troops would cross the northeastern corner of Alabama and become a real threat to the Confederates at Dalton.

By the last week in April Johnston knew that the opening of the campaign was not far distant, and he began to prepare his army for active operations. As early as April 19 he had directed Wheeler to move Maj. Gen. Will T. Martin's cavalry division from its winter camps to the Rome area, and he posted two brigades of recently arrived cavalry reinforcements at Resaca, the midpoint on his long Dalton-Rome front. He instructed the commanding officer at Rome to rush work on the fortifications there, using slave labor to help with the construction. On April 24 the infantry brigade of Brig. Gen. James Cantey, come from southeastern Alabama to reinforce Johnston, reached its newly assigned post at Rome. For the moment, Johnston believed, he could do no more to protect Rome against what he saw as only possible danger. The very real threat at Dalton seemed too great.

Convinced that Sherman's main effort would be in Crow Valley, Johnston focused almost all his attention on that area. In the last days of April and into the beginning of May his scouts brought an almost steady stream

of reports, most of which indicated a massive Federal concentration before the northern end of Rocky Face Ridge and in Crow Valley.[2]

Schofield's army shifted down from Knoxville, moved through Cleveland,
Tennessee, and Red Clay, Georgia, and by May 6 had deployed in front
of Johnston's Crow Valley fortifications. The IV Corps of the Army of the
Cumberland, which had been posted at Cleveland, preceded Schofield
through Red Clay and then sidled westward to confront the Rebels on
the northern tip of Rocky Face Ridge. At the same time, the massive
XIV Corps lurched out from its winter camps to Ringgold about twelve
miles northwest of Dalton and the point where the Western & Atlantic
Railroad passed through Taylor's Ridge. Meanwhile, the XX Corps left
its camps in the valley west of Lookout Mountain, moved through Chattanooga, turned south along the western side of Taylor's Ridge, and then
passed eastward through the ridge to Trickum in the valley west of the
Rocky Face.

Those movements had been completed by nightfall on May 7. As a
result, Sherman had brought the armies of Schofield and Thomas into a
line that began with Hooker's XX Corps on the right in the valley west of
Dug Gap and curved around the northern end of Rocky Face Ridge to
Schofield's XXIII Corps on the left in Crow Valley. A division of cavalry
was on Hooker's right; another protected Schofield's left. (The other two
divisions of Yankee cavalry, delayed by horse procurement problems, were
on the way to the front from Kentucky.) Of all those movements Johnston
had timely and reasonably accurate reports.

As the Union advance developed, Johnston posted the Army of Tennessee to meet the enemy. He entrusted what he believed to be the
most important sector of his Dalton line—the right—to John Bell Hood,
which probably indicated that he regarded Hood as his more reliable
infantry corps commander. Hood, in turn, placed the division of Maj.
Gen. Alexander P. Stewart with its left at Mill Creek Gap and its line
running north along Rocky Face Ridge. Hood's other divisions, those
under Maj. Gens. Carter L. Stevenson and Thomas C. Hindman, held
the Rebel lines in Crow Valley. Johnston even detached two of Hardee's
divisions, commanded by Maj. Gens. Benjamin Franklin Cheatham and
William B. Bate, and sent them to Hood to bolster his defenses on Rocky
Face Ridge. Johnston kept Hardee himself, with the other divisions of
his corps (those of Maj. Gens. Patrick R. Cleburne and William H. T.
Walker) in reserve near Dalton. Wheeler placed almost all his available

cavalry at Tunnel Hill, about four miles northwest of Mill Creek Gap. When the Yankees drove his horsemen back, Wheeler shifted most of them to join his troopers in Crow Valley. Johnston had his army well in hand, strongly fortified, and admirably placed to defend the northern end of his position.

The great weakness in the Rebel commander's situation was his very skimpy knowledge about Federal activities on, and to the southwest of, his left. In early May, while skirmishing flared at Tunnel Hill, around the northern end of Rocky Face Ridge, and along the lines in Crow Valley, Johnston received very little in-depth intelligence from the southwest. To a large degree this dearth of information was owing to Wheeler's poor deployment and use of his cavalry. Wheeler was far more interested in massing his troopers for a great mounted battle than in using them for routine scouting and patrol duty. Johnston, however, must bear the responsibility. He did not insist that his cavalry commander make better use of his horsemen, and he seems not to have had much interest in events on his left. As a result, he did not get the vital intelligence he needed. Johnston's fixed conviction that if McPherson moved into Georgia he would march on Rome blinded him to other possible meanings of reports he did receive from the south and west.

As late as May 4 Johnston took time to wire Lt. Gen. Leonidas Polk, commanding Rebel forces in the Department of Alabama, Mississippi, and East Louisiana, "Should McPherson advance from Gunter's Landing instead of Decatur toward Rome, will your troops operate against him?" The difference was crucial. If McPherson crossed the Tennessee River at Decatur, he would enter the part of Alabama for which Polk was responsible. If, on the other hand, he shifted east to cross at Gunter's Landing (at the southernmost bend of the river), he would bypass Polk's area of responsibility and enter a small part of northeastern Alabama that Johnston was supposed to defend.

Meanwhile, with Sherman's advance under way, the Confederate government bestirred itself to reinforce Johnston. Several small units from the South Atlantic Coast and others from the Mobile area were ordered to the army at Dalton. The Rebels in North Georgia, however, needed much more help, and on May 4 Johnston dispatched an urgent telegram to Richmond requesting that some of Polk's troops join him from Alabama "until the enemy can be met."

Bragg, in Richmond, reacted to the emergency by ordering Polk to send to Johnston the infantry division of Maj. Gen. William W. Loring, then near Montevallo in Central Alabama. Meanwhile, President Davis—without coordinating with Bragg—directed Polk to join Johnston in person and to take with him all the troops who could be spared from the defense of Alabama and Mississippi.

By that time Polk had concluded that McPherson's Federals along the Tennessee River would not strike directly southward. Removal of that danger meant that it was no longer necessary to hold large numbers of troops to defend Alabama. This consideration and the fact that Davis had ordered him to Georgia in person led Polk to take with him most of the troops of his old command—three infantry divisions and a cavalry division, in all more than twenty thousand men. (The total includes Cantey's troops, other units from the Mobile area, and Loring's Division.)

Even though it had been obvious for some time that the campaign would soon open, Polk still had his units scattered all across Alabama. When Davis's order reached him, he began to collect them and put them in motion for Blue Mountain (Anniston), some fifty-five miles southwest of Rome and the eastern terminus of the railroad which they could use for transportation to that point. Still thinking in terms of Johnston's May 4 message, Polk planned to concentrate his command at Blue Mountain to oppose what he assumed would be McPherson's march from Gunter's Landing against Rome.[3]

Johnston changed the deployment of his forces on May 5 and 6. Knowing that Polk's troops were on the way to Blue Mountain and having received reports that the Yankees in North Alabama were moving northeast up the Tennessee River toward Chattanooga rather than southeast toward Rome, he concluded that he should shift even more of his strength to the northern end of his line. He, therefore, ordered the two cavalry brigades at Resaca to join the rest of Wheeler's horsemen in Crow Valley above Dalton. He also directed Cantey to move his infantry from Rome to replace the cavalry at Resaca. Martin was ordered to assume command at Rome.

On May 7 Johnston telegraphed Polk that he should move all his troops to Rome as rapidly as possible, and he ordered Martin's cavalry from Rome to Calhoun to watch the Oostanaula between those two towns. Johnston also instructed Cantey to bring his infantry from Resaca to Dalton. Later in the day, however, the Rebel commander canceled this last order and directed Cantey to remain at Resaca, holding his troops ready to come to Dalton by rail while he watched the roads leading from LaFayette to the Resaca area.

By May 7 Johnston had received a trickle of reports on Yankee activities off to the northwest of Dalton. Lee and Gordon's Mill stood on Chickamauga Creek, west of Taylor's Ridge, some eighteen miles west-northwest of Dalton and about twelve miles north of LaFayette. As early as May 5 Johnston knew that Federal troops (reported to be Hooker's XX Corps) were there. Soon, more reports came in revealing that Hooker had moved east to confront Rocky Face Ridge but that McPherson's men were at Lee and Gordon's and then at LaFayette. Johnston, however, still focused most of his attention on events in Crow Valley and along the northern part of Rocky Face Ridge. When he did give thought to McPherson, Johnston assumed that he would march south from Lee and Gordon's through LaFayette. McPherson's objective, Johnston still believed, was Rome.[4]

Sunday, May 8, brought fierce Union attacks on the northern end of Rocky Face Ridge and at Dug Gap. At the former point, Yankees from Howard's IV Corps scrambled up onto the ridge and fought their way southward along its narrow crest (a "knife edge," Sherman called it) until they reached the main Confederate line, which at that point ran across the ridge top and eastward down into Crow Valley. They could go no farther. "We are," one Union general reported, "butt up against the enemy and may not be able to advance for some time."

Meanwhile, a division of the XX Corps stormed up out of the valley west of Rocky Face Ridge and made a heavy assault on Dug Gap, which was defended by two regiments of Arkansas mounted rifles and one of Kentucky cavalry. Four Union regiments, the 33d New Jersey, 73d Pennsylvania, and 134th and 154th New York, made it to the top of the ridge, but the Rebels soon drove them back. Fighting desperately, the Southerners managed to hold their position until reinforcements arrived to secure the Southerners' hold on the gap.

Sherman lost about four hundred men in those assaults, inflicted very few casualties on the Confederates, and gained no ground of any importance. The attacks, however, served their purpose. They kept Johnston's attention fixed on the Dalton area. Late that evening the leading units of McPherson's column—the Ninth Illinois Mounted Infantry and the Thirty-ninth Iowa Infantry regiments—reached Snake Creek Gap and found it unoccupied, unguarded, unobstructed, and unobserved. McPherson had completed one of the great strategic marches of the war. In retrospect, we can see that, in all likelihood, his seizure of the gap determined the outcome of the campaign. After May 8 Johnston could not long remain in his Dalton works unless he detached troops to regain Snake Creek Gap. Given the passive way he was determined to conduct his operations, he could not undo the damage.

McPherson's march, which took the XV and XVI Corps from North Alabama through Chattanooga, to Lee and Gordon's Mill, and on via LaFayette and Villanow to Snake Creek Gap, had not gone undetected. Over the previous few days Johnston got enough reports from his scouts to know the general position and route of the Army of the Tennessee, but he persisted in his assumption that McPherson's objective was Rome.

Sometime in the forenoon of that eighth of May Johnston again ordered Cantey to move his brigade from Resaca to Dalton. At 12:10 P.M., however, probably in response to a report from Cantey that Federal troops were at Villanow, Johnston countermanded the order and directed Cantey only to "hold his brigade ready" to move by rail to Dalton while watching the "approaches from Villanow and LaFayette." That evening Johnston instructed the cavalry brigade of Col. J. Warren Grigsby, one regiment of which had spent the day fighting at Dug Gap, to move south to Snake Creek Gap.

A civilian guide unintentionally led Grigsby's horsemen astray, and they did not reach the gap until dawn of May 9. As the leading units approached the southern mouth of the gap, they ran into a small band of Yankee cavalrymen. Charging, the Southerners chased the Federals back into the gap, where Union infantrymen interrupted their breakfast to repulse the attack. Snake Creek Gap was in Yankee hands, and the Confederates were not strong enough to wrest it away.[5]

Later that morning a happy, optimistic McPherson pushed his column out from the mouth of Snake Creek Gap to cut the railroad near Resaca, some eight or nine miles to the east. Dodge with the XVI Corps took the lead; Logan's XV Corps protected the rear. Poor roads, rough terrain, and stout resistance from Grigsby's troopers slowed the advance.

Not until early afternoon did the head of Dodge's column reach a crossroads some two miles west of Resaca. There, in obedience to orders, Dodge left one division of his corps to guard against any Confederate force coming from the north. With his other division he pushed on to the east. McPherson's column, originally scheduled to consist of nine divisions, then reduced to seven, then to five, had been whittled down to one as its advance closed on its objective.

It was not enough—not even when units of the XV Corps came up and relieved Dodge's reserve division so it could join the advance. McPherson, with the lead units, saw to his front the Rebel fortifications at Resaca and to his left (north) good roads running south from Dalton. Isolated from other Federal units, not knowing how many Secessionists were at Resaca (it was Cantey with about four thousand men), and fearing that Johnston might have sent troops from Dalton south to strike the left flank of his column, McPherson decided that the risk was too great. He would preserve what he had gained. Accordingly, he halted Dodge's advance, the leading units of which were within two hundred yards of the railroad. Soon he drew back to the southern end of Snake Creek Gap to entrench. A small party of Northern horsemen had managed to reach the Western & Atlantic a short distance north of Resaca but had been unable to do more than cut the telegraph wires and burn a wood station.

Sherman's great effort to cut Johnston's supply line had come very close to success, but it had failed. Then and later, Sherman, typically and ungraciously, sought to blame the failure on others. McPherson, he wrote on several occasions, had been "timid" and had not acted with the necessary vigor. In truth, the failure rested squarely on Sherman. He had chosen to send a relatively weak column to Snake Creek Gap. (Any one of Thomas's three massive infantry corps was almost as strong as McPherson's total force.) Sherman had not provided McPherson with adequate cavalry. As a result, the column often had to halt while infantrymen performed scouting duties that should have been handled by mounted units. Two of Sherman's four cavalry divisions had not yet come up from the rear, but there was no good reason why at least some of the mounted units on Hooker's right in the valley north of Villanow could not have joined McPherson's once he cleared Taylor's Ridge, thereby providing him with the horsemen he needed. Sherman's failure to strengthen McPherson adequately is even more puzzling because as early as May 6 the Federals knew that Polk's troops were moving from Alabama to Georgia. Still, from a larger perspective, McPherson had given Sherman a great success. With Snake Creek Gap in Northern hands, Johnston and the Rebels could not long remain at Dalton.

For the Southerners it could have been much worse. Johnston had been completely fooled. Only the weakness of McPherson's column and that general's unwillingness to push on to the railroad had saved the Rebels from a calamitous defeat at the very opening of the campaign.

The Confederate commander had guessed wrong in two major respects. He had concentrated far too many of his troops in the Dalton area, and he had remained fixated much too long on the possible threat to Rome. He had left Snake Creek Gap completely open, and his defenses at Resaca were suited for protecting the bridges there from a cavalry raid, not for holding off a major attack by a large force. The place to have defended Resaca against such a force as Sherman sent against it from the northwest was Snake Creek Gap. Johnston's failure to guard that passage was one of the great mistakes of the war.

(The gap, we should remember, runs from north to south and leads around rather than through the southern end of Rocky Face Ridge. It is several miles from Resaca, and it cannot be seen from the town or from any point on the railroad. Its importance to the defense of Resaca would, therefore, not have been apparent to those in the town, although anyone who went over the ground would immediately realize that the Rebels had to hold the gap if they wanted to stay in Dalton.)

When Johnston transferred Cantey and his troops from Rome to Resaca, he did not inform Cantey of the existence of the gap or alert him to its importance. At the same time, Johnston shifted the cavalry brigades that had been at Resaca to Dalton. Cantey was unfamiliar with the Resaca area, and those horsemen would have been a great help to him. Deployed in the valley west of the southern end of Rocky Face Ridge or at Villanow and along Taylor's Ridge, they would have rendered far more valuable service to the Confederacy than they could ever have done at Dalton.

Cantey did not reach Resaca until, at the earliest, sometime on May 5, and on the seventh he received orders to move his troops to Dalton as soon as the brigade of Brig. Gen. Daniel H. Reynolds, then en route from Mobile, arrived at Resaca. Johnston soon changed that order and held Cantey at Resaca, but as late as 12:00 M., May 8, he had him under instructions to move to Dalton. Even when Johnston countermanded the order a few minutes after noon, he instructed Cantey to keep his troops ready to rush to Dalton by rail. Little wonder that Cantey and the Rebels at Resaca paid slight, if any, attention to Snake Creek Gap. Almost all the orders Johnston sent to the forces at Resaca would have drawn their attention toward the north, not the west. Clearly, Johnston did not grasp the importance of the gap or understand the objective of Sherman's movements.[6]

The Northern commander was disappointed ("much vexed," according to one of his officers) when he learned that McPherson had failed to break the railroad, but he wasted little time pining over the lost opportunity. Realizing the great advantage he had gained, Sherman soon decided to move most of his other units to join McPherson. On May 10 one of Hooker's divisions and the cavalry division that had been on the right of the Army of the Cumberland marched to reinforce the Army of the Tennessee. All day on the eleventh troops, wagons, and guns crowded the roads west of Rocky Face Ridge. Heavy rains and poor roads slowed the march somewhat, but by nightfall on the twelfth almost all of Sherman's troops except the IV Corps and two divisions of cavalry that remained in front of Dalton were in or near Snake Creek Gap.

While Sherman's soldiers plodded southward, the Confederate high command continued its efforts to determine Yankee intentions. On May 9 the Rebels received a scout's report that "Logan & Dodge under McPherson [are] on an expedition to Resaca." Other sources, however, reported Hooker's troops menacing Cantey at Resaca. Many Southerners seem to have viewed the abortive thrust out from Snake Creek Gap on May 9 as simply a raid, not a major effort intended to sever their line of supply and communication with Atlanta and force them out of Dalton.

Johnston himself spent at least part of May 9 with Hood in Crow Valley. He did not return to his Dalton headquarters until 9:00 P.M. When he did, Hood accompanied him. After studying the reports that had come into his headquarters, Johnston ordered Hood with three divisions (two of them detached from Hardee) to Resaca. Early the next morning Hood sent word from Resaca that the Yankees had retired from before the town and advised Johnston to "hold on to Dalton" and to "look out for Dug Gap." That afternoon Hood was back in Dalton. One of the divisions he had taken to Resaca returned and went to Dug Gap. The other two halted at Tilton on the railroad about halfway between Dalton and Resaca.

On May 11 the Confederates at Dug Gap reported an "immense wagon train" toiling southward in the valley west of Rocky Face Ridge. That afternoon Hood, who had returned to Resaca, reported "no enemy within 4 miles," but a scout telegraphed Johnston from Calhoun, "30,000 [Federals] between S. Ck Gap & Resaca." Fortunately for the Rebels, the leading units of Polk's reinforcements from Alabama reached Resaca that day, as did Polk himself. Johnston instructed Polk to have all his men move on from Rome to Resaca as fast as possible.

Polk's arrival brought changes in the army's high command structure and its organization. The infantry units that came from Alabama eventually constituted a third infantry corps in the Army of Tennessee (although for a while, Polk's command remained technically a separate army operating with Johnston's force). The cavalry division that Polk brought remained an independent unit commanded by Brig. Gen. William H. Jackson. With Polk's arrival, the Confederate army in Georgia was organized into three infantry corps under Polk, Hardee, and Hood, a cavalry corps under Wheeler, and an independent cavalry division under Jackson. Once all Polk's troops arrived, Johnston almost always kept Wheeler's cavalry on the right flank of his army and used Jackson to guard the left.

Since Polk outranked Hardee, he became the army's second in command. The bishop's presence, however, did not alter relations among the army's high generals or between army headquarters and Richmond. In 1862 and 1863 Polk had been the leader of the anti-Bragg faction in the army. Had he lived longer than he did (he was killed a month after he got to Georgia), his presence would have complicated matters between Richmond and the army and quite likely between the old pro-Bragg and anti-Bragg factions in the army. Like Hardee, Polk had differed with Johnston over administrative, logistical, and military matters in 1863 and early 1864. Once he joined the army in Georgia, Polk, like Hardee, often found himself ignored by Johnston, who continued to consult and rely heavily on Hood.

Johnston held Hardee and Hood at Dalton on May 12. He later wrote that he elected to remain passive in his fortified lines because he still hoped to draw Sherman into an attack on his strong position and because he knew that the railroad and the roads east of Rocky Face Ridge would enable him to move to Resaca quickly. He made no effort to strike either at Sherman's obviously weakened force in front of Dalton or at the long Federal column slowly toiling southward across his front in the valley west of Rocky Face Ridge.

When a cavalry reconnaissance revealed only a single Federal infantry corps and some Yankee cavalry remaining in front of Dalton, Johnston finally realized what had happened and ordered his army to Resaca. He and Hood rode away from Dalton on the same train. Hood got off in Tilton to rejoin his corps.[7]

As Sherman rode southward on May 12 he believed the Yankees still had an opportunity to "interpose" their forces between Resaca and Johnston's army, which would soon have to retreat from Dalton. When the Unionists pushed out of Snake Creek Gap toward the railroad on May 13, they ran into stout opposition from advanced Confederate units that delayed their march while the remainder of the Rebel army deployed west of Resaca. Not only had Johnston reached the town long before Sherman had expected, but he had also determined to give battle there to gain time to get his wagons across the Oostanaula.

To cover the road and rail bridges, Johnston deployed his troops in a line that began at the Oostanaula west of the town, ran north along the valley of Camp Creek for almost three miles, and gradually curved back to the east until its right rested on the Connasauga River. Polk held the left of this line with the divisions of Cantey and Loring. (Cantey then commanded not only his own brigade but also other troops who had come from the Mobile area to reinforce Johnston.) Three divisions under Hardee manned the center of the Rebel line to the north of Polk. Hood's three divisions defended the Rebel right. Hardee's fourth division (Walker's) took post at Calhoun to guard the south bank of the river against a Yankee crossing downstream from the Confederate left.

The position had many weaknesses. In fact, it offered no advantage to the Southerners and was so "strategically untenable" that at first Sherman assumed Johnston would quickly abandon it. Should the Confederates be defeated there, they might well be trapped in the angle formed by the two rivers. A range of low hills just west of the Rebel line offered good positions from which Yankee cannon could reach the bridges at Resaca. The position's most serious weakness, however, was strategic. The Oostanaula's southwestwardly course both protected Sherman's right flank and gave the Yankees an opportunity to cross the river and threaten Johnston's rail line south of Resaca.

Skirmishing on the thirteenth soon disabused Sherman of the notion that Johnston was continuing his retreat. As the Union corps moved out from Snake Creek Gap, therefore, Sherman deployed them on a line paralleling that of the Confederates, except that its northern end bent back toward the northwest.

McPherson led the Federal column, and the units that followed moved north and took up positions to his left. Thomas's army (less the IV Corps) deployed on the immediate left of the Army of the Tennessee, Schofield on Thomas's left. When the IV Corps arrived, having followed the retreating Secessionists south from Dalton, it took its place on the left of Schofield's line. By nightfall on the thirteenth, those deployments were complete.

Sherman elected to engage Johnston at Resaca. Rejecting Thomas's suggestion that the Yankees swing infantry across the Oostanaula and make another effort to trap and destroy the Rebel army, the Federal commander issued orders to probe the Confederate position. He seems to have hoped that he would be able to pin down the Southerners and hold them at Resaca until his pontoon trains caught up and his engineers could bridge the river below the Federal right flank. Once the crossing was completed, he planned to send two cavalry divisions to try to wreck the railroad south of Calhoun.

Skirmishing erupted at first light on May 14. Sherman sent Brig. Gen. Thomas W. Sweeny's division of the XVI Corps down the Oostanaula to scout for a crossing. He also ordered a forward wheeling movement by the left of his long line. Rough terrain hampered the Federal advance, and the two armies did not come into close contact until about noon.

In the afternoon troops from the XXIII and XIV Corps assaulted the right center of the Confederate line. As was usually the case with an attacking force during the Civil War, they lost heavily and gained no important ground. At about 4:00 P.M. Hood's Rebels counterattacked, striking the Yankees' extreme left, which, the Confederates had discovered, was "in the air"—that is, neither supported by adequate reserves nor resting on an easily defensible terrain feature. Hood's men enjoyed an initial success, but Northern reinforcements rushed from the XX Corps in the Union center stymied the attack. Darkness soon put an end to the day's fighting.

The only significant changes that day came at the far south end of the battle lines. There some XV Corps troops seized a hill from which Union artillery could place fire on the Resaca bridges. During the night Johnston's engineers laid a pontoon bridge upriver, where, they hoped, it would be beyond the range of the Yankee guns.

While fighting rolled along the lines to the north, Sweeny found a likely spot for crossing the river near Lay's Ferry, a few miles downstream. Snake Creek emptied into the river about one hundred yards below the ferry. The Oostanaula's right (northern) bank was open at the ferry, but near the mouth of the creek heavy woods ran down to the river's edge. A few Rebel cavalrymen guarded the ferry. Determined to attempt a crossing, Sweeny put most of his men to demonstrating in the field opposite the ferry while his real effort took place at the creek's mouth.

Detachments of the Second and Sixth Iowa regiments carried pontoon boats down Snake Creek to a concealed point a few yards from the river.

At 5:00 P.M. those boats, loaded with men from the Sixty-fifth and Eighty-fifth Ohio regiments, pulled out into the river. Protected by fire from skirmishers on the northern bank and propelled by expert oarsmen, the boats quickly crossed the river in the face of light opposition from the Confederate horsemen and disgorged troops on the southern bank. After firing a few shots, the Rebel cavalrymen fled.

Even as his boats were in the Oostanaula, Sweeny received a report that a large party of Confederates was crossing the river a short distance above Lay's Ferry. Logically assuming that the Southerners would attempt to isolate and destroy his division before he could receive help from McPherson, he ordered his men back to the northern bank. Only later did he ascertain that the report was false.

That evening Johnston learned that the Yankees had crossed the river at Lay's Ferry. That great danger to his rail line led the Confederate commander to cancel orders he had earlier issued to renew the assault on Sherman's left the next morning. Instead, Johnston instructed Walker to move up from his post at Calhoun and drive the Federals at the ferry back across the river. By the time Walker reached the ferry, the Unionists were gone. Finding no sign of the enemy, Walker posted a small guard, notified Johnston that the reports of a Federal crossing were incorrect, and returned to Calhoun.

During the night Sherman decided to push the Confederates at two points on the fifteenth. Ordering Sweeny at Lay's Ferry to try to cross the river again, he shifted all of the XX Corps to his left center to make an attack there. Schofield, with the Army of the Ohio, moved to the extreme Federal left.

Redeployment of Hooker's men consumed most of the morning, and the XX Corps did not complete its dispositions to attack until almost noon. The three divisions of the corps advanced about that time, but the main Rebel line (Hood's Corps) threw back the assault with little trouble.

Only at a small, uncompleted dirt fort in front of Stevenson's Division did the attacking Yankees gain any success. This little work, held by Capt. Max Van Den Corput's Georgia battery, quickly became the focus of the struggle. Men from several Northern regiments, led by Col. Benjamin Harrison of the Seventieth Indiana (later president of the United States) swarmed over the battery. In bitter hand-to-hand fighting the Federals overpowered the Georgians and captured the guns. Once in the little fort, however, the Yankees found it open to the rear, and they came under such heavy fire from Hood's main line that they had to abandon their prize as soon as they had gained it. The battery's four cannon stood silent between the lines, neither side able to reach and use them. After dark, the Northerners managed to dig away the front of the fort and remove the guns.

While fighting raged along the lines north and west of Resaca, Sweeny and his division prepared for their second crossing of the Oostanaula. Sweeny decided to use the same method that had worked so well on the fourteenth. Before he could put his plan into operation, however, some of his soldiers found an old flatboat and on their own initiative crossed the river unobserved.

Once again the Southern pickets fled, carrying news to Walker at Calhoun that the Unionists were over the Oostanaula at Lay's Ferry. Walker sent word of the crossing to Johnston and tried without success to drive Sweeny's men back to the northern bank of the river.

Johnston, who, upon receipt of Walker's earlier report, had renewed his instructions for Hood to attack, now countermanded the order. Unfortunately for the Southerners, word of this second cancellation did not reach the extreme right of the Rebel line in time to prevent the Confederates there (Stewart's Division) from launching their assault as scheduled. The Yankees repulsed the attack, inflicting heavy losses on the Secessionists.

When it became clear that Walker could not dislodge Sweeny from his position on the south bank of the Oostanaula, Johnston realized that he had no option but to evacuate Resaca. Late in the afternoon of the fifteenth the Confederate wagon trains still with the army began crossing the river on the new pontoon bridge. The infantry corps withdrew after dark—Hood from the extreme right first, followed by Hardee from the center, and then by Polk. Strong details of skirmishers remained behind for several hours to keep up firing and to make enough noise to convince the Yankees that the Southerners were still present in force. As late as midnight Rebel skirmishers repulsed a reconnaissance by a division of the IV Corps. At 3:30 A.M. on the sixteenth the Confederates set fire to the railroad bridge. Shortly afterward the last men of the rear guard crossed on the pontoon bridge, taking it up as they went. Sherman's advance units reached the river in time to save the road bridge.[8]

The strategic pattern set in the campaign's first ten days was not to change until mid-July. Johnston would concentrate his army, take up a strong position on favorable terrain, strengthen that position with formidable fortifications, hold his men in the works—and wait, hoping Sherman would attack him. "Johnston," Sherman reported to the Washington authorities on May 10, "acts purely on the defensive."[9]

Johnston did not even try to pry McPherson out of Snake Creek Gap with a quick movement of troops south from Dalton. Even on May 11 and 12, when most of Sherman's army was strung out on the roads west of Rocky Face Ridge and only the isolated IV Corps and two cavalry divisions remained in front of Mill Creek Gap, the Rebel commander elected to wait supinely in his defensive works. Had he acted, or even threatened to act, against the IV Corps on either May 11 or 12, the potential danger such a movement posed to Sherman's railroad and to his base in Chattanooga might have been enough to bring the Yankees scurrying northward to protect their line of supply. A quick strike down from Dug Gap against the left flank of Sherman's long, drawn-out column would, at the least, have slowed the Federals' progress. Johnston's brief counterjabs at Resaca were not delivered with much force, and he was easily persuaded to cancel such efforts. Nor, apparently, did he ever consider reinforcing Walker for a serious effort to drive back the Unionists who crossed the river at Lay's Ferry on May 15. He did not even wreck the railroad as he retreated from Dalton to Resaca.

In all probability, the Confederates would not have been able to deliver a mortal blow to any part of Sherman's widely scattered forces. Any action on Johnston's part, however, would have inflicted losses on the Yankees and slowed their progress. With the fall elections looming in the North, every day's delay and every casualty in the Federal ranks was to the benefit of the Confederacy. If Johnston continued simply to remain passively behind invulnerable fortifications that Sherman refused to attack but could easily outflank, there was no way the Secessionists could achieve success in North Georgia—indeed, they could not long remain in North Georgia.

Sherman, on the other hand, had shown in the campaign's opening days that while he might make small-scale attacks on the Rebels and jab at their fortifications, he would not launch a massive assault. Instead, he would maneuver to outflank his enemy. By rejecting vigorous or decisive action, however, he was unlikely to achieve anything more than forcing Johnston south, where the Rebels would take up another position and the ballet would begin again. When he declined to send a strong column through Snake Creek Gap or across the Oostanaula with Sweeny, Sherman missed two excellent chances to gain a great, if not complete, success at the very opening of his campaign.

Not the least of the ironies of 1864 is the very high probability that if Grant had allowed Thomas to succeed to the command of the Military Division of the Mississippi by seniority, the 1864 campaign in Georgia would have ended two or three weeks after its opening in a crushing Federal victory that, for all practical purposes, would have ended the war in the West. The "slow and plodding" Thomas would have put such a force onto Johnston's rail line that the Rebel army most likely would have been destroyed or dispersed north of the Oostanaula. Such a smashing success, ripping open the entire center of the Confederacy, would have saved many thousands of the lives lost during the last eleven months of the war.

On the day the Battle of Resaca came to an end, a significant engagement took place at the little town of New Market in the Shenandoah Valley of Virginia. There a rag-tag Secessionist force, pulled together from all over the western part of the state, fell upon and routed Franz Sigel's invading column. The Valley of Virginia, for the moment at least, was free of danger from the Yankees.

Soon most of the victorious Confederates were moving eastward from New Market to reinforce Lee in his great struggle against Grant. Once again, the Federals had failed in their effort to prevent the Southerners from shifting troops about to reinforce threatened points. The Rebels had won the second round of the 1864 campaign.

CHAPTER SIX

On to the Etowah

The armies of Johnston and Sherman found a different environment south of the Oostanaula. The steep ridges, narrow gaps, and heavy woods that characterized the region north of the river gave way to more open terrain and gently rolling hills with much lighter vegetation. In 1864 that section of the state was a sparsely populated farming region with a few small towns. Except for the iron foundries at Rome and some mills along the Etowah, it boasted no industrial resources of note. When the armies moved into the area, most of the civilians piled a few of their possessions into wagons and sought refuge in Marietta, Atlanta, or farther into the interior.

The Western & Atlantic Railroad crossed the Oostanaula at Resaca and ran south through Calhoun and Adairsville to Kingston, where it met the branch line that stretched west to Rome. From Kingston the W&A tracks turned to the southeast, passing through Cass Station and Cartersville before crossing the Etowah River just north of Allatoona Pass. The straight-line distance from the Oostanaula at Resaca to the Etowah near Allatoona Pass is about thirty-five miles. As the railroad runs, the river-to-river distance is about forty-five miles. The few roads in the area in 1864 connected the small towns and offered several north-south routes.

When Johnston crossed the Oostanaula, he expected to find a good defensive position a few miles south of the river near Calhoun, where he could again bar Sherman's advance. In this expectation, however, he was disappointed because he soon discovered that if he took position there Oothkalooga Creek would cut through his line and make it difficult for the wings of his army to support one another. (He seems not to have realized that the same stream also would have bisected Sherman's line.)

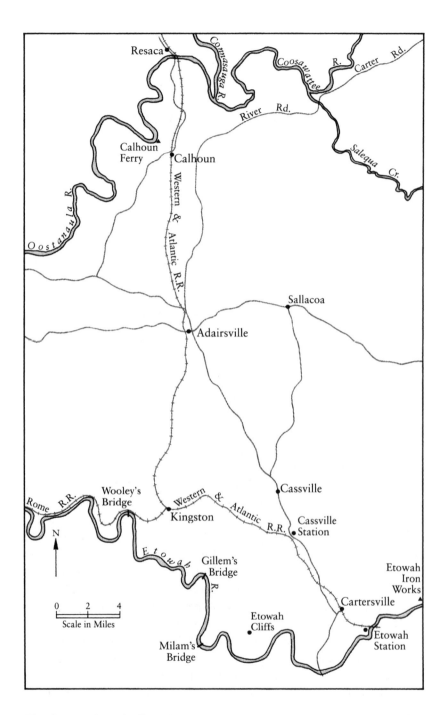

The Oostanaula to the Etowah

Concluding that he had no choice but to continue southward, Johnston fell back, hoping that once the Rebels reached Adairsville he could find a position suitable for his purpose.

By noon of May 17 advance elements of the Confederate army were in Adairsville. As Johnston approached the town, he expected to deploy his troops across a valley there to block Sherman's route south. With their flanks protected by the ridges on the sides of the valley in which the town sits, the Southerners could give battle. Once again, however, Johnston was disappointed. When he reached Adairsville, about midday, he quickly discovered that his maps had misled him. The valley was too wide to be held by the Rebel army. At Adairsville, however, Johnston was joined by more of Polk's men who arrived from Rome by rail.

For four months Johnston had been at Dalton, occupying a position he believed he could not hold. Since he had decided not to attempt an offensive movement, it therefore followed that—sooner or later—he would have to retreat. He had not bothered to survey either in person or through his staff or engineer officers the area to which he would have to fall back. Nor had he made any preparations to establish a new line south of the Oostanaula. In fact, however, it did not matter. Sherman could simply have moved down the right bank of the Oostanaula toward or to Rome and flanked any position Johnston occupied north of the Etowah.

Disappointed in not finding the type of terrain he had anticipated, Johnston again studied his maps. At a conference that night Hardee argued that the Confederates should make a stand at Adairsville even if the terrain there was not ideal. Johnston overruled him and before midnight ordered the army to continue its southward march. He did, however, develop a plan by which he hoped to draw Sherman into an ambush in which the Southerners might destroy a part of his force.[1]

While Johnston sought some position in which he might block or at least delay Sherman's advance, the Union commander indulged in his own misunderstanding of the situation. After Johnston abandoned Dalton, Sherman assumed that he would flee across the Etowah. Late on May 15, after three days' battle north of the Oostanaula, Sherman concluded that Johnston would hold his army at Resaca. Discovering the next morning that the Rebels had left the Resaca area during the night, Sherman again jumped to the conclusion that Johnston would race south to put his men below the Etowah as soon as he could.

Believing that Johnston was hastening as rapidly as possible toward the Etowah, Sherman on May 16 spread his own forces across a wide front in pursuit. Thomas with the IV and most of the XIV Corps was to cross the Oostanaula at Resaca and move south along the railroad directly after the Rebels. Schofield with the XXIII Corps and Hooker with the XX Corps were to cross the Coosawattee above the point where it joined the Connasauga to form the Oostanaula and swing into place on Thomas's left. McPherson with the Army of the Tennessee was to cross the Oostanaula at Lay's Ferry and become the western end of Sherman's line.

While these movements were under way, a division of the XIV Corps, accompanied part of the way by a division of cavalry, would move southwest, down the right bank of the Oostanaula. This movement provided some protection for Sherman's right flank and railroad against any Rebel thrust from the southwest, and it offered the possibility that the Yankees might find another place to cross the river and come in behind Johnston's army to threaten its left flank and rail connection with Atlanta.

On May 16 Thomas and McPherson pushed southward, their advance slowed to a crawl by Wheeler's skillfully handled cavalry acting as the Rebels' rear guard. Thomas's lead units did not reach Calhoun, only six miles from Resaca, until 6:00 P.M. Meanwhile, off to the northeast, Hooker and Schofield managed to get their columns tangled up and fell to squabbling over rank and the right-of-way. Their foolishness delayed the march, and only the leading division of the column had gotten across the Coosawattee by nightfall.

The seventeenth witnessed a repetition of the events of the previous day. Again the Yankee advance ground almost to a halt in the face of stiff opposition from Johnston's rear guard. Obstinate Confederate resistance convinced Sherman that Johnston intended to make a stand at Adairsville. The Yankee commander, therefore, ordered his widely scattered units to concentrate there on May 18, and he expected that his armies would then have to fight a major battle against the Rebels.

That day the lone XIV Corps division sent down the Oostanaula (the cavalry had crossed the river and moved south on the right of Sherman's wide front) reached Rome. There it skirmished briefly with the rear elements of Polk's troops, who were hastening through the town to join the Army of Tennessee. The Rebels were gone the next morning, and the Yankees occupied the town without opposition. Rome, the industrial center of northwestern Georgia and a crucial point on the line of communications between Georgia and Alabama, passed into Union hands. With it went the entire line of the Oostanaula River. In the town the Northerners captured cotton, several cannon, and large quantities of food, quartermaster stores, and hospital supplies. Central Alabama now lay open to a possible raid from Rome.

Had Johnston not been so anxious to hurry southward to a new defensive position, he might have found or made on the sixteenth or seventeenth a chance to jab at one or more of Sherman's widely separated columns. He had a fresh division (Walker's), and the Rebels might have thrown the pursuit into turmoil.[2]

On the sixteenth, as Johnston's men trudged south from the Oostanaula, Confederate troops brought to Virginia by rail from the coast of Georgia and the Carolinas met Benjamin Butler's column, which had been moving toward Richmond from the southeast. After a bitter fight, the Rebels pushed the Yankees back to Bermuda Hundred on the James River, where Butler put his men into a strongly entrenched position. There, in Grant's oft-quoted if not accurate phrase, Butler's army was "as completely shut off from further operations . . . as if it had been in a bottle strongly corked." Soon many of the Southern troops who had helped bottle up Butler were moving on northward to reinforce Lee's army in front of Grant. The Rebels had won the third round of the 1864 campaign.[3]

When Johnston decided on May 17 not to attempt a stand at Adairsville, he turned again to his maps to see what might lie to the south. From Adairsville, he observed, two roads led off to Cassville ten miles to the southeast. The main route paralleled the railroad south for about nine miles to Kingston. It then ran east some seven miles to Cassville. The other highway led directly southeast to Cassville. Those roads formed a right triangle. Kingston was the right angle, the Adairsville-Cassville road the hypotenuse.

Sherman, Johnston predicted, would divide his force at Adairsville to facilitate his march south from that town. Part of the Yankee pursuing force would move south to Kingston while the rest marched southeast to Cassville. If Sherman did use both roads, the Rebels might be able to strike one column before the other could come to its assistance. The relatively rough terrain between the two roads would make it difficult for the separated Union forces to help each other or even for them to communicate.

When the Secessionists marched out of Adairsville that night, Johnston accompanied Polk and Hood down the direct road to Cassville. Hardee, with the army's wagon trains, headed to Kingston. At Kingston he was to turn east and join the other corps at Cassville. If all went as Johnston hoped, his army would then be united between the separated wings of Sherman's pursuing force, able to strike at the weaker part.

At daybreak on the eighteenth the Unionists discovered that again the Rebels had slipped away during the night. The Northerners quickly occupied Adairsville but made no immediate pursuit. Instead, the Yankees rested until about noon while waiting for their scattered columns to arrive. After questioning some deserters, Sherman concluded that Johnston was making for Kingston. He, therefore, directed McPherson and most of Thomas's army toward that town. As Johnston had expected, he sent part of his force (Hooker, followed by Schofield) directly toward Cassville, where it was to await orders.

When the Federals went into camp about six o'clock that evening, Thomas was some six miles south of Adairsville; McPherson a few miles off to the west, about Woodland; Hooker and Schofield about three miles out of Adairsville on the Cassville Road. That night, Sherman, still hoping to catch Johnston in the relatively open country north of the Etowah, wrote Schofield, "If we can bring Johnston to battle this side of Etowah we must do it, even at the hazard of beginning battle with but a part of our forces."

By noon that day the Secessionists had reached their chosen position along Two Run Creek just north of Cassville. Johnston placed Polk's Corps across the road blocking the direct route from Adairsville. Hood held his troops off to the right and a bit south of Polk. Hardee had moved through Kingston and on east toward Cassville, where he came into position as the left of the Confederate line. With the last of Polk's reinforcements (the infantry division of Maj. Gen. Samuel G. French and Jackson's cavalry) having arrived, Johnston's army was at its peak strength—about seventy-five thousand men. Both the commander and the army were optimistic about the morrow.[4]

Thursday, May 19, was hot and muggy. For the men of the Army of Tennessee the day turned out to be one of the most frustrating and demoralizing of the war. For later historians it would prove one of the most confusing. Johnston and Hood each left a record of the day's two controversial events. It is not possible to reconcile their accounts.

In the morning, if we are to believe Johnston, the army commander ordered Hood to move out on a country road a mile or so east of the Adairsville-Cassville Road and form his corps for battle facing west. When Polk engaged the head of the pursuing Yankee column, Hood was to assail its flank from the east. Hood wrote later that he had received a report of an isolated Union force moving south a short distance east of the Adairsville-Cassville Road. He thereupon requested and received permission from Johnston to take his corps across the fields and attack it. Johnston, Hood insisted, neither ordered the attack nor instructed Polk to cooperate.

Whether at Johnston's order or at Hood's instigation, the latter marched his corps out that morning to engage the Federals northeast of Cassville. After going a short distance, Hood learned of a body of Union troops off to the right (northeast). Those Yankees constituted a great source of potential danger to the column. If Hood deployed to assault the Northerners to the west, the Unionists might fall upon the unprotected rear or right flank of his corps. Hood, therefore, halted his column and threw out skirmishers who quickly engaged the enemy. Hood soon abandoned the march and dropped back to join Polk. A short time after Hood aborted the proposed attack, Johnston scrapped all plans to fight north of Cassville and ordered the army back to a ridge below the town.

When Johnston received Hood's report, he had expressed disbelief that any Unionists were to Hood's right, although he admitted that if they were, Hood would have been foolish to continue his march. Later Johnston would insist that no Yankees were in position to menace Hood that morning. We know now that some were. (It is one of the few controversies of the day we can resolve.) Several units of Northern cavalrymen or troops from the Hooker-Schofield column had moved to the east, stumbled onto a country road leading into Cassville from the northeast, and in following that route blundered into Hood's column. For Hood to have launched an attack to the west with a Federal force of unknown strength to his rear would have been foolish in the extreme. His men could have been caught between fire from two hostile forces.

In any event, it seems unlikely that an attack by Hood would have accomplished much. By the time the Rebels abandoned the effort, Thomas's army had pushed eastward from Kingston and was threatening Hardee's Corps just west of Cassville.

That afternoon Johnston put his army into line on a ridge running from northeast of Cassville to a point about a mile and a quarter south of the town. Hood's Corps held the right of the ridge, Polk's the center, and Hardee's the left. The ridge itself seemed a strong defensive position. Johnston, as always, hoped that Sherman would assault the Confederate line.

The new Rebel position, however, had a serious weakness, and that weakness became manifest during the afternoon. Off to the northeast, Yankee gunners took position on other ridges and soon discovered that some of their cannon could deliver enfilade fire (fire coming from the side) against a segment of Polk's position at a point where the terrain forced the Confederates to make a slight angle in their line. Such a fire was often devastating to the troops subjected to it, and Polk's men in the enfiladed section of their line spent a very uncomfortable afternoon under the fire of Sherman's guns. Hood himself came under some severe shelling from the Federal artillery. So bad did the cannon fire prove that when Polk and Hood met with Johnston that night at Polk's headquarters, the corps commanders asserted that the Yankee artillery alone would make it impossible for them to hold their positions the next morning.

Johnston later wrote that Hood and Polk urged him to withdraw south of the Etowah and that only after remonstrating with the lieutenant generals for some time did he yield to their pleas. He came to fear, Johnston wrote, that the commanders' lack of confidence would spread to the troops, undermine their morale, and make it impossible for them to hold the ridge. Hood later claimed that while he and Polk agreed that the position could not be held in a defensive battle, he did think it would have made a good jumping-off point for an attack. He and Polk, he claimed, urged Johnston to strike at Sherman, but the army commander declined to do so and ordered yet another retreat.

Hardee missed the first part of the conference. When he arrived at about 10:00 P.M., Johnston had already decided to abandon the Cassville ridge. Once again finding himself left out of the decision making, Hardee protested the retreat in vain.

The spat between Johnston and Hood arose later when the two had become completely alienated and when each had had a chance to read the other's account of the meeting. No matter what happened at the conference or the degree to which Federal artillery enfiladed the ridge position, it is clear that Johnston would not have remained at Cassville on May 20. At about the time Hardee joined the conference, the Confederate generals learned that Yankee troops (some of McPherson's men moving out from Kingston) had gotten possession of Wooley's Bridge over the Etowah a few miles downriver. Had Johnston remained in his Cassville line the next day, the Yankees could simply have come up the left bank of the river and cut him off from Atlanta. On May 23 Brig. Gen. M. J. Wright, reporting from Atlanta to Bragg in Richmond, noted that "a flank movement of the enemy crossing [the] Etowah on the [Confederate] left" had been the reason for Johnston's latest retreat.

Soon after the generals' conference broke up, Johnston's staff officers went along the line delivering orders for the withdrawal. The troops began to move about midnight, but details remained behind chopping wood and making other noises to deceive the Yankees into believing that the Rebels were preparing for a morning battle.[5]

Johnston's men left their trenches with rifles at trail arms so as not to reflect the moonlight and give away their withdrawal. Many of the troops were depressed by the day's events. They had been maneuvered out of a very strong position at Dalton and then fallen back from Resaca, Calhoun, and Adairsville. Now, once again, they were withdrawing under cover of the night.

That morning, as he anticipated battle, Johnston had issued a bombastic order announcing that the army's retreat had ended and the Confederates would turn on their pursuers. The order had aroused great enthusiasm among the retreat-weary troops. That night their disappointment at abandoning yet another position was great. The spirits of many of the Rebels would revive over the next few days, but for many others their once-high confidence in Johnston would never quite be the same again.

Yankee morale soared on the morning of May 20 when Federal skirmishers reported that once again Johnston had retreated. In less than three weeks the Unionists had forced the Rebels back about half the distance to Atlanta, capturing several strongly fortified positions, occupying much valuable territory, and taking many prisoners.

Sherman had not brought Johnston to battle, but he seems to have been well satisfied with the progress he had made. Having secured a crossing of the Etowah, the Yankee commander decided to give his men a few days' much-needed rest. A small column went upriver to destroy the ironworks and corn mills there, and the rest of the Federals settled into their camps to sleep and clean up as best they could. Thomas's men were near Cassville, McPherson's at Kingston, and Schofield's near Cass Station.

One of Hooker's brigade commanders wrote, "Johnsons [*sic*] retreat from Resaca, leaving his dead and wounded in our hands, shows that he was whipped. His retreat from this place [Cassville] after fortifying it very strongly, shows that he is afraid to risk another engagement."

A few days later, on the other side of the Etowah, a Confederate officer penned a note to his wife: "I have seen so much beautiful country given up [to the enemy] as to be made unhappy by it. You can not imagine how disheartening it is & at the same time humiliating to see the apprehension of the people of a country abandoned to the enemy. I had rather have the agony of defeat as far as my own feelings are concerned."

The officer who wrote that letter was Joseph E. Johnston.[6]

CHAPTER SEVEN

Into the Hell Hole

The Confederate retreat from Cassville was marked by some confusion, but on the twentieth Johnston got his entire force south of the Etowah and removed or destroyed the bridges near Cartersville. The Rebels continued on southward along the Western & Atlantic to Allatoona, a small village just south of Allatoona Pass. The pass, a man-made cut (in places more than eighty feet deep), carried the railroad through the Allatoona Hills. The heights offered the Secessionists a very strong defensive position at the railroad itself. A few miles downstream, however, the river veered off to the northwest and flowed away from the high ground to the south and east. Johnston hoped that Sherman would follow directly along the tracks and make a frontal assault on the strong Confederate position in the Allatoona Hills.

The Federal commander, of course, had no more intention of attempting to storm the new Rebel position than he had had of making a major attack on Buzzard's Roost at Dalton. He remembered the Allatoona area from his travels through it two decades earlier, and he was well aware of the likely fate in store for his troops should he be so foolish as to launch an assault on such a position.

Soon after his armies secured the northern bank of the Etowah, Sherman turned to his next step. His attention quickly focused on the little town of Dallas, about fifteen miles south of the river and approximately the same distance west of the railroad. Within a short time Sherman had decided to swing his three armies across the Etowah west of Allatoona Pass and push rapidly south to Dallas. Occupation of the town by the Federals, Sherman believed, would compel the Rebels to abandon their Allatoona position. Once they did so, Sherman convinced himself, the

Confederates would fall back across the Chattahoochee River to the outskirts of Atlanta.

Before undertaking this maneuver, however, the Yankees needed a few days to prepare for the next phase of the campaign. Sherman would be taking his soldiers away from their railroad line of supply, and before doing so he wanted to accumulate necessary stores and ship his sick and "worthless" men to the rear. Fortunately for the Unionists, Johnston had not seriously damaged the railroad as he retreated. Federal construction crews had quickly rebuilt the burned bridge over the Oostanaula at Resaca and repaired the slight damage the Rebels had done to other parts of the line.

This brief delay gave the men of both armies a few welcome days of rest while Sherman's trains hauled supplies south and carried wounded, worn, sick, and exhausted men northward. By May 23 Sherman had completed his preparations.

The Federal commander planned for his armies to execute another great wheeling movement around to the west. McPherson, on the circumference of the wheel, would cross the Etowah near Kingston. Thomas with the IV and most of the XIV Corps would cross southeast of Kingston at Gillem's Bridge. Hooker with the XX Corps would cross on a pontoon bridge about four miles upstream from Gillem's and then join Thomas. Schofield would follow Hooker over the river but remain on the left flank of the army group.

Once across the Etowah, McPherson was to move to Van Wert, about a dozen miles northwest of Dallas, and then swing in to the latter town from the west. Thomas, moving along an interior arc, would approach Dallas from the northwest. Schofield would make an even smaller circuit and guard against any effort Johnston might make to interfere with the movement.

Rebel cavalry, patrolling downstream from the Allatoona area, reported Sherman's march almost as soon as it began. Instead of fleeing for the Chattahoochee as Sherman confidently expected, Johnston reacted quickly by shifting the corps of Hardee and Polk southwest from Allatoona toward Dallas. The Confederates had the advantage of using better roads and of moving along the chord of the arc while the Federals trudged along poorer roads on the circumference. For the moment, Johnston held Hood's Corps at Allatoona to guard against the possibility that Sherman might also launch a thrust directly down the railroad.

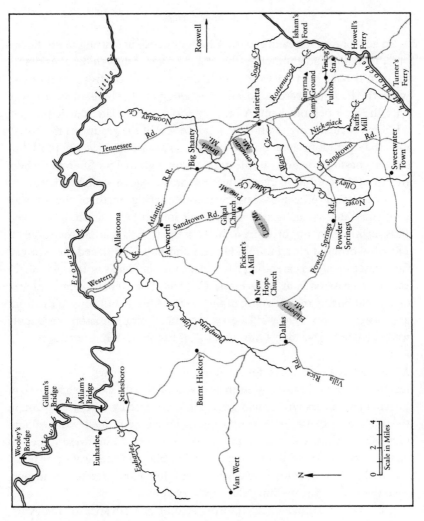

The Etowah to the Chattahoochee

In addition to retreating to the Chattahoochee or shifting to the Dallas area, Johnston had another option which he apparently never considered. He could have hurried west from Allatoona and confronted Sherman while the Federals were on low ground along the left bank of the Etowah with the river behind them. A century and a quarter later participants in a United States Army "staff ride" who went over the ground of the North Georgia operations concluded that such a ploy would have offered Johnston his best opportunity of the entire campaign to fight Sherman where the ground would have given him great advantage in a pitched battle.

On May 24 Wheeler's cavalry reconnoitering north of the Etowah confirmed that virtually all of Sherman's infantry was south of the river. Passing on a great opportunity to strike at Sherman's railroad to the north, Johnston ordered Hood to join Hardee and Polk. He placed the Army of Tennessee on a line extending from just south of Dallas north and northeast to a crossroads at New Hope Church. The Rebels were deployed along that line by midmorning of the twenty-fifth. Scouts out to the front and observers on nearby Ellsberry Mountain kept Johnston reasonably well posted on Sherman's movements off to the west and northwest.[1]

Meanwhile, the Yankees found the going hard. Heavy woods, rough terrain, and poor roads slowed their march. Even the skirmishers, one of Sherman's officers wrote, had great difficulty forcing their way through the thick underbrush. Biting and stinging insects combined with heat and very high humidity to add to the soldiers' misery. Many were forced to go for long periods without water. "For 12 miles no water was to be had," moaned an Illinois soldier. Every now and then Confederate skirmishers gave the Federals something else to worry about.

On May 25 Hooker's XX Corps, leading the advance of the Army of the Cumberland and accompanied by Thomas and Sherman, closed on the Rebel position at New Hope Church. That sector of Johnston's line ran along a low ridge and was occupied by Hood's Corps. Stewart's Division held the line at the little church itself. Stewart put three of his brigades into line on the ridge and held two others (one of them on loan from Stevenson's Division) in reserve. Along that short section of their front the Confederates posted sixteen cannon.

As his men pushed toward the church, Hooker learned from prisoners that Secessionists were present in force in his front. Alarmed and concluding that he had run into a part of Johnston's army that outnumbered his own force, Hooker halted his leading units and put the men to entrenching. Thomas sent couriers dashing through the woods with orders for his other corps to close up on Hooker. Sherman, however, insisted that Hooker's column had gotten on the left flank of the Southern army. After some heated discussion, he agreed to wait for the rest of the XX Corps to arrive before renewing the advance. "There haven't been twenty rebels there to-day," he snapped.

Hooker did not get his corps concentrated until about 4:00 P.M. Then, just as a great thunderstorm began to form, the Federals renewed their push eastward toward the church. Hooker had formed his three divisions in columns of brigades (one brigade behind another). Such a formation gave the attacking force great capability to exploit a breakthrough in an enemy line—if it could reach and break the opposing army. As the XX Corps forced its way through the tangled jungle, the right to left width of its front just about matched that of Stewart's defending division. The Southerners, therefore, were able to mass their fire against the one-brigade front of each of Hooker's divisions. Given the increased range and effectiveness of Civil War weapons, the result was predictable.

The head of each assaulting Union column encountered a withering hail of bullets and artillery fire that quickly blew it away and brought the advance to a halt. The Rebel fire, wrote one Northerner, was "most effective and murderous." In all, Hooker lost about fifteen hundred men in the short engagement. Confederate losses probably did not exceed five hundred and may not have reached that number. Among the Rebel casualties were two brothers, members of Capt. Charles E. Fenner's Louisiana Battery, shot down one after the other manning the dangerous post of rammer at the muzzle of their gun. A third brother was serving as rammer when the fight ended.

Sherman, typically, refused to admit that he had been in error and blamed the defeat on the afternoon's delay. Failure to push the advance, he asserted, had given Johnston time to bring up reinforcements. According to a rumor that flashed through the Union camps that evening, an angry Hooker retorted that about fifty more Confederates might have joined the defenders at New Hope Church during the afternoon.[2]

Dawn on May 26 found Sherman's troops scattered through the steaming woods north and west of Dallas. During the day the Federal commander managed to get his men deployed along a line paralleling that of the Southerners. McPherson, whose troops had wheeled in from Van Wert, held the Yankee right fronting Dallas. The XIV Corps division that had come up from Rome was to his immediate left. A gap of about a mile, covered only by a line of pickets, yawned between the left of the troops at Dallas and the right of Hooker's position at New Hope Church. Howard's IV Corps was on Hooker's left. The other two divisions of Palmer's XIV Corps were in reserve near the church. Schofield with the XXIII Corps was on Howard's left. Realizing that the bulk of Sherman's force was in the New Hope Church area, Johnston shifted most of his troops in that direction. Only Bate's infantry division and Jackson's cavalry remained on the Confederate left facing McPherson at Dallas.

Late on the twenty-sixth Sherman decided to attempt to turn the Rebel right flank. He selected Howard to make the effort with a division from his own IV Corps. Supported by units from the XIV and XXIII Corps, Howard was to march northeast, pass the end of Johnston's line, then turn and attack the right flank or rear of the Rebel army. Howard's column got under way about 11:00 A.M. on the twenty-seventh.

Unknown to Howard, Confederate scouts discovered his march almost as soon as it began, and Southern commanders simply extended their lines to the right along a parallel path. After going about three miles, Howard concluded that he had gotten beyond the right flank of the Southern line. He halted the column, allowed his men a brief rest, and then—at about 4:45 P.M.—ordered them forward. The Yankees were then in the vicinity of Pickett's Mill on Little Pumpkinvine Creek, northeast of New Hope Church.

Advancing over very rough terrain, the Federals soon encountered Confederate cavalry. Brushing aside the Rebel horsemen, the attackers crossed several ridges and then started up a long slope. At the top, calmly awaiting the Yankees, stood the veteran infantrymen of Patrick Cleburne's division. Artillery from off to the Federal right and vicious infantry fire from the front tore into the Union ranks. Within a few minutes the leading Yankee brigade had lost five hundred men and reeled back out of the fight. Supporting units pushing forward in its place met the same fate. Quickly the attackers lost all formation and cohesion, but many of them advanced bravely in small, isolated groups that had no chance for success.

By the time the Pickett's Mill fight ended late that night, more than fifteen hundred Northerners had been killed, wounded, or captured. "Our men were slaughtered terribly," wrote one unhappy Federal that evening. "Such piles of dead men were seldom or never seen before on such a small space of ground," recorded an Alabama soldier. Some of Howard's units took especially heavy losses. One company of the Forty-first Ohio lost 20 of its 22 men. The Forty-ninth Ohio took about 400 men into the fight and lost 203 of them. The Eighty-ninth Illinois lost 154.

Cleburne reported a loss of 35 killed and 363 wounded. Unreported casualties in the Rebel cavalry, which continued in the fight after being pushed aside by the Northern advance, probably raised total Secessionist losses at Pickett's Mill to about 450.[3]

That night the Confederates attempted a counterstroke of their own. When Rebel cavalry found the Yankee left to be vulnerable, either Hood requested permission to move his corps out to do to Howard what Howard had attempted to do to the Confederates or Johnston decided to seize the opportunity to strike the Unionists on their flank and ordered Hood to sally out and assail Howard's exposed position. (The two generals left conflicting accounts.) No matter who originated the scheme, Hood's men moved out some time during the night. Early on the twenty-eighth, as the flanking column neared its objective, Hood learned from scouts that the Northerners had pulled their exposed line back and were building earthworks to protect their flank. Calling off the projected attack, Hood dropped back to the Rebel line. Once again, as at Resaca and Cassville, the Secessionists had been frustrated in their effort to strike back at Sherman.[4]

The Federal line now stretched very thin, and another large gap had opened, this one between the forces near New Hope Church and those at Pickett's Mill. Three clusters of Union troops stood in the heavy woods north and west of Dallas—McPherson in front of the town itself, Thomas's force at New Hope Church, and Howard's column near Pickett's Mill. Johnston, meanwhile, had strongly fortified his position, and Sherman realized that he could not overrun it by assault. Nor could he continue south to reach the Chattahoochee. He did not have the logistical capability to support such a thrust at so great a distance from the railroad, especially since heavy rains in late May had made the roads very difficult. Indeed, many Yankees on the Dallas–New Hope Church line were suffering from a shortage of food. Even if Sherman had had the wagon transportation to continue to the south, he would have left Johnston in a heavily fortified line on the left flank of the Union column, ideally positioned to cut the Northerners off completely from the Western & Atlantic.

Sherman, in summary, had no choice but to get back to the railroad as quickly as he could. To do so, he would have to strengthen his line, close the gaps, and work his way eastward. He, therefore, ordered his units to shift to the left (northeast) while some of his cavalry pushed ahead to seize Allatoona Pass and thereby regain the railroad south of the Etowah.

Johnston guessed what Sherman would attempt, and over the next several days he jabbed out in a series of small-scale spoiling attacks designed to hold the Federals in position or at least to delay their movement toward the railroad. Although none of those assaults was a major effort, some of them turned into vicious little fights in which casualties among the attacking Rebels ran into the hundreds.[5]

Despite Johnston's efforts, McPherson was able gradually to extricate his men from their trenches at Dallas and to shift them northeastwardly, building new fortifications as he went. Once he had done so, Thomas and Schofield were free to move. On June 1 McPherson's men were settled into the lines at New Hope Church, and on that day some of Sherman's cavalrymen reached Allatoona Pass, which they found unguarded. Johnston had no choice but to move eastward, paralleling the course followed by the Yankees.

On June 3 some of Sherman's advance infantry units occupied the little village of Acworth, on the W&A about five miles south of Allatoona Pass. Three days later almost all the Federals were back on the railroad, and Sherman gave them a few days' rest to allow time to rebuild the bridge over the Etowah and to resupply his men and animals.

Few orders have been more welcome than those for the men to take several days to recuperate. One Northerner called the time he and his comrades spent near Dallas "probably the most wretched week of the campaign." Many of Sherman's soldiers would always afterward refer to the struggle on the Dallas–New Hope Church–Pickett's Mill line as the "battle of the hell hole."

Although he had not been able to reach the Chattahoochee River as he had so optimistically expected to do and had suffered clear tactical defeats on May 25 and 27, Sherman had won yet another crucial strategic victory. Once again Johnston had proved unable to halt the Yankees' advance. Once again another slice of North Georgia had passed into Sherman's hands.[6]

In late May and early June, as the armies grappled in the woods around New Hope Church, three important changes took place in the campaign. One concerned the day-to-day fighting. Beginning in late May both armies built fortifications on a scale not seen before in the war except in siege operations. Earlier in the campaign the men had constructed simple breastworks when and where it appeared that a battle was imminent. Rebels had piled up loose stones on Rocky Face Ridge to protect themselves. At Resaca they dug trenches and used fence rails. Near Cassville the Confederate line ran through a cemetery, and the men overturned tombstones as shelters from Yankee fire. On many occasions men of both armies scraped out slight trenches or piled up branches, fence rails, church pews, or even the bodies of dead comrades for protection. On most days in the early part of the campaign, however, the main armies were not in contact, and the men gave no thought to fortification.

This situation changed in late May. Sherman could not take his army farther to the south of Dallas with Johnston on what would have been his left flank and with his supply situation so precarious. Johnston was happy simply to remain in his works and frustrate Sherman's movements as much as possible. As a result, the armies settled into a routine of sharpshooting, artillery fire, and occasional limited assaults. Men on both sides responded by burrowing deep into the earth to protect themselves in the new kind of relatively static warfare.

Realizing that they would be in the same area for some time, the soldiers quickly learned to improve on the improvised works of logs, rails, stumps, and rocks they had thrown up when they first arrived. Most of the rest of the campaign was marked almost as much by digging as by marching and fighting.

Men scooped out a basic trench often while under fire, using bayonets, tin plates, boards, bare hands, and on occasion picks and shovels furnished by their army. Within a short time the soldiers had made a usable fortification—a trench with the dirt piled on the side toward the enemy. Usually the next step was the addition of a headlog. The men put a green log (less likely to splinter) atop the earthen breastwork and scooped out small openings beneath it. The log protected the soldiers' heads as they fired on an advancing enemy through the openings under the log. The headlog rested on skids to keep it from falling on the men in the trench should it be dislodged by a cannonball. Troops fighting in such works had "but little more than the eyes . . . exposed" to hostile fire. Both their chance for survival and their ability to repel an attack increased exponentially in such circumstances.

For a hundred yards or so in front of the main trench the defenders, if time permitted, cut away the underbrush to clear a field of fire. Young trees, felled with their tops toward the enemy, formed an abatis to impede the attackers and hold them under the defenders' fire. Left partly attached to the stumps, the trees could not be pulled aside by attacking troops. If time and resources permitted, the defenders strung telegraph wire between the trees and stumps to trip attackers and make it even more difficult for the enemy to remove obstacles. If the distance between the lines was great enough, the men would build rifle pits or skirmish pits in front of their main position. Each of those small works sheltered three or four men whose mission was to give warning of an attack and fire a few rounds to slow the enemy. That accomplished, they scurried back to the main trench to join the defenders there.

From New Hope Church in late May through the end of the campaign in early September the armies constructed fortifications when they halted after a day's march. By August, the fields where they fought resembled the blasted landscape of the Western Front in World War I half a century later more than they did the traditional open areas across which brave men marched in mass formations. The defense, which already had the upper hand on Civil War battlefields because of the new rifled weapons, became even more dominant.[7]

A second change in the campaign in late May concerned Johnston's relations with his chief subordinates. When John Bell Hood reached Dalton in late February, Johnston considered him the more reliable of the army's infantry corps commanders. In the early days of the campaign Johnston had entrusted Hood with the defense of the part of the Dalton position that he regarded as the most important—the Crow Valley line. When the Yankees appeared at Resaca, Johnston sent Hood to that area. On both those occasions, Johnston took troops from Hardee and put them temporarily under Hood's command. At Resaca Hood had made the attacks on Sherman's left. At Cassville Hood had been sent to strike the Yankees on the Adairsville-Cassville Road. Hood had taken the lead in arguing the weakness of the Cassville ridge position. On the twenty-eighth of May Hood had made the aborted effort to strike at the Federal left.

Hood, however, for all his opportunities, had not produced any results, and the advice he had sent Johnston from Resaca on May 10 had been, at best, misleading. By early June, too, Johnston may have known that Hood had criticized his commander's conduct of the campaign in Georgia to some of his Richmond friends. At the same time, Johnston's opinion of Hardee was rising. As early as May 16 Johnston had written his wife, "His

[Hardee's] conduct in our recent difficult operations has been admirable, his bearing in danger high & in council fair & candid, between our Selves would not give him for both his compeers."

Gradually, over the weeks that followed, Hood continued to sink in Johnston's estimation. By mid-July the two differed greatly, and after that time they became and remained very bitter personal and professional enemies. Beginning in June or July, the gap between Johnston and Hardee slowly closed as they came to see Davis, Bragg, and Hood as their common enemies. Eventually Johnston and Hardee became steadfast professional allies, and that new relationship endured for as long as they lived.[8]

The third and most important change developed during or immediately after—and in large part as a result of—the fighting on the Dallas–New Hope Church–Pickett's Mill line. When the campaign began at Dalton in early May, Johnston was hopeful of carrying out the idea he had expressed to the Rebel government during the winter debate over Confederate strategy, "to beat the enemy when he advances and then to move forward." The enemy had advanced at Rocky Face Ridge, Resaca, Calhoun, Adairsville, Kingston, Cassville, and New Hope Church. Although the Confederates had repulsed several attacks of greater or lesser severity, Johnston had not beaten the enemy.

Because Sherman refused to make the great, massive, all-out assault that Johnston anticipated and because Johnston was unwilling to seize the initiative and maneuver against the Federals, it had become very unlikely that the Confederates would be able "to beat the enemy." Instead of following up a victory by moving forward, Johnston had been compelled to fall back. By early June his army was only about twenty-five miles from Atlanta.

While admitting to his wife that his predicament was "due . . . partly to my own [fault]," Johnston complained that had the reinforcements sent to him after the campaign opened been with his army earlier, "the condition of things now [May 20] would, probably, have been different." Sherman, he grumbled, "is the most Cautious [general] that ever Commanded troops." "Events beyond my control have prevented my attacking the enemy on two occasions," he explained in late May. The Federal commander "is so Cautious that I can find no opportunity to attack him except behind intrenchments." Clearly, Johnston was becoming frustrated and, perhaps, a bit demoralized. "I have never been so little Satisfied with Myself," he wrote on May 23. "Have never been so weak—so little governed by my own opinions."

The problem, of course, was that Johnston had never found and never seriously attempted to create an opportunity "to beat the enemy." If he did discover what he thought was such an opening, something happened to prevent the Rebels from taking advantage of it. When such a problem arose, Johnston simply did not have the psychological strength to overcome the obstacle. It was easier just to cancel the effort and renew the retreat.

By the second week of the campaign, it had become obvious that Sherman was not going to launch a massive assault against Johnston's strong fortifications. It soon became equally clear that Johnston was not skillful, bold, or daring enough to compel him to do so, to make for himself some opportunity that the Southerners could exploit, or even to block Sherman's flanking maneuvers. In short, the strategy that Johnston had confidently set out to pursue had failed completely, and there did not seem to be much possibility that he could make it work any better in the future than he had made it work in the past.

Johnston's pessimism, however, did not last long. Sometime in the last week or ten days of May the Confederate commander came to view the campaign he and Sherman were waging in a new light. As he mulled over the first month of his operations in Georgia, Johnston convinced himself that—appearances to the contrary—his efforts had been a great strategic success. In headquarters conversations he and members of his military "family" concluded that the Rebels had made Sherman pay a very high price for his success. Some of Johnston's officers estimated Yankee killed and wounded through late May at more than forty-five thousand. Such losses (a casualty rate in excess of 40 percent) along with the men Sherman had had to detach to guard his railroad as he moved south would greatly reduce the Northerners' numerical advantage. "We have thus far succeeded in making him [Sherman] pay three or four [casualties] for every one of ours . . . , if we can keep this up, we win," wrote Johnston's chief of staff on May 30.

In late May Johnston's intelligence picked up evidence that Sherman's men and animals were short of food and forage. The Yankees' horses, one prisoner reported, had become so weak that they could hardly move the army's wagons. "Eny on half rations & stock starving," an officer at Johnston's headquarters noted in his pocket diary on May 30.[9]

Those estimates of casualties in the Yankee ranks were wildly inflated, more than double the true numbers, and the reports of shortages in Sherman's camps reflected the suffering of the Union forces while they were away from the railroad and had to haul their supplies over muddy, rain-soaked roads from Kingston to the Dallas–New Hope Church–Pickett's Mill front.

Johnston, however, convinced himself that the casualty estimates and intelligence reports accurately reflected conditions in Sherman's ranks. He then jumped to the conclusion that he, in fact, was winning a great strategic success despite his failure to achieve the anticipated battlefield victory. "He seized upon this notion the way a drowning man seizes a life ring," wrote Craig Symonds, his most recent and best biographer.

Johnston's new interpretation of the campaign led him to attach even more importance to what had earlier been but an ancillary facet of his strategic thinking. Sherman's forces depended on the railroad for supplies. If that line were so seriously damaged that it could not be used for several weeks, the Yankee armies in Johnston's front, already weakened by very heavy casualties and suffering from a shortage of supplies, would be compelled to abandon their flanking maneuvers and slow, siegelike operations. The Union commander, Johnston assumed, would then have but two options. He could give up his effort to penetrate into Georgia and fall back at least as far as Chattanooga or he could change his strategy and make a direct assault on the Rebel fortifications in an effort to decide the campaign before a shortage of supplies forced him to retreat.

Should Sherman choose the former alternative, Johnston could claim a victory and pursue him northward as far as possible. If he opted for the latter course, he most likely would be defeated with heavy casualties and then forced to retreat with the victorious Southerners in pursuit.

Having come to this point in his revised strategic thinking, Johnston turned to the key question: How could the Rebels get at Sherman's railroad? The mission seemed obviously one for cavalry. Just as obviously, the cavalry had to come either from Johnston's army or from some other command.

Since Johnston believed himself overwhelmingly outnumbered (even though, he thought, Sherman had lost a large percentage of his men), he dared not detach any significant part of his own cavalry for such a mission. He did send a few small parties that managed to wreck a train now and then and occasionally to pry up some rails, but they were too weak to achieve the results Johnston wanted. Similar efforts by small commands based in northern Alabama were no more successful.

Instead of launching a large part of his own mounted force against Sherman's railroad, Johnston reasoned that the large cavalry units then committed to the defense of Alabama and Mississippi should be so employed. Johnston, however, had no authority over those horsemen. His administrative command, the Department of Tennessee, included North Georgia and northeastern Alabama. Maj. Gen. Stephen D. Lee commanded the Rebels in Alabama and Mississippi. (Lee had succeeded Polk when the bishop left the department to join Johnston in Georgia.)

If the cavalrymen in Alabama and Mississippi were to be of any help to Johnston, he would have to persuade Lee to commit them against the rail line that supplied Sherman's force or prevail upon the Richmond authorities to order them used for such a purpose. Lee was willing to send his horsemen to help Johnston, but his first concern, naturally, was for the defense of the area entrusted to him.

Expecting the Southerners to attempt to disrupt his line of supply, Sherman ordered raiding expeditions out from occupied Memphis into Mississippi. (One of the advantages Sherman enjoyed was command over all Union forces between the Appalachians and the Mississippi River and, therefore, the ability to wage a coordinated campaign across the West without having to negotiate with some other officer as to how his troops should be used.) Time after time those raids met with failure as Lee's horsemen, brilliantly handled by Maj. Gen. Nathan Bedford Forrest, turned back one of them after another. The forays, however, served their purpose. While he was chasing Union raiders in Mississippi, Forrest could not attack Sherman's railroads in Tennessee or Georgia. By the time Forrest could rest and resupply his men and horses after defeating one Yankee raid, another was under way.

Sherman's success in keeping Forrest employed in Mississippi forced Confederate authorities to make a decision. Should Forrest and his horsemen be held to protect Mississippi or would they render greater service to the Confederacy by attacking the railroads that supplied the Yankees in Georgia? Jefferson Davis would make that decision, and he neither liked nor trusted Joseph E. Johnston.

As was usually the case when dealing with the Davis government, Johnston proved his own worst enemy. He did not explain his changed view of the campaign to the Richmond officials nor did he keep them posted on the details of his May operations. Late in the month, when his wife voiced the opinion that he should keep the government better informed about his situation, he termed her suggestion "judicious" and commented, "I do report in a general way . . . but the people of Richmond take no interest in any partial affairs [engagements] that may occur in this quarter."

Consideration of how best to employ Forrest's cavalry quickly degenerated into an argument between Johnston on the one hand and Davis and Bragg on the other. The issue was whether Johnston's own mounted arm was strong enough that he could detach a large portion of it to send against Sherman's railroad. On April 30 Johnston had reported 8,062 officers and men in his cavalry corps, only 2,419 of whom were what Confederate army regulations termed "effective" (that is enlisted men "present for duty, equipped"). Most of those not classified as "effective" were men without serviceable horses. Johnston's June 10 return showed 13,546 cavalrymen serving with his army, and 10,903 of them were "effective." (See appendix 3.)

Such a mounted force, Davis and Bragg concluded, was ample both to cover Johnston's flanks and to strike at the Yankee supply line with enough strength to break it, especially if Sherman sent troops away from his main body to help protect his railroad. Johnston's cavalry chief, Wheeler, did not help his commander's case when he wrote Bragg that he could wreck the Unionists' supply line if only Johnston would allow him to ride north to do so.

This impasse continued all through the remaining weeks of Johnston's command. As with the winter discussion of strategy for 1864, Johnston in Georgia and Davis in Richmond were unwilling or unable to trust each other. Nothing was decided on; nothing was resolved; nothing was done.[10]

CHAPTER EIGHT

On the Kennesaw Line

While exhausted Federal soldiers enjoyed a few days' rest in their camps about Acworth, Yankee repair crews labored to rebuild the railroad bridge across the Etowah River. They completed that task ahead of schedule on June 11, and once again supplies flowed southward to Sherman's troops without interruption. Meanwhile, on June 8 the Federal commander had the pleasure of welcoming to his army group 9,000 men of the two long-absent divisions of Frank P. Blair's XVII Corps. Those reinforcements, Sherman calculated inaccurately, made up for the casualties he had lost in the campaign's first month. (Incomplete reports show that the Army of the Cumberland alone suffered 8,774 casualties in May.)

Johnston had shifted his army eastward from the New Hope Church area along a line south of and parallel to Sherman's route. When they regained the railroad, the Rebels had gone into position on a line that ran generally from east to west a few miles south of Acworth.[1]

Several isolated heights dominate the area north of Marietta and offered excellent vantage points above the roads leading southward from Sherman's camps. The more prominent of these heights are Lost Mountain, west of Marietta and about five hundred feet high; Pine Mountain, northwest of Marietta; Brush Mountain, north of the town; and Kennesaw Mountain. Both Pine and Brush Mountains rise about three hundred feet above the surrounding plain. Kennesaw (often, especially in the 1860s, spelled "Kenesaw") is a ridge some two miles long and broken into three segments. "Big Kennesaw," the northeastern end of the ridge, is about eight hundred feet in height; "Little Kennesaw," in the center, is some four hundred feet high; Pigeon Hill, the southwestern end of the ridge, is about two hundred feet in elevation.

Brush Mountain, Pine Mountain, and Lost Mountain form a slightly bent line running roughly from northeast to southwest, with Pine Mountain a bit in advance (northwest) of a line connecting the other two heights. The Kennesaw Ridge is parallel to and two or three miles south of the right center of this line. On those elevated positions in early June Johnston's men built signal stations and emplaced artillery batteries. They constructed long lines of formidable trenches on, around, and between the commanding heights. Once again, Johnston had his army solidly in place. Once again he hoped that the Yankees would attack his fortifications.

Sherman, meanwhile, sat in his Acworth headquarters pondering his next move. The Western & Atlantic Railroad stretched south from Acworth, passing through Big Shanty (now Kennesaw), and then running almost due south toward the Kennesaw Ridge. Just north of the ridge the tracks made a right angle turn to the east and paralleled the ridge until they passed its northeastern end. There the railroad turned south around Big Kennesaw to reach Marietta.

The railroad's route compelled Sherman to move directly south from Acworth. Were he to shift his force off to the east, where he would find more favorable terrain, he would expose both the railroad and his recently established supply depot at Allatoona to a quick strike by the Rebels. For that reason the Sandtown Road became (and would remain for a month) the axis of his advance. This crucial highway ran south from Acworth to Gilgal Church between Pine and Lost Mountains. Thence it continued south, passing along to the west of the Kennesaw Ridge to reach Sandtown on the Chattahoochee some nine miles downstream from the W&A bridge. On its southward path the Sandtown Road zigged and zagged, crossed numerous creeks, and intersected several routes leading east or northeast into Marietta.

As usual, Sherman expected Johnston to fall back and make his next stand along the Chattahoochee, although the Rebels, he thought, might offer slight opposition at some points north of the river. "I think he [Johnston] will oppose us lightly all the way to the Chattahoochee and defend that line with all his ability," Sherman informed Schofield on June 6. On the following day he wrote, "I want to go to Marietta on Wednesday or Thursday [June 8 or 9] and feel down to the Chattahoochee next day." One optimistic Yankee happily predicted that the Unionists would celebrate the Fourth of July in Atlanta.[2]

Not until June 10, however, did Sherman's armies leave their camps. Thomas followed the Sandtown Road. McPherson marched on his left, Schofield to his right. By then cavalry reconnaissance had revealed that the Rebels were present in force to the front and holding a fortified line stretching from the railroad southwest as far as Lost Mountain.

Soon after beginning their advance, the Yankees ran into Confederate skirmishers. Over the next several days small-scale fighting erupted here and there along the line of contact between the opposing forces, but there was no general engagement. Sherman's attention soon focused on Pine Mountain, which stood a short distance in advance of the Secessionists' line.

Johnston had posted William B. Bate's division of Hardee's Corps in the forward position on Pine Mountain and had connected that outpost to the rest of the Rebel works with a network of trenches. Pine Mountain thus became a salient, or projecting angle, in the Confederate line. A Rebel punster quipped that Johnston was setting a trap for Sherman, using the troops on Pine Mountain as the "bate."

By June 12 Thomas had the Army of the Cumberland deployed in front of the Pine Mountain salient, and Sherman had realized that he might break Johnston's line by thrusting some of his force in between Pine and Kennesaw Mountains. On that and the following day Thomas worked his army around to the east of Pine Mountain, and it appeared that the Yankees might isolate Bate's Division, cutting it off from the rest of the Rebel army.

On the morning of June 14 Johnston and Hardee went to Pine Mountain to study the salient and decide if they should withdraw Bate's troops from so endangered a post. Polk accompanied them to avail himself of the height to study the ground in front of his own line to the east. Foolishly disregarding warnings that Yankee artillery had the exact range of the mountaintop, the generals climbed onto the breastworks to get a clear view of the area below. A large group of Bate's soldiers soon gathered to watch the high-ranking officers.

Sherman, too, was out on the lines that morning. When he observed a crowd of Rebels on the summit of Pine Mountain, he ordered nearby artillery to disperse the group with a few shots. The Confederate generals had just begun to walk away from the summit when the first round fell near them. Quickly the group scurried for cover, and all but Polk soon reached places of safety. The bishop-general did not want to set a bad example for the men. As he walked deliberately away from the exposed area, something attracted his attention, and he stopped for a better look. As he did, a cannonball passed through his body. He was the second highest-ranking Confederate killed in the war (after Gen. Albert Sidney Johnston, who died at Shiloh April 6, 1862).

Johnston and Hardee wanted to rush to Polk's assistance, but wiser men restrained them. Polk's body was carried off the mountain and sent to Augusta for burial (it was moved to New Orleans in 1945). In the bishop's pockets the Southerners found four copies of a religious tract, three of which he had inscribed for presentation to Johnston, Hardee, and Hood. All were soaked with his blood. Maj. Gen. William W. Loring, the ranking officer in the corps, took temporary command. By Johnston's order, Bate withdrew from Pine Mountain that night.

Hood's Corps held the right of this "first Kennesaw line," Polk's the center, and Hardee's the left. Jackson's cavalry division had to stretch all the way from Hardee's left to Lost Mountain. The weak part of the position was the left, and on June 16 some of Schofield's troops, moving around to the south on the far right of Sherman's front, seized high ground from which their artillery could enfilade Hardee's line off to the east.

Schofield's success forced Hardee to reposition his corps. That night, therefore, he abandoned much of his line and pulled his left back to a ridge east of Mud Creek. This stream rose near Pine Mountain and flowed almost directly south, passing between Lost Mountain and the Kennesaw Ridge. Johnston's position (the "Mud Creek line" or the "Second Kennesaw line") now resembled the upper left corner of a doorway. Hardee's new trenches ran north to south; Loring's and Hood's troops held a line running west to east. Hardee's withdrawal behind Mud Creek forced the Rebels to abandon Lost Mountain.

On the seventeenth Thomas discovered that the angle in the Confederate line permitted his guns to enfilade Hardee's new position from the north. Obviously the Southerners could not long remain in the second Kennesaw line, and Johnston put his engineers to building another set of fortifications nearer Marietta. This "third Kennesaw line," however, would not be ready until the nineteenth. The Rebels had no choice but to grit their teeth and endure two days of furious shelling.

Finally, the engineers completed the new line, and during the night of June 18–19 Johnston moved his troops back to it. Hardee's infantry remained on the left, with Jackson's cavalry to his left. Loring occupied the formidable Kennesaw Ridge itself. Hood's troops held the right of the line east of Big Kennesaw, with Wheeler's horsemen covering their right. In this new line Hardee's and Jackson's men faced to the west, Loring's to the northwest, and Hood's and Wheeler's more to the north.

When Sherman's men found the Mud Creek trenches empty, their commander again leaped to the conclusion that his opponent was fleeing to the Chattahoochee. Within a few hours, however, Yankee skirmishers, pressing forward, learned that once more the Southerners had simply pulled back to another line—this one much stronger and anchored on the Kennesaw Ridge itself. Since the angles in the new Rebel line were at the Kennesaw Ridge, the looming bulk of the mountain shielded both ends of the position against enfilade fire. Except for Rocky Face Ridge at Dalton, the third Kennesaw line was the strongest position Johnston occupied during the campaign. As was the case with the Dalton position, however, the Rebels could not hold the third Kennesaw line if they simply sat passively in their trenches. To stay on Kennesaw Mountain, Johnston would have to conduct an active defense. If he did not, it would be only a matter of time (and, as it turned out, weather, since it rained almost every day from late May to late June) until Sherman once again maneuvered the Confederates out of their fortifications.[3]

The heavy rains that fell almost daily beginning in late May had turned roads into ribbons of mud, fields into lakes, and the area's many small creeks into rivers. They filled trenches with water and soaked men, animals, wagons, and equipment. They also slowed Sherman's progress, and it took a day or so for the Yankees to work their way up to confront Johnston's men in their new line. McPherson remained on the left of the Union forces, facing the Confederates on the Kennesaw Ridge and in the area north of Marietta. Thomas was to the right of McPherson, facing Hardee's trenches that extended south from the southwestern end of Kennesaw Mountain. Slowly the whole Yankee force oozed to the south. On June 20 Hooker's corps on Thomas's right approached the Powder Springs Road about four miles southwest of Marietta. Meanwhile, Schofield, who had been off in the Lost Mountain area, had moved along the Sandtown Road to Nose's Creek. Late on June 21 his advanced elements made contact with Hooker's right flank a mile or so west of Kolb's Farm on the Powder Springs Road.

Rebel observers atop Kennesaw Mountain had watched the southward extension of Sherman's right. During the night of June 21–22, Johnston countered by shifting Hood's Corps from the right of the Confederate line to the left. On the morning of the twenty-second Hood's divisions slipped into position on Hardee's left, facing Hooker and Schofield and extending the line of Rebel infantry south across the Powder Springs Road. Jackson's horsemen patrolled the area to Hood's left. Wheeler's cavalrymen took over Hood's old trenches east of Kennesaw Mountain.

Early on June 22 Schofield and Hooker resumed their push eastward along the Powder Springs Road. In midafternoon some of Schofield's leading elements captured several prisoners from the Fifty-eighth and Sixtieth North Carolina regiments of Hood's Corps. From those men the Unionists learned that Johnston had reinforced the left of the Confederate line. This change in the Rebel forces, the Yankees concluded, meant the Secessionist commander was concentrating to strike the right of the Federal position.

Quickly Schofield and Hooker closed up their units, and their men went to work to construct basic field fortifications using logs, fence rails, and any other material they could find. The generals threw forward two regiments—the 123d New York of Hooker's corps and the 14th Kentucky of Schofield's command—as skirmishers to delay the anticipated Rebel advance as long as possible.

Moving cautiously into the open field to their front, the Kentuckians and New Yorkers advanced slowly against stout resistance from Rebel skirmishers. As the Yankees reached a wooded area, they encountered a massive force of Secessionists. With a long line of Confederates threatening to lap around their flanks, the two Union regiments had to fall back to their main line.

Given plenty of warning, the Northerners were ready to meet the attack that followed hard on the heels of the Federal skirmishers. Johnston, of course, had not intended to launch an assault by his left. Hood seems to have taken the advance of the two regiments as an attack on his new line. When the Northerners fell back, he decided to send two divisions of his corps forward in immediate "pursuit," doubtless hoping to catch the Federals before they could regain their own position.

The Southerners advanced to the west, some charging across an open field north of the Powder Springs Road and others struggling over much rougher terrain to the south. Federal guns along Hooker's line to the north had a clear field of fire against Hood's right and shredded the Confederate line. South of the road the terrain helped break the force of the attack. "I think it was the heaviest fire I ever was under," wrote one Rebel. Soon the Southerners abandoned the effort and fell back to the positions from which they had begun the assault. Hood lost about a thousand men that afternoon and gained nothing. Northern losses totaled about three hundred, mostly in the two advanced regiments that first encountered the Confederates.

After the fight at Kolb's Farm, Hood took up his new post as the left of the Rebel infantry. In a few days his trenches extended Johnston's line southward to Olley's Creek. Jackson's cavalry to his left held the south bank of the stream. For several days there was little movement along the lines.[4]

The Kolb Farm fight led to another flare-up between Sherman and Hooker. That afternoon the Federal commander sent a message directly to Hooker asking how he was faring. "We have repulsed two attacks and feel confident, our only apprehension being from our extreme right flank," came the reply. "Three entire corps are in front of us." Sherman reacted to this exchange in a way that reveals one of the least savory aspects of his personality and character.

The two men had long despised each other, and Sherman may well have been seeking an excuse to rid himself of the commander of the XX Corps. The morning after the Kolb's Farm fight, Sherman visited the right of his long line and fell into a confrontation with Hooker. The commander of the Military Division of the Mississippi berated his subordinate for communicating directly with him rather than following the prescribed chain of command and sending the message through Thomas. Since Hooker had done no more than answer a query put directly to him by Sherman, the accusation was patently unfair. Hooker was no more outside the chain of command than was Sherman.

The Federal commander also asserted that Hooker had falsely accused Schofield of failure to protect his right flank. Hooker's message, however, read "*our extreme* right flank" and, by any fair reading, referred to the flank of the army group—the right end of Schofield's line. Finally, Sherman asserted, Hooker had been wildly irresponsible in stating that all three corps of Johnston's army had concentrated in his front. It seems that the statements of prisoners, or Federal interpretations of those statements, indicated that "the whole Rebel army had concentrated" against the

Bridge over the Tennessee River at Bridgeport, Alabama. When repaired, this structure was a crucial link in Sherman's supply line.

Tunnel Hill on the Western & Atlantic Railroad northwest of Dalton.

Depiction of the early May skirmishing at Mill Creek Gap. Sketch by Alfred R. Waud.

Yankees of the XX Corps assaulting Dug Gap, May 8. Sketch by Alfred R. Waud.

The death of Lt. Gen. Leonidas Polk, Pine Mountain, June 14. Generals Johnston and Hardee at left. Sketch by Alfred R. Waud.

The June 27 assault on Kennesaw Mountain. William T. Sherman on horseback, facing right. Sketch by Alfred R. Waud.

Pickets trading coffee for tobacco between the lines—a common practice during the campaign. Sketch by Edwin Forbes.

Union skirmishers. Sketch by Edwin Forbes.

Federal troops in a captured Confederate fort near Atlanta.

Captured Confederate fort outside Atlanta.

View of part of Atlanta after the city fell. The rail cars are U.S. Military Railroad rolling stock. The Lard Oil Factory was destroyed by a fire ignited by Federal artillery shells.

Ruins of the ordnance train burned when the Confederates evacuated Atlanta.

Federal right. Thomas believed it probable that Johnston would mass as many men as he could to block the progress of the Union right. In truth, the Yankees did encounter men from the left of Hardee's Corps, as Sherman himself later admitted.

Hooker's conduct on July 22 fell well within the boundaries of proper behavior, and his comments were not unreasonable. Sherman's indictment of his best corps commander was unfair and unbecoming.[5]

After the Battle of Kolb's Farm, Sherman faced a difficult situation. His army group was stretched along a wide north-south front, and Schofield's units on his far right were about seven miles from his railhead. The roads were still in bad condition, and even after the rains stopped on June 25 the country would need days to dry enough that an army could maneuver across it. Once the roads became passable, Sherman could renew his push to the south, hoping eventually to pry his enemy out of the Kennesaw position. He could also attempt an assault at some point or points on Johnston's long line hoping to make a breakthrough that would shatter the Rebel army. What the Union commander could not afford to do was to sit in his own trenches. Such a passive course would free Johnston to send part of his army to reinforce Confederates elsewhere or to use it against Sherman's precious rail line which lay just behind the Federals' left flank. Even if Johnston did nothing—his most probable course—the Rebel commander would gain merely by waiting as the days wore away.

If Sherman elected simply to extend his line southward, he would have to wait several days to allow the roads to dry and to accumulate supplies and distribute them to his troops. An attack, on the other hand, would probably entail heavy casualties but, if successful, could mean the destruction of Johnston's army. On second thought, however, an attack might not be as hopeless as first appeared. Johnston, like Sherman, had stretched his line very thin. It might be weak enough to break at some point. Besides, if the assault failed, Sherman could still resume the effort to extend to the south once the roads dried. He thus could try one option. If it failed and his losses were not crippling, he could try the other. After weighing the situation, he decided to make the attack.

Two days after the Yankees repulsed Hood's men at Kolb's Farm, Sherman directed that his troops make an assault against three points on Johnston's fortifications at 8:00 A.M., Monday, June 27. McPherson would assail some point, to be selected by him, on the Rebel line near the southwestern end of the Kennesaw Ridge. Thomas would make his attack to the right against a point south of the Dallas-Marietta Road. Schofield was to strike the Confederate position near the Powder Springs Road while demonstrating to the south along Olley's Creek near Johnston's far left flank. On the twenty-fifth, however, Sherman visited Schofield's front and, after studying the enemy fortifications there, canceled Schofield's attack and directed him to place more emphasis on the Olley's Creek operation. Sherman ordered the demonstrations for June 26, hoping they would mislead Johnston into rushing reinforcements to his left, thereby weakening the points to be assailed the following morning.[6]

McPherson decided to send the XV Corps against the portion of Johnston's line on and just south of Pigeon Hill. Should the attack succeed, the Federals would pour through the broken Southern line and cut off the Secessionists on the mountain to the north. Meanwhile, the XVI and XVII Corps would demonstrate against the Rebels along the rest of the Kennesaw Ridge.

Thomas chose to assault a salient in the Confederate line about three-quarters of a mile south of the Dallas Road on what came to be called Cheatham's Hill after the general whose division defended it. He would also launch another attack against the Southern trenches a short distance to the north. He seems to have doubted that the assaults would succeed and to have selected those objectives because the attacking troops would have to advance a shorter distance under enemy fire than at other points on his line.

At the appointed hour on June 27 Federal artillery began to pound the Rebel line. Soon afterward the attacking columns lurched forward. Bullets flew out from beneath the headlogs on the Confederate earthworks. All the assaulting forces quickly met with defeat, although most of the soldiers performed well. Some of the attackers got to within a short distance of the defenders' line before being forced to halt. A handful of men from the 55th and 111th Illinois regiments of McPherson's army managed to reach the Confederate earthworks before they were shot down. At Cheatham's Hill the color-bearer of the 52d Ohio got to the Rebel line and started up the earthen parapet in front of the trench. A Southern officer leaped out to wrest the flag from him. In the struggle that followed, the Ohioan killed his enemy and then fell with the flag he had carried so far and defended so well.

At all points, it quickly became obvious that the Yankees could not break through Johnston's line. The Federals either fell back to the positions from which they began the attack or burrowed into the earth at the point to which they had advanced. At Cheatham's Hill some Northerners, unwilling to try to recross the open area between the lines, clung for five days to a position under the brow of the hill only a few yards from the Confederate trenches. Eventually they began to dig a tunnel into the hillside, hoping to reach a point beneath the Rebel fortifications and blow them up.

Unfortunately for the men in the attacking units, their generals had chosen to make the assaults against the portions of Johnston's line held by the divisions of Cheatham and Cleburne and the Missouri Brigade of Brig. Gen. Francis M. Cockrell (Pigeon Hill)—three of the best and toughest infantry outfits in the entire Confederacy. The attacks cost Sherman a total of about three thousand men. Johnston's losses (including an estimate for all parts of his army) probably totaled about one thousand.[7]

Although the Rebels had repulsed the direct attacks on their fortified line, Sherman did gain a great strategic victory as a result of the operations of June 26 and 27. On the twenty-sixth, in hopes of inducing Johnston to withdraw troops from points to be assaulted the next morning, Schofield detached a brigade from the right of the Yankee line and sent it south along the Sandtown Road to Olley's Creek. There the Federals skirmished with Jackson's defending Rebel horsemen but made no serious attempt to cross. While the two sides traded bullets at the Sandtown Road crossing, another of Schofield's brigades reached the creek a mile or so upstream. Finding no Confederates defending the creek in his front and discovering that his men could easily cross, Col. Robert K. Byrd, commanding the brigade, quickly moved to the south bank, advanced to a small hill just beyond the creek, and put his men to entrenching.

Early on the twenty-seventh more Yankees crossed Olley's Creek. By the time the attacks to the north got under way, the equivalent of a division of Federal infantry was south of the creek and had chased off defending Confederate cavalry. Soon those infantry units, joined by some Union horsemen, had pushed another mile or two southward along the Sandtown Road. In so doing they put the extreme right flank of Sherman's force closer to the Chattahoochee than was the left of Johnston's army. Unless the Confederate commander were willing to detach a strong force of infantry to drive back Schofield's men, the Southerners could not remain in the third Kennesaw line. Johnston was unwilling to take such a risk because, he feared, Sherman might attempt another assault on the Confederate trenches. Sherman's plan succeeded in reverse. The demonstrations intended to draw troops away from the points of attack achieved a great strategic success because the attacks prevented Johnston from sending men to oppose the demonstrations.[8]

Tactically Johnston had won a minor defensive triumph on Loring's and Hardee's lines. Schofield's success, however, gave Sherman a great advantage, and the Federal commander quickly decided to exploit it. Before he could do so he had to wait a few days for the roads to dry completely and to distribute supplies to his troops so they could operate for a while out of contact with the railroad. By July 1 all was ready.

That night McPherson's troops quietly pulled out of their lines on the Federal left and marched away to the south, passing behind Thomas's fortifications. By noon on the second, the lead units of the Army of the Tennessee had joined Schofield south of Olley's Creek, and the combined armies of the Tennessee and of the Ohio were pushing on toward the Chattahoochee. They encountered "stubborn" resistance from Jackson's cavalry supported by a small division of Georgia militia that Governor Brown had called into service and placed at Johnston's disposal.

Almost immediately after the repulse of the assaults on the twenty-seventh, Johnston had anticipated that Sherman's next effort would be against the left of the Confederate line. Realizing that Jackson's cavalry and the militiamen could not long delay the massive force moving south along the Sandtown Road, believing it unwise to extend his own line farther, and unwilling to run the risk inherent in detaching a portion of his veteran infantry or of Wheeler's cavalry either to meet the flanking column or to strike at Sherman's railroad north of Marietta, Johnston concluded to abandon the third Kennesaw line and fall back to a new position near Smyrna that his engineers had been constructing for several days.

At nightfall on July 2, the Confederates again began their familiar ritual of retreat. As each Rebel division evacuated its portion of the line, it left behind a detail of men to answer shots from Sherman's outposts. Not long after midnight the Southerners' fire died out. Soon Federal pickets, curious about the silence to their front, began cautiously to creep forward. Only the curses of Northerners who tripped over roots or rocks or bumped into a stump broke the night's quiet. They found the Rebel trenches empty, and word soon went back to their own units and thence up the chain of command. When Sherman learned that Johnston had gone, he ordered a pursuit, hoping to catch the Southerners before they could get into another fortified position. One gleeful Unionist wrote that the

Secessionist works at Kennesaw Mountain had been too strong to carry by assault, but "we flanked them though, and they had to skedaddle."[9]

Six weeks had passed since Sherman had taken his armies across the Etowah. During that period he had flanked Johnston out of the strong position at Allatoona, back from the Dallas–New Hope Church area, and out of the three Kennesaw lines. The armies had fought no major battle. Even the attack of June 27 was not a large engagement by 1864 standards. Altogether Sherman lost about twelve thousand men during those six weeks, Johnston approximately nine thousand. (By contrast, in the fighting on May 5–6 in the Virginia Wilderness Lee and Grant lost a combined total of about thirty-two thousand men.)

The operations of late May and June demonstrated yet once again that Sherman was not about to shatter his army in large-scale assaults on Johnston's fortifications. Those same operations also showed once more that Johnston was not about to do much more than remain passive behind those works and concede the initiative to his enemy. The Rebel commander might make an occasional halfhearted and ineffective effort to strike at the Yankees, but he was unwilling to attempt any serious maneuvering to thwart Sherman's flanking movements.

In late May and June Johnston once again missed several good chances to punish his opponent. When Sherman crossed the Etowah, Johnston could have moved west from Allatoona to threaten the Yankees' left flank and, perhaps, challenge them on the low ground immediately south of the river where the Unionists would have had their backs to the stream. Johnston did not spot either of the two wide gaps that yawned for several days in the Federal line at Dallas and New Hope Church (or, if he did, he chose not to try to take advantage of them). In late June he elected not to detach infantry from his main line to try to drive the Unionists back across Olley's Creek. At no time did he send a sizable force of cavalry to operate against Sherman's railroad, even in late June, when he knew the great bulk of Sherman's force to be miles away, moving south to flank him out of the third Kennesaw line. He did not even inflict serious damage on the railroad behind his own position before he evacuated Marietta. It would be unfair to expect Johnston to have seized all those opportunities, but an alert, confident, aggressive commander could at least have attempted *something* to get at his enemy during those six weeks. A more thoughtful general would have destroyed the railroad thoroughly as he retreated.

Johnston, of course, would have responded that if, for example, he sent an infantry division against Schofield's force south of Olley's Creek, Sherman would have seized the opportunity to attack the weakened portion of the main Rebel position. We are justified in wondering, however, how Sherman would have determined so quickly which part of Johnston's line had been weakened and how he would have been able to concentrate his own extended forces against it quickly enough to have made a successful assault. Surely Johnston's observers on Kennesaw Mountain would have spotted some indication of a Yankee concentration had it taken place in daylight. If Sherman waited until after dark to concentrate his assaulting columns, he could not attack until the following morning. By then, Johnston's detached infantry would have had time to deal with the Yankees beyond Olley's Creek and return to its old works.

In truth, Johnston should have invited and welcomed such an assault on his lines. His initial strategy for the campaign had been based on the premise that Sherman would attack the Confederate fortifications and be defeated. If Johnston desired to draw Sherman into an attack, perhaps he should not have fortified his positions so strongly. Weaker Rebel defensive works might have lured Sherman into a frontal assault in which the odds would still have been very much in favor of the defending Rebels. Conversely, Johnston might have relied more on his strong fortifications to hold the Yankees at bay while mobile columns from his main body marched to meet Sherman's flanking forces. If Johnston simply held his men in their trenches and waited for Sherman to make massive attack after massive attack—something that by mid-May it was obvious the Yankee commander was not going to do—it would be impossible for him to prevent the Federals from flanking the Secessionists out of every position they took.

CHAPTER NINE

Across the Chattahoochee

When word reached Sherman's headquarters that the Southerners had abandoned the third Kennesaw line, the Yankee commander's characteristic optimism surfaced again. Convinced yet one more time that Johnston was hastening to get his army south of the Chattahoochee as quickly as possible, Sherman ordered his forces forward to strike the Confederates "in the confusion of crossing the . . . [river]."

Thomas with the Army of the Cumberland swept into Marietta from the west and turned southward. The XIV Corps in the center moved along the railroad, the IV Corps to its left, the XX Corps on its right. McPherson and Schofield with the other elements of Sherman's army group continued southward along the Sandtown Road. The Federal commander hoped they might strike the flank or rear of Johnston's retreating column.

Thomas's men encountered a small Rebel rear guard just south of Marietta, and skirmishing erupted at once. The Northerners made slow progress against stout Confederate opposition. By late afternoon on July 3, as the Yankees neared Smyrna four miles from Marietta, Southern resistance so stiffened that the Unionists deployed a division for battle. It was, however, too late in the day for further combat. Secessionist skirmishers also slowed the Federals' progress off to the west on the Sandtown Road.

Unknown to Sherman, Johnston had prepared two major lines of fortifications between Marietta and the Chattahoochee. The Rebels had constructed their northern line along an east-west ridge that crossed the railroad at Smyrna. Its right flank was protected by Rottenwood Creek, its left by Nickajack Creek. The second line had been built in a semicircle with its ends resting on the river some distance above and below the railroad bridge.

The main body of Johnston's troops reached the Smyrna line early on July 3. Loring's Corps held the right, guarding the main road to Atlanta. Hardee's men occupied the center. Hood's troops stood on Hardee's left, with the Georgia militia on their left. As usual, Wheeler's cavalry covered the right of the Confederate force, Jackson's horsemen the left.

At 6:45 P.M. on the third Sherman wrote to Thomas, "The more I reflect the more I know Johnston's halt is to save time to cross his material and men. No general, such as he, would invite battle with the Chattahoochee behind him." (Somehow Sherman managed to forget that the Rebel commander had fought with his back to the Oostanaula and Connasauga and had tried to make another stand with the Etowah but a short distance in rear of his army.) Again believing that Johnston was attempting to escape across the Chattahoochee, Sherman asserted that the Northerners had "the best chance ever offered" to catch the Rebels at the riverbank or in the confusion of crossing the stream and inflict heavy casualties upon them.

A day's skirmishing along the line on July 4 produced relatively few casualties but an important result. McPherson's Yankees on the western end of Sherman's front pushed across Nickajack Creek and gained a position from which they threatened to cut the Georgia militia off from the main body of the Rebel army. Faced with this danger on his left, Johnston abandoned the Smyrna line during the night and marched away to the south. By the next morning the Rebels were safely in the heavy works of the Chattahoochee line.

On July 5 Federals, pushing southward in pursuit, came up to the new Confederate position. The wings of Sherman's army group—Howard's IV Corps on the left, McPherson's army on the right—reached the river above and below Johnston's fortified line. Once again the Secessionist commander had chosen to make a stand with a river behind him. Skirmishing that afternoon soon demonstrated that the Chattahoochee line was far too strong to be carried by assault. With their own flanks securely on the river, the Yankees, too, were safe from attack. The Chattahoochee was still high from the massive June rains, but it was falling rapidly.[1]

While he studied the situation and waited for the river to drop, Sherman pulled Schofield's army out of the line and sent it back to Smyrna. There it could both act as a reserve and be positioned to march quickly to some point on the river to effect a crossing. The Yankee commander also dispatched Brig. Gen. Kenner Garrard with his cavalry division east from Smyrna to Roswell, an important little manufacturing town on the Chattahoochee some sixteen miles upstream from the right end of Johnston's line.

Sherman knew full well the futility of assaulting the Confederates' massive fortifications ("by far the strongest we have yet encountered," his chief engineer called them; the Federal commander himself labeled them "the best line of field intrenchments I have ever seen"). Realizing that he would have to cross the Chattahoochee to force Johnston out of the river line, Sherman concluded to strike above the Rebels' position. A crossing there offered several advantages to the Northerners. Union armies operating above the Southern works would be better positioned to protect their own all-important railroad. They would also be able to cooperate with Garrard's cavalry, already at Roswell. An upstream crossing would not place Sherman so that Johnston's army was between himself and the operations in Virginia, thereby opening the possibility that the Rebels might shift troops from one area to reinforce their army in the other without his knowledge. Finally, Sherman believed—correctly— that Johnston expected him to attempt to cross the river in the Sandtown area, below the railroad bridge. Had Sherman not moved against the Confederate left to flank the Rebels out of every prepared position— Dalton, Resaca, Allatoona, Kennesaw Mountain, and Smyrna? Ever since the June 27 attack Sherman had aggressively pushed his right (Schofield and McPherson) southward along the Sandtown Road.

Believing his enemy would continue operating to the west, Johnston anticipated an attempt to cross downriver from his fortified line. Accordingly, he strengthened his guards on the left bank at the fords and ferries below his fortifications. Only small detachments of militiamen watched the upriver crossings. (Later Johnston claimed that he did not post strong forces along the river above his fortifications because had he done so Peachtree Creek would have divided his army and made it difficult for one part to support the other. Again, he overlooked the fact that the same creek—and the Chattahoochee too—would have divided Sherman's forces.)

To keep Johnston deceived, Sherman directed McPherson and the cavalry with him to demonstrate along the right bank of the river at several points downstream from the Confederate fortifications as if seeking a place to cross at or below the mouth of Nickajack Creek. To Thomas went instructions to press against Johnston's works to fix the main body of Rebels in position. While McPherson and Thomas thus distracted Johnston, Schofield was to march his small army from its Smyrna camps to the river at any point between Thomas's left and Roswell that he believed offered a good chance for success and there attempt a crossing.[2]

Sherman's plan worked perfectly. As Johnston kept his attention focused downriver, Schofield reconnoitered the northern bank upstream from the Rebel position and selected a point near the mouth of Soap (or Sope) Creek as the best place to attempt a crossing. The Southerners had destroyed the bridge there, but the Yankee general found the submerged ruins of an old dam a short distance above the creek's mouth. A few unsuspecting Confederates stood guard opposite the mouth of the creek.

On the morning of July 8 Schofield moved his army to Soap Creek. At 3:30 P.M. one of his brigades splashed across the river on the unguarded dam and became the first sizable body of Sherman's troops to set foot on the Chattahoochee's left bank. (Small parties had crossed earlier.) Thirty minutes later the Twelfth Kentucky crossed at the mouth of the creek under cover of fire from Yankees on the northern bank and chased off the Rebel guards. By nightfall Schofield had a couple of brigades across and deployed along a ridge where they went to work entrenching. Soon after dark his engineers completed two pontoon bridges, and an entire division quickly crossed.

The next morning Garrard's cavalrymen got across the river at Roswell. The men who made that crossing were armed with repeating rifles that fired metallic, waterproof cartridges. To avoid Rebel bullets as they waded the river, they stooped down in the water, stood up to fire, and then ducked again beneath the surface. The defending Confederates, accustomed only to single-shot weapons and bullets that came wrapped with powder in paper tubes, were amazed by the "guns that could be loaded and fired under water." Some of the Secessionists simply ceased shooting and remained to surrender, eager to see the novel weapons used by their enemies. By 7:00 A.M. the Yankees had a second bridgehead on the Atlanta side of the Chattahoochee.

Sherman lost no time hastening reinforcements to Soap Creek and Roswell. By nightfall on July 9 an infantry division had reached Roswell, crossed the river, and relieved Garrard's cavalrymen. Early the following afternoon part of the XXIII Corps had also reinforced the Roswell bridgehead and by eight that night the Yankees had a footbridge in place there.

Meanwhile, other Federal units made additional crossings. The First Tennessee (U.S.) Cavalry reached the river above Soap Creek before dawn on July 9. The men spread out along the riverbank and at daylight began to exchange shots with a small party of Confederates on the opposite bank. Northerners who attempted to wade the river found it too deep. Finally, Lt. Col. James P. Brownlow took eight men a mile upstream where they constructed a small raft on which to float their weapons. The men stripped and swam the river, pushing the raft. Once across, they donned their belts and cartridge boxes and received instructions for the attack. (One Yankee was heard to mutter, "I'll be durned if this ain't baring our breasts to the foe for a fact.")

After the party deployed, it moved down the bank, the men suffering a great deal from rocks, underbrush, and insects. "Cuss low" came the order. Finally, they reached a point behind the Rebels, who were still engaged with the Yankees across the river. Brownlow formed his men into line and charged. Taken by surprise, the Southerners turned and bolted off through the briers where—Brownlow's Federals soon discovered—the Yankees could not pursue. "It was," reported one of Sherman's officers, "certainly one of the funniest sights of the war, and a very successful raid for naked men to make."

Once the Federals had secured their river crossings and fortified bridgeheads, Johnston felt that he had no alternative but to evacuate his massive fortifications north of the Chattahoochee. He rejected the possibility of detaching part of his army to attempt to push the Yankees back into or over the river, and during the night of July 9–10 he crossed the stream, burning the wagon bridge, the railroad bridge, and some of his pontoon bridges that he could not remove. In so doing, he left Sherman master of the entire region from Chattanooga south to the Chattahoochee.

In abandoning the right bank of the Chattahoochee, Johnston gave up another valuable industrial area. From Roswell on the river above the railroad bridge to the mouth of Sweetwater Creek below stretched a twenty-mile strip of land where streams flowing into the river from the north powered many mills, most of which produced cloth for the Confederate army. Some of the establishments continued in operation until Yankee cavalrymen walked in the door and ordered the workers to leave. The Federals then set fire to the buildings. Destruction of the Chattahoochee mills, coupled with the loss of Rome and the ironworks along the Etowah, constituted a severe blow to the Rebels.[3]

Once over the river, Johnston pulled his army back to a line south of Peachtree Creek, only about three miles from downtown Atlanta. The stream flowed roughly from east to west, passing north of the city, to join the Chattahoochee. Johnston seems to have hoped that the creek would present a serious obstacle to Sherman's advance. If so, perhaps the Confederates could find an opportunity to attack the Yankees. Wheeler's cavalry took position in front of this new line; Jackson's horsemen held their usual post on the left of the infantry. Hood's Corps manned the right of the army, Hardee's men the center. Johnston entrusted the left to Polk's old corps under its new commander.

After Polk's death on June 14, Johnston informed President Davis that he wanted Alexander P. Stewart (whom he called the "best qualified" of the infantry major generals then with the army) as the bishop's replacement. Twelve days later, probably because he feared the delay indicated that the president had rejected his recommendation, Johnston asked for Lt. Gen. Richard S. Ewell to take Polk's place. Owing to Ewell's poor physical and mental health, however, Davis eventually acquiesced in Stewart's selection.

Stewart assumed his new post on July 7, replacing Loring, who returned to the head of his division. To succeed Stewart as division commander in Hood's Corps, Johnston asked for his old friend Maj. Gen. Mansfield Lovell, who had been serving with the army in a supernumerary capacity. Again, Davis ignored Johnston's wishes and selected Henry D. Clayton, one of the brigade commanders, to head the division. (Davis may have decided on Clayton before receiving Johnston's request for Lovell. Even so, he once again had made a major personnel decision about Johnston's army without consulting Johnston.)[4]

On July 6, while the armies were still north of the Chattahoochee, Sherman had telegraphed Federal authorities that once he was over the river, "I propose to make a circuit [of Atlanta], destroying all its railroads." The Federal commander realized that if the rail lines radiating from the city were cut, Atlanta would be useless to the Confederates even if they managed to retain possession of it.

With both banks of the Chattahoochee in his grip, Sherman could operate against Atlanta in either of two directions. He could shift downriver to campaign below the city against the railroads running to Macon and West Point. If successful, such a maneuver would carry the contending armies into a comparatively open area where the terrain would favor the

Unionists. The probable result, however, would be to force Johnston to transfer his main line of supply to the Georgia Railroad, which ran east from Atlanta to Augusta. If the Federals then managed to compel Johnston to quit the city, he could easily fall back to the east. Such a development would be undesirable for Sherman because it would place the troops of Johnston in Georgia and those of Lee in Virginia squarely between the two main Union forces and expose one or both of the latter to possible defeat should the Southerners quickly reinforce one of their armies with troops from the other. Sherman, therefore, elected to pursue his second option. He would extend his left north of Atlanta seeking to destroy the Georgia Railroad so thoroughly that no large body of Confederate troops could rush via that route from one Secessionist army to the other.

Before shifting his forces to the east side of Atlanta, however, Sherman wished to cripple Johnston's rail connections with Alabama. To do so, he planned a two-pronged raid. A mounted force from Tennessee would undertake a long-range strike to cut the railroad in eastern Alabama between Tuskegee and Opelika while the cavalry division of the Army of the Ohio struck at the tracks a short distance southwest of Atlanta. Maj. Gen. Lovell H. Rousseau would command the former effort, Maj. Gen. George Stoneman the latter.

Rousseau set out on July 10, leading a column of some twenty-five hundred troopers south from the Tennessee River. Skirmishing occasionally with Alabama militiamen and small parties of Confederate soldiers as he went, Rousseau reached Talladega on July 15. There his raiders captured and destroyed quantities of salt, sugar, flour, and bacon. Turning eastward, the Yankees devastated the railroad as they marched. By the time Rousseau abandoned his work on July 17 and marched northeast to join Sherman in Georgia his men had burned buildings and rolling stock, destroyed bridges, and torn up thirty miles of track. By striking the line west of Opelika, the raiders cut both railroads from Georgia into Alabama since the two lines joined at Opelika. Rousseau and his horsemen had seriously damaged Rebel communications between Georgia and the Alabama-Mississippi area. The Confederates would need at least three weeks to get the lines back into full operation.

Stoneman's raid, by contrast, turned into a fiasco. On July 13 his cavalrymen captured a partially wrecked bridge over the Chattahoochee thirty-five miles below Atlanta. The next day Stoneman's troopers crossed in force. Once a nearby party of Confederates opened fire with artillery, however, Stoneman panicked, beat a hasty retreat across the river, and burned the bridge. When Sherman learned of the debacle, he ordered Stoneman to abandon the effort. Rousseau's success, however, meant that Sherman could focus his attention on the railroad east of Atlanta.[5]

Sherman's plans for his operations about Atlanta called for McPherson to pull the remainder of the Army of the Tennessee out of its position on the Chattahoochee below the city and swing upstream, passing behind Thomas's lines, to Roswell. From the bridgehead there McPherson would move out to the east, arcing around to reach the Georgia Railroad between Stone Mountain and Decatur. As McPherson advanced from Roswell, Schofield and Thomas would swing forward on parallel courses, the former in the center of the Federal force, the latter to the west acting as the hinge, with his right on the river. McPherson thus would become the left of the advancing Union line, Schofield the center, Thomas the right. By July 17 McPherson's army was concentrated at Roswell, and the Yankees were poised to resume their advance.

Pushing out from the river that day, the Federals ran into stiff opposition from Wheeler's cavalry. By evening, however, Schofield had reached the little settlement of Cross Keys, and the other armies were closing on their objectives. The day's operations had advanced the Union line from the Chattahoochee to Nancy's Creek, roughly halfway between the river and Peachtree Creek. Sherman was hopeful that his men would reach and cut the Georgia Railroad on the eighteenth.[6]

CHAPTER TEN

On Other Fields

In the afternoon of July 9, the day after Schofield's men splashed across the Chattahoochee near Soap Creek, another army forced its way across another river some 550 miles to the northeast. A Confederate force under Lt. Gen. Jubal A. Early had erupted from the Shenandoah Valley, crossed the Potomac River into Maryland on July 5, and four days later routed a hastily assembled body of Federal troops at the Monocacy River near Frederick. Two days after fighting their way across the Monocacy, Early's veterans were in the suburbs of Washington.

The Rebel raid into Maryland came after two months of campaigning in Virginia. In early May, when Sherman moved against Johnston's army at Dalton, Grant had taken the Army of the Potomac across the Rapidan and Rappahannock Rivers to grapple with Lee. While Sherman jabbed and feinted at Johnston and flanked him out of one position after another and while Johnston sat and waited for Sherman and then fell back time after time, Lee and Grant waged a titanic series of battles across the Old Dominion. Their armies clashed in the Wilderness, at Spotsylvania Court House, on the North Anna River, at Cold Harbor, and along the heavily fortified lines in front of Petersburg and Richmond. This great "Overland campaign" ended in mid-June when Grant's battered army reeled back in defeat from the first attempt to take Petersburg. By that time—after six weeks of fighting—Grant had suffered some sixty-five thousand casualties. He had lost more men than Lee had had in his army when the campaign began.

Strategically, Lee had won a great victory, keeping Grant on the circumference of a circle that centered on Richmond. If the two great antagonists had been fighting on the face of a clock, they had started at twelve and fought their way down around the side past one, two, and three to four. More important, Lee had punished the Army of the Potomac more severely than any other Civil War army had—or any other large American army has—ever been punished.

In mid-June Grant found himself bogged down before the formidable Confederate works that protected Richmond and Petersburg. He could make no more assaults on Lee's position. The flower of his army had been left behind in shallow graves in the Wilderness or on one of his other battlefields or sent off to hospitals in the rear. The men who remained and the green troops who had been called forward from rear echelon units to replace casualties would not have tolerated further attacks even had Grant wanted to make them. Nor could the Yankees continue on around the clock south of Petersburg to six or seven without exposing their flank and supply lines to Lee and leaving Washington uncovered. Grant could not pull back and start over someplace else without doing great psychological and political harm to the Union cause. In summary, Grant had been checked. He had not taken Richmond. He had not inflicted a significant and visible defeat on Lee's army. His own forces had suffered staggering losses. He was, in a word, stalemated.

Grant had not even been able to prevent Lee from detaching a large number of Rebel troops to go elsewhere. Secure in his strong fortifications, Lee in mid-June had sent Early off westward with about one-third of the Army of Northern Virginia. Early originally had gone to dispose of a new Yankee force advancing from the Shenandoah Valley but Lee soon expanded his mission, and he quickly moved north through the Valley and across the Potomac.

Early could not stay long in the Washington area after his victory at the Monocacy because Grant detached reinforcements from the army at Petersburg and Richmond and rushed them north to protect the national capital. The Confederates fell back to the northern end of the Shenandoah Valley, where they remained both a threat and an embarrassment to the Federal government. To add insult to injury, some of Early's cavalry burned Chambersburg, Pennsylvania, on July 30.

A stalemate on the Richmond-Petersburg front, horrific casualty lists, the smoldering ashes of a Pennsylvania town, and a potent Rebel force lurking about the Lower Shenandoah Valley were not the sorts of things that Lincoln and Grant had anticipated back in March when they laid plans for the summer's military operations. Confederate victories over Banks in Louisiana, over Sigel at New Market, and over Butler at Bermuda Hundred, along with Grant's clear failure to achieve any of his objectives and Early's obvious triumph in the valley, made it impossible for Northern officials to claim any degree of military success as of midsummer. Clearly, as June wore along, the Secessionists were well on their way toward winning—indeed, they probably already had won—the fourth round of the 1864 campaign.

The battlefields of Louisiana, Georgia, and Virginia were not the only points at which the Federal and Confederate governments clashed in 1864. The Northern elections scheduled for that fall opened up another front on which the two antagonists struggled throughout most of the year.

The United States Constitution mandated that a president be elected in November 1864. When the year opened it was by no means certain that the Republican Party would renominate Abraham Lincoln or that he could win reelection if it did. No president had won a second term since Andrew Jackson in 1832, and no political party had even nominated an incumbent chief executive for another term since the Democrats put forth Martin Van Buren in 1840.

During the first three years of the war many of Lincoln's policies had generated great opposition within the ranks of his own party. As 1864 wore along, many Republicans who disagreed with their president's policies became restless and fearful that his unpopularity would drag them and the party down to defeat that fall.

The "Radical" wing of the party (extreme antislavery men) had been disenchanted with Lincoln and what one of them called his "timid and almost proslavery course" almost from the beginning of the war. The Radicals regarded the president as much too conservative and faulted him for not being zealous enough in using the war to strike at the institution of slavery, for being too lenient in his proposed postwar treatment of the Southern states, and for vetoing several of their pet legislative measures. Such conservatism as the president exhibited, they believed, both hampered a full prosecution of the war effort and threatened the Republicans' control of the Federal government. If the seceded states simply resumed their antebellum status, their politicians, in all likelihood, would reunite with Northern Democrats to regain control of the Federal government.

Rallying first behind Secretary of the Treasury Salmon P. Chase and then (after Chase's presidential boomlet had been torpedoed by Lincoln) behind Maj. Gen. John Charles Frémont, the Radicals moved to deny Lincoln the party's 1864 nomination. Frémont had been the Republicans' 1856 candidate, and in 1861 when he commanded in Missouri, he had issued a proclamation granting freedom to the slaves of Confederate sympathizers in the state. Lincoln had quickly overruled his general lest Frémont's ill-conceived measure drive pro-Union slaveholders to join the rebellion. Frémont's act, however, made him a hero to the Radicals. On May 31, 1864, a group of Radicals met in Cincinnati and nominated him for president on a platform calling for racial equality and the confiscation of land owned by Confederates.

Lincoln, with an incumbent's firm grip on the party machinery, secured renomination on June 7 at the Republicans' regular convention in Baltimore. Even so, many in the party (one-third of the Republicans in Congress by the historian James M. McPherson's estimate) were displeased with their party's action. Many of them diligently went to work behind the scenes to pry the president out of the nomination and to replace him with a candidate more acceptable to the Radicals. Some, for example, plotted to nominate Benjamin F. Butler so as to win the votes of Democrats who supported the war. They hoped to persuade Frémont to switch his support to Butler and withdraw from the race. Then Lincoln, they assumed, would have no choice but to do the same.

Northern Democrats also hoped to deny Lincoln a second term, but they, of course, did not want to replace him with some other Republican. Many conservative members of the opposition party were appalled at the government's suppression of the writ of habeas corpus, its use of the military to arrest and even to try civilians, its suppression and censorship of newspapers, and its imprisonment of citizens (including even some state legislators) without trial. Many "Peace Democrats" had never favored a war against states that chose to leave the Union, and many others had become so sickened by the conflict and its attendant casualties and suffering and so weary of the struggle that they were willing to acquiesce in independence for the South if doing so would put a stop to the killing. Many Peace Democrats—perhaps a majority—so differed with Lincoln's policies on emancipation and race that they would not support a war for preservation of the Union after it became also a war against slavery. Finally, there were many "peace men" in the Democratic Party who believed sincerely that reunion could be achieved more efficaciously by peace (which would allow the two sections to resume their traditional relationship) rather than by war (which, by definition, drove North and South apart).

George B. McClellan was the leading candidate for the Democratic nomination. A former commander of the Army of the Potomac, McClellan had advocated a very conservative war effort with the sole objective of restoring the status quo antebellum. He favored preservation of the Union but opposed Federal efforts to abolish slavery. By 1863 McClellan had broken completely with the Lincoln administration over the war, and he wanted to secure the 1864 Democratic nomination and win a victory at the polls to vindicate his long-standing opposition to the president's war policies. The Democratic Party also embraced other interests and factions. One of the more visible was a vocal peace-at-any price-because-the-war-is-a-bloody-failure group. Clement L. Vallandigham of Ohio was the leading spokesman for that faction of the party.

The Democrats, James M. McPherson has written, were therefore "half opposed to the war and wholly opposed to emancipation." If war-weariness grew in the North that summer, they might pose a real threat to Lincoln's reelection, to the movement to abolish slavery, and perhaps even, unintentionally, to the effort to preserve the Union itself.

The Democrats had scheduled their national convention to meet in Chicago on July 4. Thinking they would take full advantage of whatever might develop that summer and also to allow as much time as possible for resentment over war taxes, conscription, and other measures to grow, the Democrats postponed their gathering until August 29–31—the latest date at which they would have enough time to get their political machinery cranked up and running for the November election. By late August, they expected, the military situation would have clarified to the extent that they could then adapt their party to whatever posture would most advantageously position them to run against Lincoln.

As the summer wore along, the casualty lists lengthened, and the Federal armies failed to win any great, obvious victory, the number of those in the North who favored peace increased. So too did the number of Republicans who regarded Lincoln as a failed war president. Through June and July, many came increasingly to believe that Lincoln could not be reelected in November.[1]

This unstable political situation in the North offered the Confederates an opportunity to enhance their chances for independence. If the Rebels could act to strengthen the Democrats in general and the peace faction of that party in particular, they would weaken their great, implacable enemy—Lincoln. To accomplish that goal, the Secessionists had to do several things. First and foremost, their armies must avoid the massive military defeat that would vindicate Lincoln's conduct of the war. So long as they achieved that goal, they bolstered the peace faction's arguments that the administration's war policies had failed and could not be made to succeed. At the same time the Secessionists had the opportunity to devise and execute a covert program to strengthen some of Lincoln's political opponents—but it had to be a program so subtle that it did not result in the peace men being tarred as disloyal even as it weakened the Union war effort. Such a program required great diplomatic and political skills and a difficult balancing act. The task of devising the effort and seeing to its execution fell squarely onto the shoulders of Jefferson Davis.

Long aware of the potential benefits the Confederates might derive from possible political turmoil in the North, Davis had dispatched agents to Canada from which sanctuary they were to implement several steps designed to enhance the prospects of peace candidates. The Southerners especially hoped to influence the balloting in the northwestern states, where, they believed, antiwar sentiment was strongest. The Rebels might, for example, furnish money to help finance the campaigns of peace candidates. They could also subsidize pro-peace, pro-Democratic, anti-Lincoln newspapers that would help spread the message that the Federal government had not achieved, was not achieving, and could not achieve its military goals. They could purchase gold in Northern markets and ship it abroad to drive up its value relative to the paper money issued by the Federal government. (During the war, the value of gold was an oft-cited indicator of Northern success—the higher the price of gold relative to paper money, the lower seemed the prospects for Union victory. In July 1864 gold soared to "284," meaning it took $2.84 in paper money to purchase $1 in gold. By buying gold and sending it out of the North, the Confederates would reduce the supply of the precious metal and thereby raise its price.)[2]

Davis, however, made a fundamental miscalculation in his appraisal of and his approach to Northern politics. The Rebel president accurately viewed himself as far more skilled in dealing with military affairs than he was at the intrigues and subtleties of politics and diplomacy. Although he sent commissioners to Canada to do what they could to undermine Lincoln and further the cause of Confederate independence, he tied their hands with the instructions under which he required them to act and he sometimes worked at cross-purposes with them. The impossibility of Davis and his agents communicating on anything like a regular basis also hampered greatly Rebel efforts to dabble in Northern politics.

After talking with several peace men, the Confederate commissioners —Clement C. Clay, Jacob Thompson, and James P. Holcomb—came to understand something of the complexities of the antiwar and anti-Lincoln movements. They realized that many of those who desired peace and opposed Lincoln's policies, especially emancipation, also wanted desperately to preserve the Union. Many of the most sincere peace men were, in fact, motivated by a deep conviction that an end to the war would restore the Union. They, therefore, were willing to accept an armistice which they saw both as a means of halting the slaughter and of opening the road to reunion.

As the Rebel agents developed an understanding of the Northern peace movement, they realized that their best hope was to play on this desire for peace and reunion. In doing so they chose to emphasize the desirability of an immediate end to hostilities and a cooling-off period to allow sectional animosities to die down. They hinted at but never promised that the ultimate outcome of such a course could be reunion. The Southern agents reasoned that once the war had been halted, public opinion in the North would not permit its resumption. The Confederacy, therefore, would have both peace and de facto independence. By dangling the reality of immediate peace and the vague prospect of future reunion before Northern voters, the Rebels might strengthen the popular appeal of peace candidates.

President Davis, on the other hand, had neither a clear picture nor an accurate understanding of the complexities of the Northern peace movement. He almost certainly overestimated its strength (his habit of wishful thinking?) and underestimated its fragility. Nor did he appreciate the longing for reunion among many of the peace men in the North. Davis also had to worry about a similar peace faction in the Confederacy. Its adherents might prove all too anxious for an armistice and all too unwilling to resume fighting should a need to do so arise. Many of them would be agreeable to some outcome short of Confederate independence if they could preserve their "rights" (especially slavery). Out of contact with his commissioners in Canada, Davis decided sometime that spring or summer that Northern recognition of Confederate sovereignty must be the indispensable precondition for an end to the war.

Davis's agents in Canada came to view negotiations as a potential means of helping achieve Confederate independence, and they sought to pursue a course based on that strategy. The Confederate president believed that negotiations should be an acknowledgment that Rebel independence had been won. In mid-July he publicly rejected cooperation with Northerners who were not willing to recognize the Confederacy as an independent nation.

In summary, Davis insisted that the point in dispute—Confederate independence—be yielded before he would agree to negotiate. His agents saw negotiation as a potential way of gaining that point. By taking the stand he did, Davis undermined the work of his commissioners, weakened the peace movement in the North by making it impossible for loyal Northern peace men to work with the Confederates, played (unknowingly) into Lincoln's hands, and severely limited his own options.

Davis believed that Confederate military success would influence the outcome of the Northern elections far more profoundly than could any actions that the Rebel government might undertake through manipulating the price of gold or subsidizing Democratic newspapers and peace candidates. As was the case so often in his life, Davis was absolutely correct in the abstract and completely wrong in the real world. He failed to see that the policy favored by the commissioners might win a de facto independence that, with time, could be converted into the sovereignty he was pursuing. Even worse for the Rebels, Davis placed all his hope on military victory. If the Secessionists won all of the year's military campaigns, his policy stood a excellent chance of success. If, on the other hand, the Southern armies suffered a major defeat anywhere, the president had nothing to fall back on. He, in fact, staked everything on his armies.[3]

As the hot July sun roasted the opposing soldiers across the land, Davis could rejoice at the obvious victories his armies had won in the Red River valley, at New Market in the Valley of the Shenandoah, and at Bermuda Hundred on the James, and he could view with great hope and confidence the accomplishments of Lee and Early in Virginia. Only in Georgia did there seem much doubt about Confederate success. In mid-July Davis acted to strengthen the Rebel hand there.

CHAPTER ELEVEN

Hood Takes Command

The cheerful new interpretation of the campaign in Georgia to which Johnston and his military family had come in late May and early June created a hopeful outlook at the headquarters of the Army of Tennessee. Few Southerners outside the army shared that optimism, however, and even many of Johnston's own soldiers lost heart with every southward step the army took.

When veterans of the Army of Tennessee sat down in the postwar decades to pen their memoirs, autobiographies, and reminiscences, they declared—almost to a man—that in 1864 they had believed that "Old Joe" had followed a successful strategy of drawing Sherman deep into Georgia where the Rebels would be able to defeat him. The long retreat from Dalton, they insisted, did not impair their morale, and they retained complete confidence in their beloved general.

Many of the letters and diaries that Johnston's men wrote in the summer of 1864 tell a different story. When the soldiers composed those documents, they did not know what the future held for them and their cause. Their contemporary writings make it clear that a significant (but undeterminable) percentage of the soldiers in Johnston's army did, in fact, lose faith in both Johnston and the Confederacy as May turned into June and June into July and the army continued its long retreat toward Atlanta. Some deserted to the Federals; others simply went home. Most, however, confined their feelings to remarks in their letters and diaries and grimly soldiered on as best they could, hoping that somehow the Confederacy could win its independence.

For example, Capt. W. L. Trask wrote after the Rebels abandoned Adairsville on May 17, "I notice many men demoralized and disheartened. Several of the Kentuckians, no doubt disgusted by the prospect, threw their guns into the bushes as they marched along and no doubt sought the first opportunity to fall out and hide themselves, for the purpose of falling into the enemy's hands and getting a chance to go home." On July 6 Celathiel Helms, a Georgia soldier, wrote, "The men is all out of heart and say that Georgia will soon have to go under and they are going to the Yankees by the tens and twenties and hundreds a most every night. Johnson's [*sic*] army is very much demoralized as much as a army ever gets to be." Five days later a member of the Fifty-sixth Georgia remarked, "Sister I am getting a little Scared about home. . . . there are prospects of us leaving Atlanta and if we do I will be a little demoralized for if we cant Stop them at . . . [the Chattahoochee River] it is not reasonable that we can stop them any other place and an other thing 1/3 or 2/3 of our men will desert and go home."

Northerners also commented on drooping morale among Johnston's soldiers. One recorded that on May 18 about three hundred deserters from Johnston's army came into the Federal lines. A Union general wrote in early June, "A good many Rebel stragglers and deserters have been taken on each abandonment of Rebel camps. . . . These deserters have no special love for us, but are tired of war, discouraged, and after years of absence anxious to see home, which is generally within our lines."[1]

Discontent with Johnston's conduct of military operations in Georgia also bubbled up in civilian and political circles. Jefferson Davis (to be sure, not a disinterested commentator) wrote after the war that a "clamor" for removing Johnston from command of the Army of Tennessee "commenced immediately after it became known that the army had fallen back from Dalton, and it gathered volume with each remove toward Atlanta."

In Richmond as early as May 21, Col. Josiah Gorgas, of the army's Ordnance Bureau, noted in his journal, "Johnston is falling back as hard as he can. . . . It is surmised that he will reach Macon [one hundred miles south of Atlanta] in a few days at the rate he is retreating. I trust the country will sooner or later find out what sort of General he is. I don't think he will suit [in] the emergency." On the following day Robert G. H. Kean, a War Department clerk, wrote in his diary, "Johnston has retreated still further. . . . The Secretary [of War, James A. Seddon,] is dissatisfied. He told me this morning that General Johnston's theory of war seemed to be never to fight unless strong enough certainly to overwhelm your enemy, and under all circumstances merely to continue to elude him. This is a very just criticism upon all of General Johnston's campaigns."

Four days later, as the armies clashed along the lines at New Hope Church, Gorgas again commented on the situation in Georgia. "Johnston verifies all our predictions of him. He is falling back just as fast as his legs can carry him. . . . He is falling back behind the Chattahoochie [*sic*] and will I fear give up Atlanta. . . . Where he will stop only heaven knows." On May 30 Kean noted that "the loss of material, manufactures, and skilled workmen by his [Johnston's] retrograde movements has been among our most serious disasters." A month later Gorgas wrote of events in Georgia, "I have little confidence in the State [*sic*] of affairs in that quarter. I fully expect to hear of his [Johnston's] retreat behind Atlanta, probably in the direction of West Point[, Georgia]."

Johnston's long retreat from Dalton to the outskirts of Atlanta aroused so much concern in Richmond because it threatened to undo all the Confederates had done—at such great cost—that summer. Unless Johnston could find some way to defeat and drive back Sherman, or at least to block his further progress, he would lose Atlanta, hand the Yankees the great success they had been unable to win elsewhere, render useless the enormous sacrifices the Rebels had already made, reelect Lincoln, and doom the Confederacy to defeat and destruction. (Indeed, in retrospect, we can see that he may well have done so when he lost Snake Creek Gap— two months before he pulled his army across the Chattahoochee.)[2]

Late on June 24 a visitor appeared at Johnston's Marietta headquarters. Senator Louis T. Wigfall, a bitter critic of President Davis and his policies and (not coincidentally) a friend and political ally of Johnston, was en route home to Texas following adjournment of the Rebel Congress. When he reached Atlanta, the senator left his wife and daughters in the city while he paid a visit to the army. The news he brought could not have come as a surprise to Johnston.

Wigfall informed his friend that rumors were then circulating in Richmond to the effect that Davis was so dissatisfied with the situation in North Georgia that he intended to relieve Johnston from command and name Hood to replace him. Of course, the senator added, should Johnston defeat Sherman, the president would not take such a drastic step.

In reply Johnston put forth the same arguments he had been making in much less detail to the government. He was, he said, facing an enemy force, which, despite the high casualties it had suffered, still greatly outnumbered his own. Since the Yankees always fortified each new position immediately upon occupying it, the Confederates could not attack the enemy with any hope of success. If, however, the Rebels could cut Sherman's supply line, they would force the Federals to abandon their thrust into Georgia. Since he needed all his own cavalry to protect the flanks of his army, Johnston maintained, he could not spare any large mounted force to send against Sherman's railroad. The only way to defeat Sherman, therefore, was to use Forrest's horsemen from Mississippi to wreck the rail line that supplied the Yankees in Georgia. This, Johnston concluded, should be done even if it necessitated "temporarily" abandoning Mississippi. To Johnston and Wigfall it seemed obvious that the perverse Davis was again denying the means of victory to a general who was his personal enemy.

Promising to keep up political pressure on the administration, Wigfall departed. His visit certainly strengthened Johnston's conviction that the government cared little about him and his army. It doubtless undermined further his relationship with Hood. It may well have led him a short time later to dispatch to Richmond the only substantive piece of correspondence he sent to the government during the campaign. In that letter, dated June 27 but probably written the day before or perhaps long after the Yankee attack of that morning, Johnston attempted to explain why he thought the enemy's superior numbers made it impossible for him to stop Sherman's advance with his own army and that it was necessary to order Forrest to operate against the Yankee railroad. His own cavalry, he asserted, was so weak compared to Sherman's that he had not been able to detach any sizable part of it to try to cut the Yankee line of supply. Johnston closed the letter with yet another plea to the government to use mounted troops from other areas against the railroad that brought supplies to his opponent.[3]

A week after Wigfall's visit, another Confederate politician called on Johnston. Senator Benjamin H. Hill of Georgia, understandably alarmed at the deep Federal penetration into his state, came at the urging of Wigfall and Governor Brown to learn from Johnston himself what the military situation was and what the Confederate commander planned to do. To Hill, Johnston repeated the assertions he had made to Wigfall, but he added several other comments and recommendations.

There were, Johnston told Hill, two bodies of Rebel cavalry that could easily cut Sherman's rail line and thereby save Georgia. Brig. Gen. John Hunt Morgan was poised at Abingdon, Virginia, with five thousand men. Forrest could strike with four or five thousand of the sixteen thousand

Confederate cavalrymen then in Mississippi. Either of those officers—or, better, both of them could get on Sherman's rail line and make it impossible to supply the enemy in Johnston's front. Success by either would wreck the Union offensive in Georgia. Sherman's cavalry, Johnston claimed, numbered about twelve thosuand men, but it was "very inefficient and would not fight our cavalry except with infantry support." Finally, Johnston told Hill, the Rebel horsemen should destroy the railroad south of Dalton to cut Sherman off from his advanced base there as well as from the larger depots in Chattanooga and Nashville.

Once Johnston had presented his case, Hill asked if there was still time for such a strategy to be effective. Johnston replied that there was. Hood—apparently the only other person present—expressed skepticism. When Hill asked how long Johnston could hold the Yankees north of the Chattahoochee, the general led him to believe that he could do so for at least a month. Again, Hood voiced doubts, pointing out that once the Secessionists left the third Kennesaw line they would find no other naturally strong position north of the river. Johnston responded that he had already prepared several such positions between Marietta and the Chattahoochee where he would be able to delay Sherman for a long time.

Before leaving Johnston's headquarters, Hill vowed to go to Richmond immediately and advise the president to direct the cavalry in Mississippi to operate against the Federal rail line. Hill was a friend and political ally of the president. His views, therefore, were far more likely to receive a friendly hearing than were those of an administration critic such as Wigfall (who in any case had continued on his way to Texas). Meanwhile, Governor Brown (a frequent and often intemperate critic of the administration) and Maj. Gen. Howell Cobb (commanding Georgia's reserve forces and a pro-Davis political figure) joined in the deliberations, urging the government to commit Forrest's cavalry to the defense of Georgia.[4]

Jefferson Davis and Braxton Bragg were not stupid men. From the beginning of the spring's military operations they had been well aware that destruction of the railroad north of Sherman's army group would hamper the operations of that force and might even result in its defeat. They had also seen that Rebel horsemen in Mississippi might be able to carry out such a mission. Unlike Johnston and Brown, however, Davis and Bragg had to concern themselves with the entire Confederacy—with Mississippi as well as with Georgia—and they had to weigh factors that Johnston and Brown could not, or would not, see.

The governor and the general in Georgia could urge the "temporary" abandonment of Mississippi to save Georgia. From his Richmond perspective, Davis saw that even a "temporary" loss of Mississippi could have disastrous consequences for the Rebels. For example, loss of the Tombigbee River valley in western Alabama (easily reached by Yankee raiders once they had possession of Mississippi) would result in the loss of foodstuffs for Johnston's army. "The interior of Alabama and the Tombigbee Valley are our best reliance for supplies in the coming campaign," Davis had written on February 15. The Federals might even push on eastward and wreck the great munitions complex at Selma, capture Montgomery, and take Mobile. They could even go on into Georgia to operate against Johnston's army there. Besides, Davis knew, the Confederates had *never* permanently regained any area once it had been occupied by the enemy. If an invasion of Georgia demoralized that state's soldiers and citizens, what impact would abandoning Mississippi and an invasion of Alabama have on the troops from those states and their civilian populations?

To the president and his chief adviser it was clear that the Confederates *had* to defend *both* Georgia and Mississippi. They, therefore, turned their attention to the question of how those objectives could be achieved. In late May and June, as Johnston frantically importuned them to loose Forrest on Sherman's rail line, they considered the options. Eventually, they arrived at what seemed to them the best course for the Rebels to pursue.

Both Johnston in Georgia and Stephen D. Lee in Mississippi were outnumbered. Both were menaced by strong enemy forces. Already more than twenty thousand troops had been shifted from Lee's department to reinforce Johnston (the divisions of French and Loring, Jackson's cavalry, and the troops from the Mobile area who were organized into a division commanded first by Cantey and then by Maj. Gen. Edward C. Walthall).

Davis and Bragg decided that Lee's primary responsibility was the defense of Mississippi and Alabama. Once those areas were secure, he could use his cavalry to operate against Sherman's line of supply. Meanwhile, Johnston would have to do the best he could with the forces under his command in Georgia.

To Davis and Bragg this policy seemed reasonable because, they concluded, Johnston was much stronger relative to the enemy in his front than was Lee relative to the Yankees who menaced Mississippi. On June 10 Johnston had reported that he had 6,538 officers and 63,408 enlisted men present for duty (with 60,564 effectives). Of this total, 1,218 officers and 12,328 enlisted men were assigned to his cavalry (10,903 effectives).

Looking at those numbers, Davis and Bragg concluded that Johnston's own horsemen should go after Sherman's railroads.[5]

On July 10, after some delay, Senator Hill reached Richmond and met with Davis in the Clay Street house that served as the Confederacy's Executive Mansion. Davis listened patiently as Hill described conditions in Georgia and recounted the July 1 conversation with Johnston and Hood at army headquarters. The president then explained the situation from a national perspective. Morgan did not have five thousand men. He had recently taken his two thousand troopers (eight hundred of them on foot) into Kentucky and had suffered a stinging defeat at Cynthiana. He fled back to Virginia and was then encamped at Abingdon with a demoralized command and weakened, broken-down horses. The Rebels defending Mississippi and Alabama, Davis told Hill, totaled only thirteen thousand troops, including Forrest's cavalry. Stephen D. Lee had reported that they were menaced by thirty-five thousand Yankees. (Lee exaggerated the threat, but Davis had no way of knowing that.)

After explaining the Confederacy's manpower situation in the West, Davis asked his visitor how long he had understood Johnston to have implied that he could hold Sherman north of the Chattahoochee. Hill answered that the general had led him to believe he would keep the Federals north of the river at least until late July. The president then read to Hill Johnston's telegram of that morning reporting that the Yankees had gotten across the Chattahoochee and, as a consequence, the Confederates had abandoned the northern bank of the stream and fallen back to the outskirts of Atlanta.

A few days later Hill—doubtless much disgusted at this turn of events —dashed off a quick telegram to Johnston: "You must do the work with your present force. For God's sake do it." At about the same time Josiah Gorgas noted in his diary, "Everybody has at last come to the conclusion that Johnston has retreated far enough."[6]

The day after Hill's visit, Davis sent two communications to Johnston. One, a telegram, told the general that as the former commander of Confederate forces in Mississippi, he should know that the Rebels did not have sixteen thousand cavalry there. The president also made an obvious point, noting that "if it be practicable for Forrest to reach Sherman's railroad from Mississippi it must be more so" for Wheeler's cavalry, which was much nearer the objective. Davis also wrote Johnston a letter detailing the situation in Mississippi and pointing out that removal of Confederate cavalry from that region would free the Yankees to seize Selma and to shift thousands of troops eastward to Georgia to reinforce Sherman and to guard his railroad. (Johnston did not receive this letter until July 24.)

Doubtless the president hoped his messages would jolt Johnston into realizing that the Confederacy could spare no more troops from other areas for his army and that his own horsemen under Wheeler and Jackson should be used against Sherman's rail line. At the same time Davis acted to learn more about the situation in Georgia than Johnston was telling him and to gather information that would help him decide two weighty matters he then had under consideration.

On July 10 the president dispatched Bragg to Georgia to report on the situation there. Bragg reached Atlanta early on the thirteenth. Over the next three days he scurried about the city, meeting with Johnston and the army's corps commanders and sending a stream of messages to Davis in Richmond. Although there was a bit of vacillation in Bragg's reports, the overall impression they created was very detrimental to Johnston. "Indications seem to favor an entire evacuation of this place," he tele-graphed upon reaching Atlanta. "Our army sadly depleted. . . . I find but little encouraging," he reported soon after. On July 15 Bragg commented of Johnston: "I cannot learn that he has any more plan for the future than he has had in the past. It is expected that he will await the enemy on a line some three miles from here, and the impression prevails that he is now more inclined to fight."

Johnston later implied that, during the visit, he and Bragg had had almost no substantive conversation on the military situation in Georgia and his visitor had led him to believe that his main task was to confer with Rebel commanders in Alabama and the Trans-Mississippi about securing reinforcements from those areas for the army in Georgia. It is difficult to credit the former assertion given the situation in which the Confederates found themselves in mid-July 1864 and the latter because of Davis's decision that no more troops could be transferred from the Department of Alabama, Mississippi, and East Louisiana to Johnston. (If the former assertion is true, Johnston missed yet one more excellent chance to explain his situation to the Richmond authorities.) Bragg's July 15 message, quoted above, clearly implies that he had tried to get information from Johnston about the army's operations. Either Johnston was not being truthful when he wrote his memoirs, or Bragg was using his visit to push his own agenda by meddling in the affairs of the army to strike at his old enemies and secure rewards for his allies by sending misleading reports to Davis, or both. We shall never know. As with Hill's account, however, the important thing is what Davis was told, not what was actually the case.[7]

In dealing with the crisis in Georgia the chief executive faced two related but quite different questions: Should Johnston be removed from command? If so, who should take his place? The telegrams Bragg sent to Richmond dealt mostly with the former question. He also wrote a letter that dealt with the latter. This document, dated July 15, was carried to the capital by one of Bragg's staff officers. In this letter Bragg reported that Polk, Hood, and Stewart had opposed Johnston's constant retreats while "Hardee generally favored the retiring policy." Johnston, Bragg wrote, "has ever been opposed to seeking battle, though willing to receive it on his own terms in his chosen position."

Those facts, Bragg concluded, meant that simply removing Johnston and allowing Hardee to ascend to army command by seniority "would produce no change in the policy." (Bragg's statements regarding Hardee run contrary to all the evidence about the early stages of the campaign.) Instead, opined Bragg, "Hood would give unlimited satisfaction" although he was not "a man of genius, or a great general, but . . . [would be] far better in the present emergency than anyone we have available." In addition to this communication, Bragg's messenger carried a letter that Hood had written on July 14. In this self-serving document Hood reported to Bragg that he had frequently urged Johnston to stand and fight and implied that Hardee had supported Johnston's strategy of avoiding battle.

It seems clear that Bragg had picked up those details in conversations with Hood. Did Hood feed Bragg false information in hope of denying Hardee Johnston's place, thereby clearing the way for his own promotion? Did Bragg come to Atlanta wanting to deny his old personal enemy Hardee command of the army? If Bragg came to gather evidence to justify the removal of Johnston, did he solicit comments from Hood—perhaps holding out promotion as a reward if Hood would provide justification for removing Johnston and reasons to deny Hardee the command? It is unlikely, however, that Bragg's messenger reached Richmond in time for the letters to have affected Davis's decision. If the documents did reach the president before he made his decision, they certainly did not play a significant role. Clearly Davis had pretty much made up his mind to remove Johnston. As Wigfall told Johnston on June 24, Richmond rumor mills then had it that the president was considering Hood as the new commander for the army.[8]

By July 16 Davis had had enough. He sent Johnston a telegram that day: "I wish to hear from you as to present situation, and your plan of operations so specifically as will enable me to anticipate events." Johnston's reply, also dated the sixteenth, read: "As the enemy has double our number, we must be on the defensive. My plan of operations must, therefore, depend upon that of the enemy. It is mainly to watch for an opportunity to fight to advantage. We are trying to put Atlanta in condition to be held for a day or two by the Georgia militia, that army movements may be freer and wider."

Johnston's message is a mind-boggling document. He knew that the government was very dissatisfied with events in Georgia. Yet, when asked to explain his plans "specifically," he sent merely a vague general statement. On July 10 he had reported his army's "present for duty" strength as 59,000. He thus told Davis that Sherman's army group had a strength of 118,000 men. Later he claimed that Sherman had suffered 60,000 casualties in North Georgia. He thus credited Sherman with having a total strength of 178,000 men. If Johnston believed his own statements, we are justified in wondering how he expected the old men and boys of the Georgia militia to keep Sherman's 118,000 battle-hardened veterans out of Atlanta no matter what condition he put the city in. The militia then with the army did not number more than 5,000 and would not number more than 15,000 even in the unlikely event that Governor Brown fulfilled his promise to raise additional state troops for the defense of Atlanta. We are also justified in wondering why, if the militia could hold Sherman's force at bay, the veteran infantry of the Army of Tennessee could not have held the third Kennesaw line "for a day or two" while Wheeler attacked Sherman's railroad. In summary, it is impossible to conclude that Johnston had any other plan than the hope that Sherman would assault the Rebel fortifications—which the Federal commander obviously was not going to do—or that the Confederate government would abandon Mississippi and Alabama in order to use Forrest against Sherman's rail lines—a strategy that Davis had already rejected for good reason (see appendix 3).[9]

On July 17 Davis had all the information about conditions in Georgia that he was going to get and the advice of all those he would consult (with the probable exception of Bragg's July 15 letter and its inclosure). Perhaps he thought back to the spring of 1862. Then Johnston, commanding the principal Rebel army in Virginia, had retreated (without keeping the government informed as to his plans) to the very outskirts of Richmond. When he attempted to make an attack on the Federal army, he was seriously wounded. Davis had selected Lee to replace Johnston, and within a month Lee had driven the enemy away from the capital and soon followed that success with other victories. In 1864 the decision rested solely on the Rebels' chief executive.

Certain facts were obvious. The Secessionists must hold Atlanta. Johnston had given no indication that he would even make an all-out effort to do so. His campaign in North Georgia had already been a logistical, and possibly a political, disaster as well for the Confederacy. Hardee, so it had been reported to Davis, had agreed with Johnston's policy. Hood, Davis had been told, had favored giving battle in an effort to hold the city. Johnston's only plan seemed to be to abandon Mississippi to concentrate that state's defending cavalry to attack Sherman's railroad—a proposal that Davis had rejected because the Rebels could no more afford to give up Mississippi than they could stand to lose Georgia or Virginia. Johnston absolutely refused to use his own horsemen against the Yankees' railroad despite his repeated assertions that cutting the enemy's supply line was the only way to defeat Sherman. Now, it seemed, he was contemplating leaving Atlanta in the none-too-strong hands of the Georgia militia.

Sometime that Sunday Davis came to his decision. Soon a message clacked over the wires from Adjutant and Inspector General Samuel Cooper to Johnston at Atlanta: "Lieut. Gen. J. B. Hood has been commissioned to the temporary rank of general. . . . I am directed by the Secretary of War to inform you that as you have failed to arrest the advance of the enemy to the vicinity of Atlanta, far in the interior of Georgia, and express no confidence that you can defeat or repel him, you are hereby relieved from command of the Army and Department of Tennessee which you will immediately turn over to General Hood."

The message reached Johnston about 9:00 P.M. Almost immediately he wrote out an order relinquishing command and prepared to leave Atlanta.

Whatever his feelings, the telegram could not have come as a surprise to him. It probably came as a relief.[10]

Davis's two July 17 decisions—first to remove Johnston and second to replace him with Hood—were among the most controversial he made as Confederate president. Ever since the summer of 1864 Johnston, his friends and relatives, and later his supporters and disciples argued that his approach to the operations in Georgia had been the only realistic policy for the Rebels and had Davis not removed him just as he was about to strike the blow that would have defeated Sherman, the Confederates would have held Atlanta and gained their independence. These assertions are based on blind faith, not any indication visible at the time or since.

A calmer look at the matter makes it clear that if Atlanta had to be held, Davis was fully justified in removing Johnston from command of the army—indeed, he would have been justified in doing so much earlier than he did. The president's selection of Hood to replace Johnston was more questionable but logical considering the information he had and probably the best choice that could have been made under the circumstances. Time alone dictated that the new commander had to come from within the army and be familiar with the area in which the Army of Tennessee was then operating. Had Davis acted a week or two earlier, he could have sent in someone from the outside. (Beauregard was probably the only realistic choice.) Within the army the only conceivable options were Hardee and Hood. Davis knew that Hardee had declined command of the army the previous December, and the president had been told that he had favored Johnston's 1864 strategy of retreat. Hardee had also been a leader in the army's old anti-Bragg faction, and his appointment could well widen the gulf between army headquarters and Richmond and rekindle the destructive feuding within the army between pro-Bragg and anti-Bragg generals.

Jefferson Davis's real problem in July 1864 was the rot he had allowed to develop and fester in the army's high command in 1861, 1862, and 1863. It simply was too late to do anything about that in July 1864.

By midnight of July 17–18 the die had been cast. The fate of Atlanta and the Confederacy's chance for independence rested on the shoulders of John Bell Hood.

CHAPTER TWELVE

The Rebels Strike Back

Rarely has a general assumed command of an army under more inauspicious circumstances than those facing John Bell Hood on the morning of Monday, July 18, 1864. His army was backed up to a city it had to hold—a fact that limited his strategic options and room to maneuver. He also had to keep his force positioned to cover the prisoner-of-war camp at Andersonville, some 120 miles to the south. There thousands of captured Yankees sweltered in the July heat and humidity. Should one of Sherman's raiding parties reach that prison and liberate those Northerners, the resulting panic among civilians in Central and South Georgia could both undermine Confederate morale and result in massive damage to some of the farms, factories, and railroads that helped feed and supply Secessionist armies in Georgia and Virginia. At the least, Hood would have to detach large numbers of troops from the Army of Tennessee to pursue the fugitives and to protect the lives and property of the area's civilians.

To his front Hood found a confidant, vigorous enemy force numbering some ninety-five thousand men. Johnston's retreat across the Chattahoochee had removed the last major natural obstacle between Sherman's army group and Atlanta. Two of the four railroads radiating from Atlanta were either in possession of the Federals or damaged (the Western & Atlantic from Chattanooga and the Montgomery & West Point, torn up west of Opelika by Rousseau's raiders). On the day Hood assumed command of the Rebels, McPherson reached and cut the Georgia Railroad east of Decatur. With that line severed, Atlanta lost its importance as a rail hub, and the tracks running from Columbus through Macon became the Confederacy's only east-west rail route. After July 18 only the Macon

& Western linked Atlanta and its defending army to the rest of Rebeldom. Should Sherman break that railroad, the Secessionists could not remain in the city.

Much of Atlanta's industrial importance had been lost with Johnston's retreat over the Chattahoochee, and Union artillery would soon wreck much of what industry remained in the city itself. Almost all movable machinery and government supplies had been sent to other cities in early July. Most of Atlanta's civilian population had fled. Hood, in fact, was fighting to hold a city that had been reduced to a symbol, not a place that was itself any longer of value to his country.[1]

Hood's own army was hardly in shape to wage a great struggle on which the life of its nation depended. Casualties, sickness, and desertion had reduced its strength to below sixty thousand. The long retreat from Dalton had sapped the morale of many of the Confederate soldiers. Many others who had retained their faith in Johnston were demoralized by his departure. Still others who regarded Johnston as a failure also doubted Hood's fitness to head the army.

The Army of Tennessee also suffered from several serious problems in its high echelons—some of long standing, some created or exacerbated by the campaign of May and June. Brig. Gen. William W. Mackall, the chief of staff and a devoted friend of Johnston's, remained at his post for the first week of Hood's tenure as army commander. Mackall clearly resented Hood's elevation to a post he believed rightfully Johnston's. When he was relieved from duty on July 24 after refusing to shake hands with Bragg at army headquarters, he petulantly took many of the chief of staff's office records off with him. Hood chose as his successor Brig. Gen. Francis A. Shoup, who had been the army's chief of artillery.

Hardee, now Hood's senior subordinate, remained at the head of his corps. Like Mackall, but for different reasons, he very much resented Hood's promotion. He soon made it clear that he wished to leave the army to avoid serving under Hood. Hardee's bitterness, however, seems to have been owing less to any fondness for Johnston then to the fact that a much younger officer, once junior to him and whose competence he clearly doubted, had been chosen as the army's new commander. President Davis denied Hardee's request for a transfer. Had Hardee left, Hood would have lost his only experienced corps commander. Stewart, now the army's third-ranking officer, had been at the head of a corps for less than three weeks and had never handled a force larger than a division in combat.

Serious general officer personnel problems also cropped up in what had been Hood's Corps. When Hood ascended to army command, Carter L. Stevenson, the senior major general then with the corps, took his place. Hood and the Confederate authorities, however, did not regard Stevenson as qualified for the post. They selected Stephen D. Lee as the new corps commander. Until Lee could arrive from Mississippi, however, they preferred that the corps be commanded by someone other than Stevenson. Hardee suggested and Hood approved the temporary assignment to the post of Maj. Gen. Benjamin Franklin Cheatham. Cheatham's record was mixed. Beyond question, he was a hard fighter, and he was popular with the men of his division—second only to Cleburne's in quality in the Army of Tennessee. Cheatham, several officers had alleged, had on various occasions been drunk on duty. Cheatham's selection was based on his reputation as a troop leader, his seniority, and the fact that the assignment was only temporary. Cheatham, however, was an ally of Hardee and a longtime foe of Bragg. He was also an admirer of Johnston. He may have resented Johnston's removal and Hood's elevation to army command. Later, when Stewart and Loring, his senior division commander, were wounded on July 28, Hood placed Cheatham in command of Stewart's Corps for about two weeks.

The army's new commander thus had to defend Atlanta with one infantry corps commander (Hardee) who clearly resented the new command structure of the army, another (Cheatham) who may have, three (Cheatham, Stewart, and Lee) who were new to the responsibilities of corps command, and one (Cheatham) who had given serious cause to doubt his fitness for a high position.

Under such circumstances the head of the army would have to shoulder far more of the load of command than usual. Hood's crippled condition, however, militated against his playing a physically more active command role. Nor was the army's chronically weak staff able to take up the slack—even had the chief of staff been willing to cooperate fully with the new commander. After Mackall's departure, Shoup, the new chief of staff, was inexperienced in his role. So, too, was the new chief of artillery, Col. Robert F. Beckham.

The army's general officer personnel problems rippled below corps level. Loring was Stewart's senior division commander—indeed, the senior Confederate major general in the West. He had commanded the corps for more than three weeks after Polk's death and was, in the words of a surgeon in his division, "deeply chagrined" at being bypassed so

Stewart could be brought in from the outside as the new lieutenant general. Thirty-four of the corps's high-ranking officers, including a major general (Samuel French) and eight brigadier generals, had petitioned to request Loring's promotion and his retention in command of the corps.

Similar pools of resentment and frustration may have existed elsewhere in the army, but the known records are silent on the matter. French, another of Stewart's division commanders, had outranked his new corps chief when the latter was a major general. In late July, when Stewart and Loring were wounded, he was passed over as even a temporary corps commander. Carter Stevenson would have been less than human had he not felt slighted. He, too, had outranked Stewart as a major general and was, in fact, the senior West Point–trained major general in the army. In July 1864 he had thrice been denied promotion and a higher command (first as Polk's successor and twice as Hood's).

The army had other division-level personnel problems at the time Hood assumed command. On July 4 Thomas C. Hindman had suffered a severe eye injury that forced him to leave active duty. Brig. Gen. John C. Brown was shifted from his brigade in Stevenson's Division to fill Hindman's place until Maj. Gen. James Patton Anderson could arrive from Florida as Hindman's permanent successor. Anderson himself was wounded soon after he joined the army. Two days after Hindman's injury, Cantey's Division of (then) Loring's Corps was entrusted to Edward C. Walthall, who was transferred from brigade command in Hood's Corps. Cantey had given up his post because of illness (and he may have been drinking too much). Stewart's promotion necessitated selection of a new commander for his old division. On July 8 Henry D. Clayton was promoted to major general to take Stewart's old post. When Cheatham took command of what had been Hood's Corps, Brig. Gen. George Maney took charge of his division. On August 10, when Bate was wounded, Hood detailed Brown to command that division.

In summary, Hood found himself with an inexperienced chief of staff and chief of artillery newly installed as commander of an army of which two of the three infantry corps and four of the ten divisions of infantry were under officers untested at their new level of command. One other division was headed by a general who resented the fact that he had been bypassed for higher command (Loring), and at least two others (Stevenson and French) may have been.

Each change in division command, in turn, necessitated brigade-level changes. It seems likely, therefore, that the entire army was pockmarked by pools of resentment among some of its colonels as officers from other divisions or even corps were transferred to replace men elevated to division command. Brigade-level pools of bitterness, in their turn, probably created similar resentments at the regimental level. Such command turmoil in the army resulted in many troops being placed under officers whom they did not know. In such circumstances, soldiers often lack confidence in their new commander. Such lack of confidence, in turn, reduces an army's effectiveness. One consistent theme running through the Army of Tennessee's history was major reorganization on the eve of battle—or, once, *during* a battle (Chickamauga). July 1864 was no different.

When he assumed command, Hood had no time to worry about such personnel matters even had he been of a temperament to do so. With Sherman extending his left out from the Chattahoochee along an arc north and east of Atlanta, the Rebels simply did not have time to allow organizational turmoil to subside and for troops and commanders to grow accustomed to each other. The Army of Tennessee had never enjoyed great strength at either the staff or general officer level. When Hood took it into the battle for Atlanta, its command and staff were weaker than they had ever been.[2]

Early on July 18 Hood rode to army headquarters. At his request, Johnston continued to direct the Rebels' movements (in Hood's name) for most of the day while the new commander familiarized himself with the dispositions of the entire army. Meanwhile, Hood, Hardee, and Stewart wired President Davis requesting that the change of command be suspended until the fate of Atlanta had been decided. Not until late in the day did the president's reply come. "The order has been executed," he telegraphed, "and I cannot suspend it without making the case worse than it was before the order was issued."

By the next day Johnston was gone and Hood had gotten a tenuous grip on the army. Both his situation and the task the government expected him to perform were daunting. Hood had somehow to destroy Sherman's army or at least to cripple it to such an extent that it would withdraw well into North Georgia if not back to Chattanooga. Merely to shove the Yankees across the Chattahoochee would not suffice. In such a case Sherman could simply hunker down behind the river moat, dare the Rebels to attempt a crossing in the face of his superior numbers, and perhaps detach a strong column to sweep down the right bank of the Chattahoochee to the Gulf of Mexico cutting all Rebel communication with Alabama and

Mississippi and smashing (with artillery) the Secessionists' industrial and naval complex at Columbus, Georgia.

Such a force might cross the Chattahoochee below Columbus and strike eastward about fifty miles to free the prisoners at Andersonville. It would also sever Montgomery, Selma, Mobile, and the Tombigbee River valley from the eastern part of Rebeldom. In so doing, it would, for all practical purposes, pare the viable Confederacy to the Carolinas, Florida, and the Secessionist-held areas of Georgia and Virginia. That outcome would realize one of Grant's original strategic goals for 1864—the establishment of a line of Union control running from Chattanooga, via Atlanta and Montgomery, to Mobile. If nothing else, attainment of such a goal would boost Northern morale and, doubtless, enhance the Republicans' chances in the fall elections.

To drive Sherman back, Hood would have to take the offensive. Changes in military technology, however, had so increased the power of the defense that even defeating an army fighting on the defensive was no easy task. Destroying or seriously crippling such an army was extremely difficult unless its commander made a very serious error or overwhelming force could be brought against it. Obviously, the Rebels could not bring overwhelming force against Sherman. Just as obviously, Sherman was unlikely to make a great mistake. Hood would have to find some other way to deal with his enemy.

Except in unusual cases, a Civil War army acting on the offensive had to maneuver for advantage if its commander hoped to gain an edge or force his opponent to abandon a campaign. Simply launching a frontal attack usually resulted in failure and very high casualties. Successful maneuvering, in turn, required accurate intelligence about both the terrain and the enemy forces, wise decisions by the commander, competent staff work, and intelligent direction of tactical operations by subordinate unit commanders. A great deal of luck also helped.[3]

Scouting reports received at Confederate headquarters on July 18 and 19 revealed that Sherman had allowed a gap to open in his lines. As the Yankees moved out from the Chattahoochee, McPherson swung the Army of the Tennessee far to the east to reach the Georgia Railroad beyond Decatur. Schofield followed with the Army of the Ohio a short distance to the northwest. As the two columns advanced on the eighteenth and nineteenth, they veered off several miles from Thomas and the Army of the Cumberland, which moved from the river, via Buckhead, more directly toward Atlanta. Had the Yankees been on the face of a clock with Atlanta at the center, McPherson would have moved around the circumference of the dial to three, Schofield to two. Thomas was between eleven and twelve.

The gap between the left of Thomas's army and the right of Schofield's meant that the wings of Sherman's army group could not quickly support each other should either need help. After studying the scouts' reports, Hood realized that he had an opportunity to strike a heavy—perhaps a mortal—blow at a part of Sherman's force.

Peachtree Creek flows from east to west, passing some two miles south of Buckhead and about three miles north of the 1864 limits of Atlanta. Thomas's advancing army would reach that stream in a line (the corps side by side) and would, therefore, have to effect crossings at several points before it could reach Atlanta. If the Confederates could strike into the gap between Thomas and Schofield and assail the eastern end of Thomas's line after the Unionists had crossed the creek but before they had time to entrench on the southern bank, Hood concluded, they could push the Yankees off to the west—farther away from Schofield—and trap them in the angle formed by Peachtree Creek and the Chattahoochee. With the creek behind them, the river on the west, and attacking Rebels to the south and east, the Federals' only options, Hood reasoned, would be surrender or destruction.

Sherman, who had learned of Hood's elevation from an Atlanta newspaper, correctly inferred that the change meant an end to the Confederates' passive defense and that he could soon expect some sort of aggressive effort by his enemy. As usual, however, he guessed incorrectly about the Southerners' intentions. Believing McPherson and Schofield to be weaker and more exposed than was the Army of the Cumberland on his right, Sherman directed Thomas to send the IV Corps to the left to bolster the eastern end of the Federal line. The Yankee commander thus unknowingly weakened the very part of his force at the very point his new opponent had chosen to attack.[4]

During the night of July 19–20 Hood met with his chief subordinates to explain his plan. Cheatham, with Hood's old corps supported by Wheeler's cavalry and the Georgia militia, would take position east of Atlanta to shield the right of the Rebel line and the approaches to the city from McPherson and Schofield, who, Hood believed, were still well off to the east of Decatur. Cheatham would mass most of his artillery on

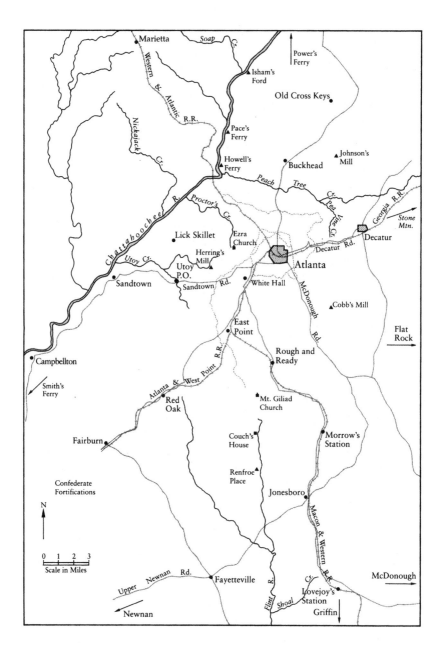

Atlanta Area

his left where the guns could fire north into the gap between the Union columns to keep the two wings of Sherman's army group apart.

The Rebel attack on Thomas would be delivered by Stewart's Corps on the left and Hardee's men, who then held the center of the Confederate line. Hood wanted the assault to open at 1:00 P.M. by which time, he estimated, Thomas would have Peachtree Creek in his immediate rear and would not yet have built formidable works covering his front. Hardee was to open the action by advancing en echelon from his right. As each division successively took up the attack, it would gradually wheel to its left. Stewart would follow Hardee, his right division moving into the battle after the division on Hardee's left had joined the assault. Each corps would hold one division in reserve to be committed to finish the victory. If all went well, the assaulting Rebels would first penetrate into the gap on Thomas's left, cutting him off from Schofield and McPherson (and the IV Corps, although the Rebels did not know that), and drive him back into the angle formed by the creek and the river.[5]

Units of the XIV Corps on Thomas's right reached Peachtree Creek on July 18. The next morning those Yankees forced their way over the stream in the face of stiff opposition from elements of Stewart's Corps. On the morning of July 20 Thomas began pushing the remainder of the Army of the Cumberland across the creek. Palmer's XIV Corps was the first to complete its crossing. The severe skirmishing on the nineteenth had convinced Palmer that he should exercise great caution. He, therefore, advanced his men to a ridge a short distance south of the creek and put them to work building fortifications. His right rested on the Chattahoochee. Hooker's XX Corps crossed to Palmer's left (east) and pushed out about a mile from the creek to the Collier Road Ridge.

Thomas, meanwhile, had modified Sherman's order and sent only two divisions of the IV Corps to join McPherson and Schofield. He retained the other division and put it into line on Hooker's left. By 12:00 M., almost all the Army of the Cumberland was south of the creek and thinly spread across a broad front. The XIV Corps on Thomas's right had thrown up some protective works. The XX Corps had not.[6]

As the army of the Cumberland struggled across Peachtree Creek, the Confederates' situation east of Atlanta began to deteriorate rapidly. McPherson had been much more aggressive on July 19 and 20 than Hood had anticipated. The Yankees occupied Decatur, six miles east of Atlanta, on the nineteenth, and the next morning they pushed forward so vigorously that Wheeler, on the Rebel right with his cavalry and the militia, notified Hood that he needed help.

To deal with the unexpected crisis, Hood, at about 10:30 A.M., directed Cheatham to shift his corps to the right (south) a distance of one division front to give more support to Wheeler and to put some veteran infantry in front of McPherson's oncoming army. To cover the gap this movement would open in the Confederate line, Hood instructed Hardee and Stewart each to move to the right a corresponding distance. After the maneuver, Hood expected, Hardee's left would have shifted one-half a division front to the right and Stewart's Corps would have moved a similar distance. Hood also instructed Hardee to maintain contact with Cheatham. This relatively simple movement, Hood assumed, could be completed in time for the Rebel attack against Thomas to begin on schedule at 1:00 P.M.

Cheatham, however, was new to corps command, and two of his division commanders were also neophytes at their posts. They mishandled the movement. When the halting, jerky effort was done, the corps had shifted about twice the prescribed distance to the south. Hardee, without consulting or even notifying Hood, followed in order to keep his right in contact (by a line of pickets) with Cheatham's left. Stewart had no choice but to tag along to keep his right in touch with Hardee's left. Cheatham did not complete his movement until about 3:00 P.M. By then he had dragged Hardee and Stewart some distance east of the position from which Hood had intended for them to launch the assault on Thomas.

Luck, however, was still with the Rebels. Although they would bicker about the movement and the resulting delay in later years, the Confederates actually benefited from Cheatham's bungling. In the new position Hardee's right extended a bit to the east of Thomas's left and was much better positioned to get into the gap in the Union line. Stewart's men were even more fortunate. Their corps had shifted from in front of the fortified position of the XIV Corps to the unprotected front of the XX Corps. By sheer luck, the Secessionists were ideally positioned to deliver exactly the type of assault Hood envisioned.

At about 4:00 P.M. Hardee, his deployment completed, ordered his troops forward. At that moment luck permanently deserted the Southerners, and their effort began to fall apart. Hardee's right division (Bate's), leading off the assault, advanced to the east of the Yankees' left flank, encountered a few small Northern units, but was unable to find either the end of the main Union line or the creek and, in effect, wandered around in the heavy woods for several hours listening to the battle raging off to the west and accomplishing nothing. Hardee's center division (Walker's) advanced and attacked the IV Corps division on Thomas's left. The Rebels briefly threatened to lap around the division's flanks, but without support on their right they eventually fell back in some confusion. Maney, commanding Cheatham's Division on Hardee's left, advanced after Walker but soon halted and pulled back. Cleburne's Division did not get into the battle at all.

Maney's go-and-stop attack meant that Stewart's men had no support on their right as they moved forward to assault the XX Corps. A Mississippian in Loring's Division described their plight: "The [Yankee] firing wuz comin' from the area where Hardee's left division wuz suppose to be, but they wuzn' there . . . we had to fall back cuz our right flank wuz bein' turned for lack of support." Stewart's troops, nevertheless, mounted a ferocious attack, and the Federals repulsed them only after a stubborn fight in which the Rebels temporarily overran parts of the Union position. Sometime between six and seven that evening the battle spluttered out. Hood ordered Hardee and Stewart back to the position from which they had advanced to attack Thomas. The Rebels' first sortie against Sherman's army group had failed.[7]

By a mixture of boldness and good luck Hood had brought a superior force to the point of battle. He had sent five divisions with two others in support to assail four Union divisions and a few small elements on the left of the XIV Corps. In all, an estimated twenty-three thousand Confederates had been available to fight some twenty thousand Yankees, most of whom were not in a fortified position. The Confederate field commanders, however—especially Hardee—had badly managed the attack. With four divisions on the field, Hardee had gotten only one of them (Walker's)—and only part of it—more or less seriously engaged. After Bate became separated from the assaulting formation, Hardee had neither gotten him back on course nor moved his reserve division (Cleburne's) up to replace him at the most important point in the attacking force. Both Bate and Maney had clearly failed in their missions. Even the commanders of the three divisions that did play a serious role in the battle (Walker, Loring, Walthall) had often allowed their brigades to fight with little or no coordination. Indeed, only six brigades, two from each of those divisions, had borne almost the entire brunt of the battle on the Rebel side.

Part of the Secessionists' problem may have stemmed from the fact that neither Hood nor Hardee sent staff or engineer officers to examine the terrain over which the attack would be made. Nor did either general find local citizens or seek men from Georgia units who might have been familiar with the area and who could have acted as guides.

Some twenty-five hundred Confederates fell at Peachtree Creek, about two thousand Federals. Although some units on both sides took very heavy losses, the overall casualties were not high by 1864 standards.[8]

While fighting raged along Peachtree Creek north of Atlanta, McPherson and Schofield continued pressing toward the city from the east. By early afternoon the Yankees were only about two and a half miles from downtown Atlanta and shells from their artillery were falling in the city. Cheatham's infantry, the militia, and Wheeler's cavalry could not stop McPherson's twenty-five thousand-man juggernaut as it moved forward from Decatur. To deal with what threatened to become a major crisis, Hood sent an urgent message to Hardee to rush a division from the Peachtree Creek battlefront to the extreme right of the Confederate line east of Atlanta (on the clock to move from eleven through the center and then out to between three and four). In response, Hardee dispatched the force he had been holding in reserve (Cleburne's Division). Fortunately for the Southerners, Sherman and McPherson—as they had done at Snake Creek Gap and Resaca—did not realize the opportunity they had and, therefore, did not push their advantage. By early on July 21, Cleburne had reached the right end of the Rebel line, and his troops extended the defensive front south of the Georgia Railroad. Later Maney's (Cheatham's) Division joined him.

All through the twenty-first vicious fighting raged along the line east of Atlanta as McPherson tried to continue his push toward the city. Thomas, off to the north, was very cautious, unwilling to resume his advance until certain that the Rebels would not again strike at him.

Hood that day discovered another opportunity to hit an unprotected part of Sherman's force. Moving westward from Decatur, McPherson had deployed his troops along a north-south line that crossed the Georgia Railroad two or three miles east of Atlanta and stretched off to the south. While McPherson's infantrymen had been working their way toward the city, Sherman had sent the cavalry division that usually covered the left flank of his army group eastward to tear up the railroad. Back on July 16 Grant had advised Sherman that he expected Lee to send reinforcements from Virginia to Georgia. Since Sherman planned to swing most of his force around to the west and south of Atlanta, he wanted to rip such a large gap in the Georgia Railroad that the Southerners could not use the line to move troops and supplies from Virginia to their army at Atlanta. By July 21 the Yankee horsemen were gleefully tearing up track many miles east of Decatur.

With the Union cavalrymen away from McPherson's left flank, Hood's scouts were able to penetrate the area. They returned with the startling intelligence that the southern end of McPherson's line was completely unprotected and vulnerable to an attack from the flank or rear.

To take advantage of this situation, Hood planned to pull Cheatham, Stewart, and the Georgia militia back to a newly constructed inner line of fortifications. Stewart would guard Atlanta on the north, Cheatham and the militia on the east. Hardee, accompanied by Wheeler's cavalry, would leave Atlanta that evening, march south, and then swing around to the east to come in at daylight on the twenty-second behind McPherson, destroy the Yankee wagons parked at Decatur, and assail the left rear of McPherson's army. Once Hardee stampeded the Federals, Cheatham would move out from the lines east of Atlanta and take up the attack. Hood selected Hardee to play the key role in executing the plan because he was the Rebels' most experienced corps commander, his corps was larger than either of the others, and it was better positioned to make the march.[9]

At dark on July 21 the Confederates put Hood's plan into motion. Hardee's divisions north of Atlanta (Bate and Walker) got under way on schedule. Cleburne and Maney east of the city—battered by a hard, vicious day of battle—could not even begin their march until almost midnight. Many of the men, especially Cleburne's, were physically and psychologically exhausted after the hurried march to the east on the twentieth and the all-day fight against McPherson on the twenty-first. A hot, humid night, deep dust in the road, and frequent halts to allow mounted units to cross the line of march all added to the delay and frustration. Hundreds of Hardee's men fell behind their units or dropped exhausted alongside the road.

Sometime that night Hood and Hardee realized that the flanking column could not possibly reach Decatur in time. Hood, therefore, directed Hardee to shorten the march and attack McPherson's left rather than attempting to get far behind the enemy army. With those modified instructions, Hardee rode off with his plodding column. By midmorning Bate's Division, leading the corps, was southeast of Atlanta, just east of Sugar Creek. The other divisions of the corps were strung out behind.

Running far behind schedule and deciding that he had come far enough, Hardee sent Wheeler on to Decatur to strike the Yankee wagons there and began to deploy his men to attack toward the north.

While the Confederates had been planning and executing their night march, McPherson had grown increasingly worried about his extreme left flank, held by the XVII Corps. Well aware that Hood—his classmate at the United States Military Academy—was a bold, daring commander, McPherson ordered the XVI Corps to his left to bolster the line there. Sherman, who was becoming obsessed with the desire to destroy Rebel railroads, instructed McPherson to use the XVI Corps to wreck the Georgia Railroad between Decatur and Atlanta. At McPherson's request, however, Sherman agreed to allow the XVI Corps to remain on the left of the Army of the Tennessee until 1:00 P.M.[10]

Once deployed late that morning, Hardee's infantrymen started north-ward toward what they believed to be McPherson's exposed left flank. They found the going difficult. Rough ground, very heavy underbrush, and a large pond combined to delay the advance and break the lines. The Southerners had procured the services of at least one local civilian as a guide, but they were again advancing over ground that their officers had not reconnoitered and against an enemy whose position was not exactly known. Not until shortly after noon did the first of Hardee's troops make contact with the Yankees. By then, many of the Rebel units had lost their formation.

As Hardee's Confederates floundered northward to launch their as-sault, the XVI Corps troops whom McPherson had ordered to his left were nearing their new position. Those men were marching west, parallel to Hardee's front. When scouts brought word of a large body of Rebels off to the south, they simply halted and faced to the left, their line perpen-dicular to that of the XVII Corps. The Yankee position thus resembled a capital L. Although there was a gap near the angle in the line, the Northerners were almost perfectly placed to meet the impending attack.

Hardee's first assaults—by Bate and Walker on his right—were deliv-ered piecemeal by brigades and were poorly led. When the advancing Rebels met an unexpected heavy fire from the XVI Corps's infantry and artillery, they halted and fell back. Walker was killed by a Yankee infantryman, and numerous brigade and regimental commanders were killed, wounded, or captured. The two divisions on the right of Hardee's line played no further organized role in the battle.

Soon afterward Cleburne's Division launched its assault. The division achieved some success near the angle in the Union line, and at about 4:00 P.M. Hood ordered Cheatham's Corps out of its works to join the battle. Attacking eastward, Cheatham's men broke through the Federal line along the Decatur-Atlanta Road and the Georgia Railroad. Yankee reinforcements, however, soon drove them back. Slowly the fighting all along the line died out.

The engagement (usually called the Battle of Atlanta)—the largest of the campaign—had no significant result. The Confederates had won an initial success and could boast of capturing prisoners and a few cannon, but they had suffered about fifty-five hundred casualties. The Unionists lost some thirty-five hundred troops, including McPherson, killed when he rode into a small party of Cleburne's men who had penetrated the gap in the Federal line. Maj. Gen. John A. Logan took command of the Army of the Tennessee and led it capably in the remainder of the battle. Sherman, however, preferred a professionally trained officer for such a high post, and a few days later he moved Oliver O. Howard from the IV Corps to replace McPherson. Maj. Gen. David Stanley succeeded Howard at the head of the IV Corps.

Hooker, angry at Howard's elevation to army command—he had once commanded an army in which Howard led a corps—resigned and went north, doubtless much to Sherman's delight. To replace Hooker at the head of the XX Corps, Sherman summoned Maj. Gen. Henry W. Slocum from his post in Mississippi. Until Slocum arrived, Brig. Gen. Alpheus S. Williams, the senior officer with the corps, took charge of it.

After the fighting died down east of Atlanta, Hardee posted his bloodied corps along a fortified ridge running to the south. There, on high ground on the extreme right (southeast) of the Confederate defenses, he could meet any renewed Federal push either directly toward Atlanta or to the southward if the Yankees attempted to move in that direction toward the Macon & Western.[11]

Sherman, concluding that it was not practicable to try to reach the Macon railroad from his position east of Atlanta and unwilling to assault Hood's fortifications, decided to implement a long-standing plan to shift his main effort to the west side of the city. He would then extend his right southward, reaching for the railroads below Atlanta. Cutting the rail line that stretched southwest to East Point and thence to Montgomery,

Alabama, and that running to Macon in Central Georgia would force Hood to abandon Atlanta.

To reach those railroads, Sherman would swing the Army of the Tennessee from his left around north of the city and then down the west side of Atlanta to the right of the Union army group. At the same time he would launch a massive two-pronged cavalry raid to distract the Secessionists from his other movements and to cut or wreck the rail lines south of Atlanta.

On the night of July 26–27 the Army of the Tennessee silently slipped out of its trenches on the battlefield of the twenty-second, and Union cavalry units took its place. A long night march carried the army around to the north, behind the lines of the Armies of the Ohio and of the Cumberland. Sherman had instructed Howard to march on south to the Lick Skillet Road west of Atlanta. Possession of that road, Sherman thought, would enable the Yankees to flank Hood's left or to move on farther south to the railroad. A cautious Howard advanced by having each of his divisions deploy facing east as it reached the end of the Union line. The right end of the Federal line thus came to resemble an unrolling capital J as units moved into position.

Hood had expected such a movement, and when Rebel scouts brought word of Sherman's maneuvers, he correctly concluded that withdrawal of the Army of the Tennessee from the east side of Atlanta meant that the Yankees would make their next attempt west of the city. On the twenty-seventh he learned that the Federals were extending their right southward toward the Lick Skillet Road.

To counter the danger, Hood pulled his old corps, commanded by the recently arrived Lt. Gen. Stephen D. Lee, out of its position on Atlanta's east side. While Hardee stretched his line northward to fill the gap, Lee would march out the Lick Skillet Road and position his men to block Howard's southward shift. Stewart, reinforced by one of Hardee's divisions, would follow Lee. Should the Yankees attack the Rebel works west of Atlanta that afternoon, Lee was to assail their right flank. If they did not, Stewart would swing around to the west and north on July 29 to strike and crush the right flank of the line which, Hood assumed, the Unionists would have established on the twenty-eighth when they found their southward progress blocked by Lee.

When Lee reached his designated position on the afternoon of the twenty-eighth, he found Union skirmishers already in the area he was to occupy. The main Federal force was still a half mile or so to the north. Apparently thinking he had a chance to strike the Yankees before they could fortify, Lee disregarded his instructions and threw his men into a series of small-scale uncoordinated assaults on the Federals. The Unionists hastily improvised protective works from logs, rails, and pews from a nearby meetinghouse called Ezra Church. Stewart, following along behind Lee, concluded that he had no choice but to join in the attacks.

The resulting Battle of Ezra Church was a simple affair, with one Confederate unit after another going forward in piecemeal attacks. The Yankees repulsed the assaults with ease. By the time the engagement ended, the Southerners had lost some 3,000 men. Union casualties totaled 632.[12]

While the infantrymen fought at Ezra Church, Sherman's cavalry raids got under way. The Federal commander planned for Brig. Gen. Edward McCook with some thirty-five hundred troopers to cross the Chattahoochee southwest of Atlanta and move east to Lovejoy's Station on the Macon & Western, about twenty-six miles below the city. Meanwhile, Maj. Gen. George Stoneman, with about fifty-five hundred men, would move from the Decatur area, use part of his command to decoy the Rebels, and ride with the rest around Atlanta to meet McCook at Lovejoy's. After wrecking the railroad there, the Yankee horsemen were to march south to Macon, an important rail and manufacturing center and the site of a prison camp for captured Union officers. Stoneman also sought and received from Sherman permission to try to go on to Andersonville fifty-five miles southwest of Macon, where he hoped to liberate the thousands of Unionists confined there.

The Federal horsemen got under way on schedule, but the raid soon fell apart. The basic problem was Stoneman, who, without notifying anyone, disregarded his orders and moved directly on Macon. As a result, three separate Union cavalry forces galloped about south of Atlanta. The decoy force detached from Stoneman's column accomplished nothing and returned to its base on July 29 after skirmishing with a handful of Rebel horsemen.

The other Yankee forces fell victim to Stoneman's irresponsibility and superbly handled Southern forces, and their mission ended in abject failure. McCook reached Lovejoy's but, of course, did not find Stoneman there. When he turned back toward the Federal lines, he got into a running battle with the Confederates. Eventually, his column was cut up and limped back in small parties. In all, he lost about one thousand men.

Stoneman fared even worse. As he approached Macon, he found that the Ocmulgee River had damaged a bridge he had to cross and he encountered a hastily fielded force of militia and home guards. He turned back only to run into pursuing Rebel horsemen. On July 31 at Sunshine Church near Clinton his exhausted men were beaten and he and more than five hundred of them were captured.

By the end of the month fragments of the commands were trickling back to Sherman's lines. Men came in, often on foot, individually and in small groups. The raids had done no serious damage to the Rebels' railroads and had wrecked two divisions of Sherman's cavalry.[13]

The end of July marked the completion of Hood's first two weeks as commander of the Army of Tennessee. In that period he had reversed Johnston's policy and had thrice struck out at Sherman in an effort to cripple or destroy parts of the opposing force. Three times he had failed to achieve his objective. Yet his efforts had not been without results. Sherman's movements became much more cautious as July came to an end.

The superb courage and fighting ability of Sherman's soldiers accounted for a major part of the Rebels' failure. Even so, however, the Secessionists' own problems had greatly hampered their efforts and may well have doomed them long before the Confederates began their assaults at Peachtree Creek. The army's command structure was weak. Incompetent implementation will doom the most brilliant plan to failure. The Army of Tennessee had *never* had a strong command structure. All during the war its generals had shown themselves unable—often unwilling—to follow instructions. They were to do so for the rest of the war as well. Hardee, whose corps played the key roles at Peachtree Creek and Atlanta, was at best an average commander. His resentment at Hood's elevation to head the army and his lack of confidence in his new chief combined with his poor handling of his troops in the two battles to weaken seriously the Rebels' efforts. Hood's infantry corps commanders—Hardee, Stewart, Cheatham, and Lee—performed poorly in the late July battles. So did many of the division commanders.

Then, too, Hood's plans had often been far too ambitious and had demanded more than his men could give. The march planned for Hardee's Corps during the night of July 21–22, even as modified, was simply too much for men who had had little rest since the nineteenth, had fought at Peachtree Creek on the twentieth, and many of whom had undergone a hard day's battle east of Atlanta on the twenty-first. In all three battles (Peachtree Creek, Atlanta, and Ezra Church) the Rebel generals on the field sent troops into assaults piecemeal and allowed their attacks to get out of control. They had not used their units very well.

Whether any of the attacks would have achieved success had they been delivered when and as Hood ordered is a matter that we shall never know. We do know that a great gap existed between what Hood expected his army to do and what it actually did. That gap is the measure of John Bell Hood's inability as an army commander.[14]

Hood, nevertheless, had held Atlanta. Sherman, in fact, had made no significant gain since his men broke the Georgia Railroad on July 18. The successes won by the Rebel cavalry at the end of the month offset in part the failures of July 20, 22, and 28. In fact, as Sherman's movements slowed over the next few weeks, many Confederates concluded that Hood's battles had been strategic victories for the Rebels because they had thwarted attempts by the Federals to flank Atlanta. If the Secessionists could hold their rail lines, they could at least remain in the city. Perhaps Hood could yet devise some bold scheme that would force Sherman to pull back into North Georgia. If he could, all might yet be well for the Secessionist cause.[15]

CHAPTER THIRTEEN

Battle for the Macon & Western

For almost a month after the engagement at Ezra Church and the failure of the McCook-Stoneman raid, the opposing armies remained in relatively stable positions about Atlanta. Their parallel sets of heavily fortified trenches and artillery positions began on the east side of Atlanta, near Decatur, curved around to the north and west, and then stretched south along the city's western side. Hood's fortifications stood between Sherman's forces and the railroads connecting Atlanta to East Point and thence to West Point, Montgomery, and Mobile to the southwest and Macon to the south. Those lines—especially the Macon & Western (M&W), which one Union soldier called "the great feeder of the Rebel army"—were Hood's lifeline to the Confederacy. So long as he could fend Sherman off from at least one of them, he and his army could remain in Atlanta. (By August the Confederates had repaired most of the damage Rousseau had done to the railroad to Montgomery, but owing to that line's proximity to the Federal forces, they no longer made heavy use of it.)[1]

In the first week of August Sherman sought to extend the right of his army group to the south to sever the Confederate rail lines. When he found that the Army of the Tennessee on his extreme right could stretch its lines no farther, the Federal commander moved Schofield's Army of the Ohio from its old position on the Yankee left northeast of Atlanta to the right end of the Union line. Only Northern cavalrymen remained in the works east of Atlanta. Sherman hoped that Schofield would be able to reach the railroad somewhere near East Point, about six miles southwest of Atlanta (a little farther as the railroad ran). Since the Atlanta & West

Point (A&WP) and the Macon & Western used the same track from Atlanta as far as East Point, cutting the line north of East Point would break both railroads. If the Federals got south of East Point, they would first reach the West Point line and then have to move overland several miles to the south and east to seize the road to Macon.

By August 3 Schofield had worked his way to the heavily wooded terrain along the north fork of Utoy Creek, about two miles southwest of Ezra Church and some four miles north-northwest of East Point. He was probing for the West Point Railroad, and to ensure success, Sherman ordered John M. Palmer and the XIV Corps to the Union right to support his efforts. Palmer had instructions to report to Schofield and to act as part of his force. The combination of Schofield and Palmer would put about twenty-five thousand Yankees in position where, Sherman hoped, they could overwhelm any Rebel force in the area and cut the railroad. In making this shift, Sherman ran into a problem.

Palmer believed he outranked Schofield. Like many officers, he resented being subject to the orders of a "junior." (Both held commissions as major general with date of rank November 29, 1862. The matter was complicated because Schofield's original appointment as major general expired in March 1863, and he had been reappointed with his old date of rank.) Palmer's pique may also have stemmed in part from the fact that he was exhausted, had come to resent what he saw as the arrogance of professional officers, had long since tired of the war, and simply wanted to go home. He may well have been seeking an excuse to leave the army. Whatever his motives, Palmer, on August 4, sent word to Schofield that he expected to receive orders only through Thomas, his commanding officer. "I will not obey either General Sherman's [direct] orders or yours as they violate my self-respect," Palmer informed Schofield. (In Palmer's defense, we should note that Thomas had told him that Sherman did not intend to give Schofield command over the XIV Corps. Palmer's foolishness during active operations, however, deserves severe censure.)

Even when Sherman personally pleaded with—and then bluntly ordered—Palmer to "report to and receive orders from General Schofield," he refused. He would do no more than merely relay instructions from Schofield to his division commanders. Those officers, not surprisingly, exhibited little enthusiasm for executing the directives they received. On August 5 Sherman ruled that Schofield was senior to Palmer. Palmer thereupon submitted his resignation and left for his home in Illinois. One of his division commanders with the unlikely name (for a Yankee general) of Jefferson Davis was soon promoted to brevet major general to take his place at the head of the XIV Corps.

Owing to Palmer's recalcitrance, the Federals wasted August 4 and 5. On the sixth Schofield sent troops of his own XXIII Corps southward in an attempt to carry out the mission he had earlier tried to get Palmer's men to perform. By then the Confederates, fully alert, had had ample time to reinforce their left and to extend and strengthen their fortifications. The Rebels, occupying a line running generally westward from the old left end of their position, easily repulsed Schofield's assault on their works and inflicted more than three hundred casualties on the attacking Yankees. The Confederates lost fewer than twenty-five men. On the following day, after taking more casualties, Schofield called off the effort. By then, the Secessionists had constructed a line of works extending south to East Point and had pulled back from their westwardly running line.[2]

Failure along Utoy Creek left Sherman in a most unpalatable situation. He could continue extending his forces to the right in an effort to reach the railroad below East Point. His line, however, was already about eleven miles in length. Consistently overestimating Hood's strength, Sherman believed the Confederate army and the Georgia militia about equal in numbers to his own force, and he had to assume that the Rebel commander would make yet another corresponding extension of his own line. "Every new trench found a fresh one opposite," wrote Oliver O. Howard.

South of East Point, moreover, the tracks of the Macon & Western curved off to the east. Any Federal force trying to reach the rail line there would both present its left flank and rear to the Confederates in Atlanta and put Sherman's whole army group on the circumference of a strategic circle with the Secessionists holding the interior position and therefore able easily to concentrate against a part of the Union line. Sherman would also face the problem of getting supplies to such a force at such a great distance from his Chattahoochee railhead. The Confederates, by contrast, could easily supply their troops via the Macon & Western.

Those factors meant that, at least for the time being, the Yankees were stalemated before the Rebel fortifications. Neither Sherman nor Hood would assault the massive works held by the army of the other. Hood—in what may have been a fatal omission—saw no need to extend his fortifications beyond East Point, and Sherman saw but little possibility of significant gain if he prolonged his trenches. In early August, then, the fighting around Atlanta settled down to sharpshooting and occasional small unit actions. On the third, for example, Federals from the XV Corps captured some Confederate rifle pits in their front. The Southerners rallied and retook the position. The Yankees then mounted a second effort and secured the pits. "The engagement was severe but of short duration," reported Logan. Union casualties amounted to 11 killed, 81 wounded, and 3 missing. The Northerners claimed to have taken about 140 prisoners. Other Confederate losses are unknown. Nothing of importance had changed. In fact, no important change was possible unless Sherman or Hood could devise some means of breaking the stalemate. Both tried because each found the existing situation unsatisfactory.

Sherman faced three potentially very serious problems. He knew that Grant was bogged down before Richmond and Petersburg. Failure of the Federal forces to gain a significant, obvious success might result in a Democratic victory in the approaching elections. By August it was most unlikely that Northern armies could gain such a triumph anywhere other than in Georgia, and even there prospects for success seemed uncertain at best.

Sherman had two other problems specific to his own situation. The three-year terms for which many of his troops had enlisted would soon expire, and those men would then be entitled to discharge. Almost ten thousand of his soldiers who had chosen not to reenlist would leave for home in August, and more would depart in the early fall. Even if he soon received new draftees, they would not equal in quality the men he would lose. Supply problems might also arise by early fall. The four-month stock of supplies with which Sherman began the campaign had not been adequately replenished. During the summer Union quartermasters watched with alarm as their ability to keep Sherman's armies supplied began to decline. Low water in the Tennessee and Cumberland Rivers hampered the delivery of supplies by boat. Meanwhile, increased demands on Yankee rail transportation as Sherman's supply line lengthened coupled with the occasional loss of a train to accident or small parties of Rebel raiders reduced the ability of rear echelon units to support the advancing armies. By mid-September, Sherman's chief quartermaster calculated, the Yankees in Georgia would begin to run short of some supplies.

Nor could Hood accept an indefinite continuation of the status quo, although his plight in that regard was not as dire as was Sherman's. The Confederates had no guarantee that Northern voters would turn the Lincoln administration out of office. Perhaps they would accept Sherman's deep penetration into Georgia as evidence of military success. Perhaps Sherman would decide to slide down the Chattahoochee to the Gulf of Mexico, slicing Alabama and Mississippi off from the rest of Rebeldom. Would the capture by Sherman of Montgomery, Selma, and Mobile be enough to swing the elections to the Republicans even if the Rebels still held Atlanta? Better, from the Secessionist point of view, to drive Sherman back into North Georgia and make certain that Lincoln's critics had another obvious military failure to add to the 1864 catalog of Union defeats in Louisiana and Virginia.[3]

Sherman acted first. He decided to try his artillery. Yankee cannon had occasionally lobbed shells into Atlanta since coming within range in mid-July, but in August the frustrated Federal commander turned to the big guns to damage the city as much as possible. He brought four 4.5-inch rifled siege guns from Chattanooga. Those heavy weapons joined the Unionists' field artillery to hurl thousands of shells into Atlanta—a thirty-pound shell every five minutes during the day, every fifteen minutes at night. Although the bombardment damaged some buildings and on occasion killed or injured soldiers and civilians, it soon became obvious that the artillery could neither cut off rail traffic into and out of Atlanta nor force Hood and the Rebels to evacuate the city.

By August 13, after several days' bombardment, Sherman realized he would have to use his infantry to destroy the rail lines that supplied the Southerners. To accomplish that goal, the Yankee commander decided to send one corps to hold a heavily fortified bridgehead where the Western & Atlantic crossed the Chattahoochee. With his railroad thus protected, he would have both a secure forward base and a place of refuge should his effort meet with disaster. Then, with his six other corps, some sixty thousand men, Sherman would abandon his trenches before Atlanta and swing out in a wide arc to the west and south to reach Hood's railroads with a force that could destroy them beyond possibility of immediate repair. His mobile column, he hoped, would be strong enough to deal with any body of Confederates it might encounter. He set the night of August 18 as the time to begin the movement.[4]

While Sherman's artillery pounded the city and the Federal commander planned his next maneuver, Hood, too, sought some means of ending the stalemate and forcing his opponent to give up his position at Atlanta. Defeat of the McCook-Stoneman raid in late July and the wrecking of so much of Sherman's cavalry seemed to present such an opportunity. Even as Rebel horsemen pursued the fragments of the raiding force below Atlanta, Hood concluded that the time had come to send some of Wheeler's mounted units to deliver a counterblow which, he anticipated, would force the Yankees to abandon their effort to take Atlanta.

By August 10 Wheeler, acting under Hood's instructions, had assembled some forty-five hundred cavalrymen (about half the army's mounted troops) near Covington southeast of Atlanta. His men had had a few days to rest themselves and their horses after their great victory over Stoneman and McCook and to prepare for their next mission. Hood's orders read that the Rebel horsemen were to cross the Chattahoochee near Roswell and ride north, striking at the Western & Atlantic Railroad as they went. Wheeler was then to move into Tennessee, attack both railroads between Nashville and Chattanooga, leave twelve hundred men to continue operations against the lines, and return to the army, hitting the W&A again on the way south. Ignoring the fact that such an ambitious undertaking would require Wheeler's troopers to ride at least four hundred miles, Hood expected his mounted troops to be away only "a few days."

The Rebel commander hoped Wheeler would do with the army's horsemen what Johnston had declared could be done only by Forrest's cavalrymen from Mississippi—cut Sherman's rail line so the Yankees at Atlanta would have to retreat or starve without exposing the Army of Tennessee to defeat. Optimistically anticipating that his opponent would soon backpeddle across North Georgia, Hood instructed his engineers to prepare materials to rebuild the railroad bridges between Atlanta and Chattanooga that, he assumed, Sherman would destroy as he retreated.

Wheeler moved north for several days, lashing out at the railroad as he went. Although he managed to tear up the tracks at several points and to capture some of the troops guarding the line, he was unable to inflict any significant damage. Sherman's railroad defenses were too strong for raiding cavalry. Yankee reinforcements arrived too quickly at threatened points and chased the raiders away. Wheeler's men could no more put Sherman's rail line out of service than Sherman's horsemen could demolish Hood's. Wheeler's only notable accomplishment was the capture near Calhoun of a herd of about one thousand beef cattle, which he sent back to the army at Atlanta. Then, not having seriously impeded the flow of supplies southward to the Federal forces at Atlanta—but having sent to Hood grossly inflated reports of his success—Wheeler rode off into East Tennessee. Nobody with the Army of Tennessee would see him again until mid-October. By then he had completely wrecked much of the cavalry of Hood's army.[5]

Sherman had been expecting Hood to launch such a counterblow in the aftermath of the McCook-Stoneman fiasco. Soon after Wheeler's raid began, the Yankee commander realized that the Rebel cavalrymen would not be able to do serious damage to the railroad and that his repair crews would quickly get the line back into operation. Wheeler's absence, Sherman thereupon concluded, gave the Federal horsemen another opportunity to cut Hood's rail line.

On August 15 and 16 some of Sherman's mounted units probed at the Rebels and returned to report meeting only slight resistance. One of the columns reached the Atlanta & West Point Railroad at Fairburn, about ten miles southwest of East Point, and reported upon its return that it had destroyed a few miles of track. Concluding that the Secessionist cavalry in his front was too weak to protect Hood's rail lines and anxious to avoid the delay and risk inherent in his planned infantry sweep, Sherman resolved to make one more effort to cut the Confederates' line of supply with his own mounted units. He suspended the order for the infantry movement and directed Brig. Gen. Hugh Judson Kilpatrick to take five brigades of cavalry (about forty-seven hundred men) and ride to the southwest, turning east to reach and sever the Macon & Western in the vicinity of Jonesboro, some fifteen miles directly south of Atlanta.

Kilpatrick got under way after dark on August 18. By five the next afternoon the Yankee raiders had reached Jonesboro, and their commander put them to work tearing up the tracks. Leaving Jonesboro five hours later, Kilpatrick rode south some seven miles to Lovejoy's Station. There, about noon on August 20, the raiders ran into a Rebel force defending the town. At about the same time a pursuing body of Jackson's horsemen struck them from the rear.

Concluding that he could do no more, Kilpatrick decided to terminate the engagement and get back to the Yankee lines. His men broke through the Southern cavalry in their rear and rode off eastward in a heavy rain. On the twenty-second his column got to Decatur, having ridden from the right end of the Union line southwest of Atlanta around the city and the Confederate army and reached the left of Sherman's fortified position.

Once back at Yankee headquarters, Kilpatrick gleefully reported that he had destroyed a total of ten miles of track on the M&W and estimated that the Rebels could not get the line back into service for ten days. He either lied or was badly mistaken. His raiders had damaged less than two miles of track, and the Confederates had the line back in operation on August 21, even before Kilpatrick's exhausted men reached Decatur. In fact, on the very day Kilpatrick reported the results of his foray to Sherman, Union signalmen observed an eleven-car train puffing into Atlanta from the south. The simple truth, Sherman concluded, was that cavalry could not do a thorough job wrecking a railroad defended by hostile troops and he had no option but to use his infantry to assail Hood's railroads. He set August 25 as the new starting date for the massive infantry sweep below Atlanta.[6]

On August 25 many delegates to the Democratic National Convention were en route to Chicago. By then most of the powerful eastern wing of the party had rallied behind the candidacy of George B. McClellan. Although a bitter foe of the Lincoln administration, McClellan was a staunch nationalist and believed that restoration of the Union must precede an end to hostilities. His most serious difference with Lincoln centered on the issue of emancipation. McClellan was not committed to the abolition of slavery in the United States; by 1864, Lincoln was.

Many Peace Democrats, however, whose strength was in the Midwest, opposed McClellan, whom they saw as both a tool of eastern interests and a general who had made war on the Southern states on behalf of a Federal government that was rapidly becoming—if it was not already—a tyranny. McClellan, some of them pointed out, had in 1861 arrested members of the Maryland legislature because he suspected them of trying to engineer the secession of the state.

All Democrats were anxious to regain control of the Federal government, but Peace Democrats, War Democrats, easterners, and midwesterners all had different agendas. If the party was to regain the White House in 1864, it would have to unite its adherents and reconcile its squabbling factions.

The convention opened at noon on August 29. The first and most important battle erupted in the Committee on Resolutions. Clement L. Vallandigham, Ohio's representative on the committee, chaired the seven-man subcommittee that wrote the party's platform. Vallandigham used his position, and almost certainly threatened a bolt by his followers, to secure adoption of an ultra-peace plank in the platform. In this document, the Democrats denounced the Lincoln administration's violations of civil rights in its quest for military victory, declared the war a failure, and—

most important—demanded "immediate efforts" to bring about a cease-fire to be followed by a convention of the states "or other peaceable means" to restore sectional harmony "on the basis of the Federal Union of the States." The party platform thus called for a negotiated settlement but did not demand that the Secessionists accept reunion in exchange for peace. The future status of slavery in the reunited country did not receive a mention.

"The western peace men," wrote August Belmont, national chairman of the Democratic Party, " . . . are very ultra." In an effort to avoid a party-destroying rupture in the convention and a probable boycott of the election by the "ultra" Peace Democrats, the party accepted Vallandigham's plank on August 30.

Having adopted their platform, the Democrats gathered the following day to choose their nominee. They selected McClellan on the first ballot. Many peace men doubtless believed that the platform, not the candidate's views, would and should determine the policy the party would follow once in power—a common nineteenth-century attitude, especially among Democrats. After choosing the general for the top spot on the ticket, the delegates turned to the selection of his running mate. Rejecting a slave-state War Democrat (former secretary of the treasury James Guthrie of Kentucky), the delegates stampeded to Representative George H. Pendleton of Ohio. If there was in public life in the North anyone more a pacifist than Vallandigham, it was Pendleton.

The Democrats thus emerged from their convention having adopted a platform in which they branded the war a military failure and proposed to terminate the conflict in the vague hope that sometime in the indefinite future the seceded states would agree to meet to see if, perhaps, it might be possible to work out some plan of reunion they would be willing to consider. Having taken their stand for what amounted to peace at any price, the delegates then nominated a candidate committed to reunion even if achieving that goal meant continuation of the war. Finally, they saddled their war candidate with the additional burden of an ultra-peace man as his vice-presidential nominee. It would be 104 years before the Democratic Party equaled its 1864 orgy of collective political self-immolation.

Still, as the delegates filtered out of Chicago and headed home, many believed their candidate had a good chance for victory in the election. Thousands across the North were still very displeased with the Lincoln administration's violation of civil rights, its high taxes, and its policy regarding slavery and with the constantly lengthening casualty lists. If such discontent continued to grow and if McClellan could somehow bridge the great gulf within his party, the Democrats might still defeat Lincoln and the Republicans—if, in the meantime, the Union armies did not win a great victory that would doom the peace movement.[7]

Even as the Democrats gathered in Chicago, Sherman's troops were on the march southwest of Atlanta. During the night of August 25–26, in accordance with their commander's orders, the men of the XX Corps pulled back to the Chattahoochee, where they fortified a position covering the railroad bridge and some nearby ferries. There the XX Corps would remain until the campaign had been decided. Its mission was to hold the bridgehead, guard the railroad, and offer a refuge for the rest of the army group should Sherman's movement meet with disaster. That same night the IV Corps abandoned its works and moved around to Utoy Creek, where it took position facing north, protecting the rear of Sherman's force against any Rebel effort to follow and attack it.

As a result of those movements, the Yankee trenches east and north of Atlanta stood empty. Except for the XX Corps at the river, Sherman's entire army group was fortified off to the southwest of Atlanta in a position that resembled the number seven (7). The first step in Sherman's plan had been executed without a hitch.

The Rebels did not learn of the Federals' change of position until the morning of August 26, and then they did not know what to make of it. Confederate units moved into the deserted works, where the men rejoiced to find large quantities of abandoned food, blankets, and other items. Some Secessionists jumped to the happy conclusion that Wheeler's attacks on the railroad had forced Sherman to abandon his effort against Atlanta. Arrival of the cattle Wheeler had captured near Calhoun boosted their spirits even more. (It did not dawn on those optimists to ask why the Federals had left so much food and equipment in their old trenches if their rail line had been severed.)

Hood, although hopeful, was less sanguine, especially when reconnaissance revealed that only the Union works east and north of Atlanta were vacant. The right of Sherman's line still held its position west of the city and parallel to the railroad to East Point. Realizing this change in the enemy's dispositions might mean that Sherman planned an effort to reach the railroads below Atlanta, Hood alerted Confederate units posted there and ordered troops on the Rebel right to hold themselves in readiness to move to the left on short notice.

While the Secessionist commander pondered his opponent's mysterious shift, Sherman put the next step of his plan into execution during the night of August 26–27. Using the XIV Corps to block the approaches from the north and holding the XXIII Corps in its fortifications facing to the east to screen the movement, he started the IV Corps and the Army of the Tennessee to the south and southwest toward the Atlanta & West Point Railroad in the vicinity of Fairburn.

By then, Confederate cavalry on the Rebel left had reported a strong Yankee force pushing to the south. Hood, therefore, shifted additional infantry down the railroad below Atlanta. He posted Hardee's Corps at East Point and ordered the Southern horsemen to be especially watchful for and to oppose any Union thrust toward the Macon & Western.

Sherman's army group was making a great wheel around to the southwest and south of Atlanta, and on August 28 the outer part of that wheel, the XV and XVII Corps, reached the Atlanta & West Point Railroad at Fairburn. Soon afterward, the inner part, the IV and XIV Corps, got onto the same rail line at Red Oak, about halfway between Fairburn and East Point. By that time Hood had sent some troops as far south as Jonesboro and had placed others at Rough and Ready (now Mountain View) on the Macon & Western about three miles southeast of East Point. Although the Confederate commander had a generally accurate picture of Sherman's location and realized the threat to the railroad, he remained uncertain as to what form that threat would take over the next few days, how massive the danger was, and where it was greatest. Would Sherman lash out with another cavalry raid from his right against the railroad far to the south? Would the Union infantry continue shifting south and west? Would the Yankees back at the Chattahoochee attempt to take Atlanta by a sudden thrust at the city? The Confederate commander had to dispose his force to guard against all those possibilities.

At Sherman's order, the Unionists spent the next day, August 29, thoroughly destroying the Atlanta & West Point Railroad. By that evening they had wrecked almost thirteen miles of track. Since the Rebels made almost no use of that line anyway and would make none at all after it had been crossed by the Northern infantry, Sherman, in effect, wasted a day.

Hood, meanwhile, still had not ascertained his enemy's intention. The Rebel commander's dispatches during those late August days referred constantly to "the left" of Sherman's line being back on the river. So, too, did Confederate news reports from Atlanta. The Secessionists seem not to have realized that Sherman had cut loose from his bridgehead with six-sevenths of his force to operate against the railroads below Atlanta. Not understanding the magnitude of the Yankee effort, the Southerners seem to have been thinking in terms of simply another extension of the enemy line to the south with, perhaps, cavalry raids lashing out against the M&W from Sherman's advanced position. The Confederates, therefore, underestimated the extent of the danger and overestimated the time they had to meet it. They wasted the day of grace Sherman gave them on August 29.

Once his men had thoroughly wrecked the A&WP, Sherman began the next phase of his wheeling movement. He directed Howard to march on August 30 for Renfroe's Plantation some ten miles east-southeast of Fairburn and only two miles west of the Flint River. Although his goal was Renfroe's, Howard had permission to continue on toward Jonesboro if he found conditions favorable for doing so. Thomas with the IV and XIV Corps would move on a parallel arc a few miles to the north, and Schofield would be to the north of Thomas. Moving eastward on a broad front, Howard and Thomas were to reach and wreck the M&W on August 31. Schofield's primary mission was to protect the left of Sherman's army group.

On the morning of August 30 the Federal armies moved to execute Sherman's plan. Marching on two parallel roads and preceded by Judson Kilpatrick's cavalry, Howard's Army of the Tennessee encountered stiff resistance from the Southern horsemen of William H. Jackson. When he reached Renfroe's in midafternoon, Howard discovered that his men would have no water if they camped there. He therefore ordered them on to the east to the Flint River. Late in the afternoon John Logan's XV Corps, leading Howard's column, reached the Flint. The Yankees' advance units managed to seize the bridge which the Confederates had set afire, extinguish the blaze, get across the river, and push the Rebels back. The Federals then moved to a ridge about one-half mile east of the stream. Because the XV Corps was some distance ahead of his other units and he did not know the terrain or the strength of the Confederates in his front, Howard directed Logan to entrench along the ridge. Logan's Yankees were only half a mile from the M&W.[8]

All through the afternoon of August 30 Hood and the Confederates did not fully comprehend the danger they faced. Although he knew that

Sherman was trying to cut the railroad, the Rebel commander still did not realize the magnitude of the threat closing in on the M&W nor did he know where the Yankees would strike. A little after 6:00 P.M., however, he received a telegram from officers at Jonesboro reporting that a Union force had crossed to the east side of the Flint and warning that the Yankees would probably reach the railroad the following day.

Knowing he must preserve his hold on the M&W to retain Atlanta and obviously assuming that the force near Jonesboro was the only immediate danger to the rail line, Hood ordered Hardee south with his own corps and that of Stephen D. Lee. Early in the morning of the last day of August the two corps were to attack the Federal force at Jonesboro and drive it back across the Flint. After the attack, Lee was to return to Rough and Ready while Hardee's Corps remained at Jonesboro. Should the attack at Jonesboro fail, Lee would then be positioned to cover the Secessionists' withdrawal from Atlanta. If the attack succeeded, as Hood anticipated, he would bring Stewart's Corps and the militia south to join Lee and the two corps would then assault Sherman's force while Hardee assailed it from the Jonesboro area.

Hardee himself reached Jonesboro about 2:30 A.M. on the thirty-first. His corps, commanded by Cleburne, was delayed by what turned out to be false reports of Union troops athwart its line of march. The last units of the corps did not arrive at Jonesboro until about 11:30 A.M. Part of Lee's Corps had to detour around Yankees, who, by then, were present on the direct road between Rough and Ready and Jonesboro, and the last of its units did not join Hardee until 1:30 P.M. It took until about 3:00 P.M. before Hardee finally had his force of some twenty thousand men deployed west of Jonesboro and ready to attack.

While Secessionist troops had been moving to Jonesboro, the rest of Howard's army had come up to support the XV Corps, and that corps had had most of the night and more than nine hours of daylight to fortify its line on the ridge and to bring up artillery. By Sherman's order, Thomas had sent troops to the Renfroe place, where they were positioned to come to Howard's assistance should his men need help.

Hardee planned to attack en echelon from his left, with Cleburne leading off the assault and swinging to the right to strike the right of the Yankee line. Lee would then take up the movement. The sound of Cleburne's attack to the south would be the signal for Lee's advance. Hardee hoped to roll up the Union line from south to north.

As happened on so many other fields, the Army of Tennessee's attack quickly turned into a fiasco. Lee mistook the first firing on Cleburne's front for the full attack and ordered his men forward. When those troops encountered heavy fire, they halted, and then many of them broke and fled. The left of Cleburne's line, coming under fire from Union cavalrymen along the Flint, slipped out of control and veered off to the west (left) to chase the Yankee horsemen across the river. Other units, finding no support to their left, made at most a feeble effort or simply halted and refused to advance. The casualty lists tell the poignant story of what the Yankees called the "killing time." Howard reported a total loss of 172 men. The best estimates put Hardee's casualties at "at least 2,000." Once again, defense had triumphed over a simple, badly managed, uncoordinated, straightforward, piecemeal attack.

The battle was a useless effort in any event. To the north, at about the time Hardee's attack got under way, Schofield's column reached and broke the railroad. Thus, even had Hardee's troops driven Howard over the river, the Yankees still had the Confederate supply line in their grip. At long last, Sherman had achieved his objective. Atlanta and Hood's defending army were cut off from the rest of the Confederacy. The Rebels could no longer remain in the city.

Sherman, however, was positioned to achieve a much greater success. Late in the afternoon of August 31, 1864, he stood with six corps, some sixty thousand elated, victorious troops, between the two weak parts of the opposing army and in position to crush Confederate military power in the West once and for all. The Yankee commander, however, had no taste for such decisive work. He dispatched orders for Schofield and the IV Corps, which had joined him to wreck the railroad south from Rough and Ready until they met the XIV Corps troops, who had reached the tracks and would destroy the line north from Jonesboro. Even when Thomas, a few hours later, proposed to use the IV and XIV Corps to trap and destroy the Rebels at Jonesboro, Sherman overruled him and reiterated his instructions to destroy the railroad, not the Confederate army.[9]

Hood, meanwhile, remained uncertain as to what had happened to the south. With Federals across the railroad below Atlanta and the telegraph wires cut, he had no direct communication with Hardee. He seems to have feared that the Yankees near Rough and Ready would turn north and attack Atlanta. At 6:00 P.M., thinking that "the enemy may make an attempt on Atlanta tomorrow," he sent couriers off to Hardee with orders to return Lee's troops to the Atlanta area and dispose his own corps to cover the railroad south to Macon. Thus, as Sherman's six corps converged on Jonesboro (three of them slowed by Sherman's foolish orders to destroy the railroad as they came), Hood made the Rebels' situation even worse. He ordered half the Confederate force at Jonesboro away. Until Lee could rejoin Hood, the Secessionist army would be split into three very weak parts: Hardee at Jonesboro, Hood with Stewart and the militia in Atlanta, and Lee on the march somewhere in between.

Not until early on September 1 did Hood receive by courier a report from Hardee about the failure at Jonesboro. Realizing he had no option, Hood began preparations to evacuate the city during the night of September 1–2. He, with the troops still in Atlanta, would move southeast on the McDonough Road, which ran parallel to, but several miles east of, the Macon & Western Railroad. When Lee could be located, he would be instructed to position his corps to cover the retreating column against a thrust from the Yankees along the railroad to the west. Hood's objective was Lovejoy's Station, on the railroad, about seven miles south of Jonesboro and some eleven miles west of McDonough. Once the army reunited, it would be positioned to cover Macon and the prisoner-of-war camp at Andersonville. Meanwhile, during the day, the Confederates would destroy what they could not take with them from the doomed city.[10]

While the Rebels in Atlanta spent September 1 preparing to evacuate the city, those at Jonesboro steeled themselves as best they could for what they knew was coming. Expecting Sherman to bring the full weight of his massive force against Jonesboro, Hardee shifted his troops into a defensive position. He deployed Cleburne's Division on his right flank, with its right bent back across the railroad north of the town. Hardee's other divisions took position west of the railroad, facing Howard to the west. Only about twelve thousand men held this two-mile line. In places Southern soldiers stood six feet apart. Much of the line, especially on the right, had slight, if any, obstructions to the front to slow an enemy attack or fortifications to protect the defenders.

Thanks to Sherman's foolish compulsion to destroy a railroad the Confederates could no longer use, the Yankees wasted the entire morning of September 1. That accomplished, the Union commander planned to bring the XIV Corps down the railroad from the north against Hardee's line. The IV Corps would move on the left of the XIV. While Howard with the Army of the Tennessee demonstrated against Hardee's left, the Northerners would envelop the eastern end (right) of the Secessionist position with Thomas's two corps.

Not until shortly after 4:00 P.M. were the Yankees ready to begin their attack. Some of their first assaults were repulsed, but after an hour several Union regiments overran the angle in the Confederate line and captured most of the defenders there. Fortunately for the Rebels, Howard to the west made no serious advance. Had he attacked in coordination with Thomas to the north, but few of the Confederates would have escaped. As it was, the Secessionists managed to pull together an ad hoc defensive line and stem the attack on the angle. Before the Unionists could regroup to do more or the IV Corps could come up on the east, darkness fell.

Soon after night halted the fighting, Hardee began to draw his troops out of their line at Jonesboro. The Rebels slipped off toward Lovejoy's without the Yankees realizing they had gone. Not until about 6:00 A.M., September 2, did Sherman learn that the Southerners had escaped from his front.[11]

During the night, as Hardee retreated south from Jonesboro, Hood with Stewart's Corps and the militia filed out of Atlanta and marched southeast toward McDonough. Before leaving the city, the Rebels opened the government warehouses to anyone, soldier or civilian, who would come and carry away the bacon, clothing, blankets, and other items with which they were filled. What was not taken for private use was burned. The Southerners also torched a collection of five locomotives and eighty-one freight cars that had been trapped in the city when the Yankees cut the rail lines to the south. Twenty-eight of the cars were filled with ammunition, and the resulting explosion leveled nearby buildings and echoed across the countryside. The last of Hood's infantry cleared the city by about 1:00 A.M., September 2. Only a few cavalrymen remained behind.

Soon after daylight Mayor James M. Calhoun, accompanied by other municipal officials, rode north from Atlanta carrying a white flag. Not far beyond the city's fortifications the mayor's party met a patrol from the XX Corps cautiously inching toward Atlanta. Slocum had sent it to try to discover the meaning of the explosions and fires in Atlanta during the night. The mayor thereupon surrendered the city and requested protection for noncombatants and private property. At 11:00 A.M. the first Union troops marched into Atlanta, chased away the few remaining Confederate horsemen, and raised the flags of the Sixtieth New York and

111th Pennsylvania over City Hall. Slocum himself reached the city early in the afternoon and soon dispatched a short message to Washington: "General Sherman has taken Atlanta."[12]

Meanwhile, to the south Sherman was attempting to organize a pursuit of Hardee's Rebels. He and the others near Jonesboro had heard the explosions to the north during the night but did not know whether they indicated a battle between Hood and Slocum, an evacuation of the city, an accident, or something else. On September 2 Sherman sent Howard with the Army of the Tennessee southward on the west side of the railroad and Thomas with the IV Corps directly south along the tracks, while Schofield with the XXIII Corps moved after Hardee on a route to the east. Sherman held the XIV Corps at Jonesboro to bury the dead, tend the wounded, and guard against a Confederate thrust from the north.

Early that afternoon the Federals came up in front of the Confederates' new line about a mile north of Lovejoy's Station. Hardee had entrenched his men in a strong position along a ridge with both flanks resting on low, marshy ground. For several hours the Yankees probed the new Rebel line. After a thorough reconnaissance, Sherman gave up all thought of an attack on it. Late that afternoon and into the evening first Stewart's Corps and then Lee's trudged into Lovejoy's, and Hood reunited his army. (The militia had gone to Griffin.) That evening Sherman concluded that he would make no more serious efforts against the forces in his front until he could learn what had happened at Atlanta. Early on September 3 he received notification from Slocum that the Confederates had abandoned the city and the XX Corps had occupied it.

Upon receiving this intelligence, the Union commander decided not to try to advance farther south for the time being. The next important point was Macon, some sixty-five miles away by rail. Hood's army stood reunited in his front. The railroad was wrecked south of Rough and Ready (thanks to Sherman) and would, therefore, be unable to supply the Unionists in an advance on Macon even if they found working locomotives and cars in Atlanta. Besides, Sherman's men were exhausted and needed rest. He ordered the troops to pull back to Atlanta.[13]

CHAPTER FOURTEEN

"Let Old Abe Settle It"

News of Sherman's success at Atlanta flew across the North, touching off massive public celebrations from coast to coast as citizens responded to the *New York Herald*'s "Let the Loyal North take heart." No sooner did President Lincoln learn of the occupation of Atlanta (from Slocum's September 2 telegram) than he hastened to tender the "National thanks" to the Federal armies in Georgia. "The marches, battles, sieges, and other military operations that have signalized the campaign, must render it famous in the annals of war," wrote the happy chief executive, who could then see that his labors to save the Union had not been in vain.

Lincoln also ordered a salute of one hundred guns fired on September 7 at the arsenal in Washington to celebrate the capture of Atlanta. To be certain that as many citizens (and voters) as possible knew about the great Union victory, the president ordered similar salutes in New York, Boston, Philadelphia, Baltimore, Pittsburgh, St. Louis, New Orleans, and elsewhere. On September 4 from his headquarters with the Army of the Potomac, Grant informed Sherman: "In honor of your great victory I have ordered a salute to be fired with shotted guns from every battery bearing upon the enemy. The salute will be fired within an hour amidst great rejoicing."

Unionists everywhere marked the occasion with fireworks, parades, artillery salutes, prayers of thanksgiving, pealing church bells, music, and speeches. No one celebrated more joyfully than did the Republicans, for the capture of Atlanta gave them, at long last, the great military success that enabled them to proclaim that Lincoln's war policy had not failed and that the national armies were, indeed, making steady progress toward suppressing the rebellion. That same success came about as close as any single event can come to locking in the outcome of a national election. It meant that the president would win in November and his party would retain control of the Federal government.[1]

Sherman's triumph put George B. McClellan in a most ticklish situation. Honestly and completely devoted to preservation of the Union, McClellan had been nominated for the presidency by an extremist-dominated political convention that had pronounced the war a failure; at least implied that, if victorious in the election, the party would seek peace at any price; and burdened its ticket with an ultra-peace man as the vice-presidential candidate.

The timing could not have been more unfortunate for the Democrats. They had postponed their convention until the last possible moment in order to evaluate the military situation as of late summer. In Chicago on August 30 and 31, the days the Democrats adopted their platform and chose their candidates, it appeared that the stalemates at Atlanta and on the Richmond-Petersburg front would continue indefinitely. No one at the Chicago convention could have known that, even as the delegates voted for the peace platform and to nominate McClellan and Pendleton, the Confederates were losing their grip on Atlanta. As the convention completed its work, Sherman's armies cut the last rail line into the Confederate citadel.

By the time McClellan received official word of his nomination, Sherman had possession of Atlanta and it was clear that the Federal armies had won a great victory that beyond reasonable doubt sealed the fate of the Confederacy. When the Democratic candidate sat down to compose his letter accepting the nomination, he had to find some way of making a case for his election that would meet the changed political-military environment created by events at Atlanta. He had both to appeal to the newly reinvigorated Unionism sweeping the North in the wake of Sherman's success and to avoid so antagonizing the rabid Peace Democrats that they would sit out the election. He had to offer voters a convincing rationale for choosing him rather than Lincoln to complete the national victory. He also had to remain reasonably faithful to his own Unionist convictions. Finally, if he were to have any chance of winning the election, he could not give the Republicans too easy a mark in pointing to his position on the one hand and to the Democratic platform on the other.

Well aware of the difficult situation in which Sherman's success and his own party's radical peace wing had placed him, McClellan labored through six drafts of his letter of acceptance. The final document, dated September 8, clearly stated McClellan's position that the seceded states must accept reunion before hostilities could cease. With anything less than that precondition, the Democratic nominee declared, "I could not look in the face of my gallant comrades of the Army and Navy, who have survived so many bloody battles, and tell them that their labors and the sacrifices of so many of our slain and wounded brethren had been in vain."

If, however, the South (or any Southern state) would accept reunion, McClellan promised to observe and preserve all its rights under the Constitution. This pledge meant that a McClellan administration would not interfere with slavery in any state that chose to permit the institution. McClellan thus argued that his election would end the war by removing the raison d'etre for secession, thereby leading to peace and a quick restoration of a Union in which the rights of all white Americans would be respected.

McClellan believed he offered Northern voters a valid choice between a quick peace with reunion and slavery or a bloody war that could drag on indefinitely as Lincoln sought both to restore the Union and to abolish slavery. McClellan and the Democrats also tried to draw the attention of Northern voters away from the conflict itself to other issues—to the Republicans as the party of "negro equality" and to what McClellan and the Democrats depicted as Lincoln's frequent violations of the constitutional rights of citizens in the Northern states. The latter charge was, in fact, potentially a major issue. In other times and under other circumstances— or perhaps even with a different Democratic platform in 1864—the charge might have been potent enough to sink Lincoln's bid for a second term.

Such was not to be the case. In August the stalemated war seemed the issue that might well drag the Lincoln government down to defeat. In September the war became the Republicans' chief hope for political victory. No matter how hard McClellan and the Democrats tried to deflect public attention to Lincoln's conduct in office or to the "threat of negro equality," Republican spokesmen would not let voters forget the gap between the peace plank of the Democratic Party's platform and its candidate's position on the war. One cartoonist depicted McClellan proclaiming, "I accept the nomination and of course stand on the platform and if you don't like the platform, I refer you to my letter of acceptance."

Nor would the Republicans let the voters forget the recent battlefield victories of the national armies. Although not the cause of other successes, the capture of Atlanta marked what amounted to the breaking of a military logjam. Events, it seemed, conspired against McClellan and the Democrats. In mid-September Union armies in the Shenandoah Valley in Virginia routed Early's small Confederate force at Winchester and again at Fisher's Hill. Republicans closed ranks behind Lincoln. On September 22 Frémont withdrew from the presidential race. Early in October the Republicans swept the crucial state elections in Ohio, Indiana, and Illinois. On October 19 the Yankees won another smashing victory at Cedar Creek near Middletown, Virginia.

McClellan made a game effort, but events had simply passed him by. Most Northern voters saw no good reason to change presidents, and many of them, in fact, saw excellent reasons for not doing so. By the fall of 1864 many, if not most, Northerners had come to believe that slavery had caused the war and that if the institution were not destroyed, it would lead to similar problems in the future. Thousands of Northerners had seen black soldiers fight and die for the Union, and hundreds of thousands had read that the Rebels had murdered captured Negroes after several 1864 battles. Should—could—those blacks who had served loyally and honorably as United States soldiers be returned to slavery? If the Southern states rejoined the Union with slavery intact, one Federal soldier observed, "we can fight them again in ten years. But let Old Abe settle it, and it is always settled."

Such logic convinced a majority of Northern voters. When they went to the polls in November, they gave Lincoln 55 percent of the popular vote, a near landslide. By the fall of 1864, Lincoln's support among the common people of the loyal states was deep and solid. Election data from the states for which it is possible to count soldier votes separately show that Sherman's men cast an almost unbelievable 86 percent of their ballots for Lincoln. In the electoral college the president won a comfortable 212-to-21-vote victory, carrying every state except Delaware, Kentucky, and New Jersey. The Federal government would see the war through to final victory. There would be no compromise with either slavery or secession.[2]

"So Atlanta is ours, and fairly won," Sherman telegraphed to Washington on September 3. When he sent that message, his success in Georgia was the only major achievement of Union arms in 1864. The capture of Atlanta came in time to relieve the gloom hanging over much of the North as the summer casualty lists lengthened and final victory seemed unattainable. It could not have been better timed to undermine the Democrats and boost Lincoln's chances for reelection.[3]

The capture of Atlanta also made Sherman a great national hero and elevated him to a position in the Union's military pantheon but little below that of Grant himself. From September 1864 to the present Sherman usually has been regarded as one of the two or three best generals of the Civil War. Indeed, in most estimations, only Grant and, perhaps, Lee rate higher.

Success and victory, however, are like spackling paste. All three can cover up a multitude of mistakes and false starts and hide errors. In so doing, they create a misleading picture of what lies beneath surface appearances. So it has been with Sherman's Atlanta campaign.

If Sherman's military reputation rested solely on his conduct of field operations from early May to early September 1864, it would be considerably lower than it presently is—probably not much above average. His greatness as a military commander and a maker of war rests on two pillars, neither of which applies to his conduct of daily operations in North Georgia. On one level, Sherman was developing by 1864 a grasp of the geopolitical-psychological grand strategy of the war that few could match. He did nothing during the Atlanta campaign to demonstrate that gift. His ability to conduct warfare on that level is much better illustrated by his great operations after mid-November 1864—the march across Georgia to the sea and the march through the Carolinas. Sherman realized that a nation could achieve victory by destroying the enemy's society and its logistical-economic-social infrastructure, and he put that doctrine into practice on a grand scale in the winter of 1864–65. He could do so, however, only because others were then fighting the Rebels he had allowed to escape from Jonesboro.

An old military saw has it that when those with but little knowledge of military matters discuss warfare, they talk about battlefield tactics. Those more knowledgeable about the subject discuss strategy. The real experts talk logistics. ("An army travels on its stomach," the Emperor Napoleon I, greatest of military commanders, is supposed to have said.) Beyond question, Sherman deserves high marks for his success as a logistician during the Atlanta campaign. In evaluating his work in that area, however, we must keep in mind that much of his success was built on the very solid foundation that Grant put in place before he went to Virginia in March 1864.

In evaluating Sherman's performance in the spring and summer of 1864, we must also remember that he held virtually all the cards. He outnumbered the opposing army about 1.35 to 1. He had no major difficulty with supplies. He exercised command over all Union forces between the Appalachians and the Mississippi and could, therefore, wage a coordinated campaign across the West. He enjoyed the firm and complete support and trust of his commander, Grant, and through Grant that of the president and the government. Most important, he faced, first, a foe unwilling even to try to seize the initiative and hampered by the distrust of his superiors in Richmond and then an opposing commander whose options were severely limited by the circumstances in which his army found itself when he took command. Neither of his opponents was an especially able general nor received the wholehearted support of his subordinates.

The Atlanta campaign itself showcased several of Sherman's weaknesses as a director of field operations. His chief shortcoming was his failure to see that the situation in North Georgia that spring and summer required him to act more as a field commander and less as a person responsible for a grand, overall war plan. His errors were ones of omission rather than of commission, matters of what he did not do that he could reasonably have been expected to do and almost certainly could have accomplished. He simply failed to realize that no single method of warfare is always best in every situation. He did not grasp the reality that sometimes armies must pursue routes to victory other than that dictated by their commanders' pet theories or personal preference. Specifically, armies sometimes have a great opportunity to win an old-fashioned, smashing military triumph on the battlefield that would be important enough to justify the risk it would involve and the casualties it would entail.

During the Atlanta campaign two opportunities to win such a great battlefield victory presented themselves to Sherman. On both occasions, he was aware of his opportunity, and on both he chose not even to try seriously to take advantage of the situation. At Snake Creek Gap he had one of the war's few real chances to trap an enemy army in the open field and destroy it. Sherman elected instead to make only a limited effort with a relatively weak force. Again, on September 1 at Jonesboro, he had a second such opportunity. He stood then with six powerful infantry corps in the midst of weakened, widely separated parts of the Rebel army. Beyond question, he that day had it in his power to destroy much or all of the opposing force. Had he chosen to pursue aggressively either of those opportunitiess, he almost certainly would have broken Secessionist power in the West for all time and hastened the end of the war by many months.

Arguably, Sherman had similar opportunities on at least four other occasions in North Georgia in 1864. One occurred on May 15 and 16 at Lay's Ferry when he might have made a serious effort to cut off Johnston north of the Oostanaula or trap him on the south side of that stream with his back to the river. Sherman's other possible opportunities came during Hood's three battles around Atlanta. On July 20, 22, and 28 it was clear that the Confederates had concentrated the bulk of their force north (July 20), east (July 22), or west (July 28) of the city. They obviously had reduced their strength in other sectors, but Sherman chose to make no real effort to try to take advantage of those opportunities.

In all those cases, we can legitimately criticize Sherman for what he failed to do. Because he did not seize any of the opportunities Johnston and Hood gave him, he left the Rebel army intact to march north in the fall after it had evacuated Atlanta. Destruction of Confederate military power in the West did not take place in North Georgia in the spring and summer of 1864. It occurred in Middle Tennessee in late November and December that year at the hands of troops commanded by John M. Schofield and George H. Thomas.

To be sure, Sherman's handling of operations in Georgia in the spring and summer of 1864 was not inept. Two of his maneuvers, in fact, rate high among the war's operations and showed considerable skill. Seizure of Snake Creek Gap at the very beginning of the campaign was one of the strategic masterpieces of the war and made ultimate Rebel success in Georgia that year very unlikely. The crossing of the Chattahoochee two months later was a well-conceived and well-conducted operation. In both those maneuvers Sherman completely fooled Joseph E. Johnston, struck where he was not expected, and by so doing compelled the Rebels to evacuate very strong positions on which they had expended much time and labor.

In summary, Sherman proved capable enough to achieve success for the Union cause. In the long run, that was what counted—except, of course, to the men killed or maimed in the subsequent operations that would have been unnecessary had the war ended nine or ten months sooner than it did.

For a century and more after 1865, Joseph E. Johnston enjoyed very high acclaim among students of the Civil War in general and of the Atlanta campaign in particular. He owed most of his renown to the facts that almost all historians of his 1864 operations evaluated them by contrasting them with those of Bragg and Hood and that they derived almost all their information about those operations from very unreliable postwar accounts. Since the Confederates had suffered no visible major defeat in North Georgia during Johnston's tenure, it was easy to assume that he had conducted a skillful campaign. The general's self-serving memoirs strongly reinforced that view.

Johnston's Georgia campaign became something of a minor subplot in the Myth of the Lost Cause with which white Southerners in the postwar decades sought to assuage the pain of their defeat. If only President Davis had not removed Johnston as he was about to turn and smite the advancing Yankee horde, the former Rebels convinced themselves, he would have defeated Sherman, saved Atlanta, and won Confederate independence. This belief became an article of faith among late nineteenth-century white Southerners. Indeed, many late twentieth-century neo-Confederates cling to it with a tenacity usually found only among the most devoted adherents of a fundamentalist religious cult.

In itself, Johnston's handling of the army's day-to-day operations was usually adequate and sometimes above average. His failure to close Snake Creek Gap and to pay adequate attention to the Villanow-Resaca area in early May, however, ranks as one of the most serious Confederate military blunders of the war. That failure, in turn, made it impossible for the Rebels to hold Dalton and probably ensured their ultimate defeat in North Georgia and in the war. In July Johnston was again completely deceived by Sherman's downriver demonstrations and allowed the Yankees a practically uncontested crossing of the Chattahoochee.

Johnston's greatest operational weakness in 1864 stemmed directly from his decision to yield completely the initiative to Sherman. "He lacked the ability to shape campaigns," wrote the historian Joseph Glatthaar, "reaction came more readily to him than action." With the Confederate commander remaining passively on the defensive, the Yankees could select the time, place, and manner of operations and could take full advantage of whatever situation presented itself. They could conduct their flank marches with no great worry that Johnston would interfere.

Johnston, in summary, began the campaign by pursuing a strategy that did not work, and he refused to abandon it and try some other means of coping with Sherman when its failure became obvious. He might, for example, have relied on his strong fortifications to block Sherman's main force and detached a portion of his army to confront Sherman's flanking columns. If nothing else, such efforts would have slowed Sherman's operations. If the Federal commander had sent, say, 20 percent of his army group off to flank Johnston's defenses, the Rebels could have dispatched 20 percent of their army to meet the flanking column without changing the relative strength of the main bodies. Such a strategy, however, would have removed many of Johnston's troops from his direct control, something that he—always a staunch advocate of concentration—was unwilling to do. The only alternative to his failed policy of waiting for Sherman to attack that Johnston ever put forth was his plea to send Rebel cavalry from Mississippi against Sherman's railroad—a move his government rejected for sound geopolitical and logistical as well as military reasons and a strategy that almost certainly would not have worked. (See appendix 3.)

Admittedly Johnston faced many difficulties. The factors listed above as advantages for Sherman were disadvantages for the Confederates. Most of them, however, were either endemic to Secessionist military operations, or exacerbated by Johnston's personality quirks, or both. To be successful, he would have had to devise some method of dealing with them. He failed to do so or even to try.

Johnston's real weakness as an army commander, however, was on a higher plane. Because he rarely thought much above the level of day-to-day movements, he simply had little or no comprehension of how his operations fit into the larger aspects of the war—something a general at his 1864 level of command absolutely must have. With his limited view confined almost entirely to his immediate vicinity and almost exclusively to the daily movements of his troops, Johnston failed to understand that abandoning North Georgia without a fight—whatever its military wisdom—was a political, logistical, and psychological disaster of the first magnitude for the Confederacy. Johnston compounded this shortcoming by his refusal to communicate with the authorities about events in his front, his plans, and his expectations.

Owing to his refusal to communicate, Johnston neither kept the authorities informed as to his operations, plans, and problems nor did he understand the government's position or its many difficulties. Had he and President Davis enjoyed full and free communication, they might have worked out some coordinated geopolitical-military grand strategy for the spring and summer to deal with developments in the West.[4]

Nor did Johnston use wisely the time he had in the winter to work with state officials and other Confederate commanders. He might, for example, have tried to develop a plan in conjunction with state authorities to have the Georgia militia activated and put in service long before late June. He could have tried to work with Polk on a joint defense plan for Georgia and Alabama. He could have pushed state and Confederate authorities about construction of the rail line across the Blue Mountain–Rome gap to facilitate a coordinated defense of Alabama and Georgia. If nothing else, Johnston might have come to understand the political and logistical importance of keeping Sherman as far to the north as he could, of delaying his progress as much as possible, and of inflicting as many casualties as he could on the Yankees.

Finally, no fair evaluation of Johnston's December 1863–July 1864 tenure at the head of the Army of Tennessee can fail to acknowledge the outstanding work he did rebuilding the army during the winter. When he reached Dalton he found a demoralized army, short of virtually everything needed for field service. When that army marched from its camps to meet Sherman in early May, it did so with high morale and was as well-equipped as Confederate armies got to be. Johnston deserves full credit for that renaissance of the Army of Tennessee. His success that winter was his greatest military work of the war and a feat few American commanders have ever matched.

In summary, Johnston did an outstanding job preparing the rank and file of his army for the campaign. His timid, unimaginative use of the army once in the field, however, reflected his fatal limitations as a commander and led to, if it did not cause, the Rebels' 1864 failure in Georgia. His refusal to cooperate with and to communicate with his government made it highly unlikely that he could achieve any success. In one very real sense, Jefferson Davis accomplished two things when he replaced Johnston with Hood. The change almost certainly resulted in Atlanta's remaining in Rebel possession a few weeks longer than otherwise would have been the case, and by obscuring the disastrous results of Johnston's operations behind Hood's later and obvious failure the change of commanders ensured that Johnston's reputation would be much higher than it should have been.[5]

Judging John Bell Hood's performance as commander at Atlanta is, in several ways, a far more difficult task than is that of evaluating Sherman and Johnston. For one thing, Hood's reputation—like Johnston's—was originally colored to a large extent by the fact that for so long he was judged based on postwar writings of Confederate soldiers. For another, Rebel options were so limited by mid-July that only a miracle, a stupendous blunder on Sherman's part, or a near-perfect performance by Hood (which many would classify as a miracle) was likely to keep Atlanta in Secessionist hands. Hood's command at Atlanta was so short, so limited by preexisting conditions, and so circumscribed by the necessity of responding quickly to Sherman's thrusts that he had no opportunity to deal then with the larger issues of administration, command, and strategy. Even had the Southerners been able to hold the city, the Federals had by mid-July destroyed its value as a manufacturing and transportation center. They, therefore, had won a great strategic success in advancing their lines from the Tennessee River to the Chattahoochee.

Hood's reputation also suffers because his efforts to hold Atlanta are usually evaluated in conjunction with—or at least in light of—his late 1864 operations in North Alabama and Tennessee, beyond question two of the worst-executed major military operations of the war. The Hood who conducted those fall campaigns was arguably a different man—bitter, frustrated, disappointed, and angry—than the officer who directed the last six weeks of the Rebels' efforts to hold Atlanta.

Many of those who have penned general accounts of Confederate military operations and even some of those who have written of the Atlanta campaign in particular have depicted Hood as, at best, simply a headstrong general who took command of the army and immediately sought to defeat Sherman by attacking him in his strongly fortified positions. Those critics have completely missed the fact that *all* Hood's July and August efforts were directed at maneuvering to catch the Yankees without earthworks—and in those endeavors he often succeeded. On July 20 it was Hood's intention to strike the Army of the Cumberland on the south bank of Peachtree Creek before the Unionists had a chance to fortify their new position. On July 22 Hood planned to assault the unprotected left flank or rear of the Northern army east of Atlanta, but the presence of the XVI Corps thwarted the plan. It was not Hood's plan to attack at Ezra Church on July 28. He wanted to block the southward extension of the Federal line there that day, fix the Yankees in position, and assail their right flank on July 29. The Battle of Ezra Church was the doing of Stephen D. Lee, not Hood. Hood hoped to strike the Unionists soon after they had crossed the Flint River west of Jonesboro, not after they had fortified.

In all those cases, the Army of Tennessee did not do what its commander planned and hoped it would. The gap between the planned and actual conduct of those operations is the measure of Hood's shortcomings. Hood simply overestimated how far tired men could march in a given time and how vigorously exhausted soldiers could fight when they reached their battleground. The first march he planned for the night of July 21–22 would have been difficult for fresh troops under the best of circumstances. Even his revised plan for that march demanded more than worn men could accomplish. The same was true for his planned movements of August 30–31 at Jonesboro. His hope that Wheeler could wreck Sherman's railroads in North Georgia and Tennessee and return to the army at Atlanta in a few days was equally unrealistic.

Why did Hood plan and undertake such operations—operations bordering on the physically impossible? Could he have been thinking back to his great days in the spring and summer of 1862, when he served in the army in Virginia with Robert E. Lee and "Stonewall" Jackson and the Rebels won seemingly miraculous victories by a combination of daring, hard marching, and hard fighting? The Army of Tennessee had never functioned with anything like the relative smoothness that Robert E. Lee's force showed in 1862 and early 1863. The rank and file of the Secessionists' western army were brave and skillful enough, but its officer corps, from full general to third lieutenant, never equaled that of its Virginia counterpart save in physical courage and had long suffered from the bitter, debilitating squabble between pro-Bragg and anti-Bragg factions. Officers who had frequently mishandled operations all through the war continued to do so in the summer of 1864 (and would do so that fall as well). In summary, Hood tried to do too much too quickly with an army that just was not capable of such operations. But, then, what choice did he have?

Hood's own style of command, perhaps patterned on that used by Lee in Virginia in 1862 and 1863, simply did not work with the Army of Tennessee and its generals in 1864. Lee had assigned a subordinate a definite task, given him the troops he would have for the mission, and then gotten out of his way, expecting him to use his own judgment in carrying out the assignment. When Hood applied that method—to Hardee at Peachtree Creek, Atlanta, and Jonesboro; to Stephen D. Lee at Ezra Church; and to Wheeler on his August raid—it had not worked. Hood's subordinates proved incapable of handling such responsibility on all the July and August battlefields. (In fairness, we should note that such a method rarely worked for Lee when the subordinate assigned the mission was not "Stonewall" Jackson. In 1864 Lee, realizing that conditions had changed after Jackson's death, took a much more active role in managing the details of his army's operations.)

Hood's crippled physical condition, along with the poor staff and administrative structure that had always plagued the army (and the latter he did nothing to try to correct during the Atlanta campaign or later), both worked to limit severely his ability either to direct operations in person or adequately to supervise his corps commanders. (Johnston's operations had also been hampered by his subordinates' poor performance— including Hood's. Since he had not attempted any major efforts, however, the results were different and almost invisible.)

Perhaps Hood's greatest failure at Atlanta was an act of omission. He could have used the weeks after the Utoy Creek affair to stake out and perhaps at least to begin construction of a line of fortifications running from East Point to the headwaters of the Flint River. Such works would have covered the Macon & Western and at least given Sherman pause. Their very existence might have dissuaded him from attempting the movement that led to Jonesboro.[6]

Finally, something needs to be said about Jefferson Davis's performance in the Georgia campaign of 1864. The Rebel president all too often focused his attention myopically on operations in Virginia and ignored those beyond the Appalachians. Davis's long neglect of the West and his refusal to face up to and resolve the personality/command difficulties that had grown up in the Army of Tennessee both poisoned that army's command structure and left the chief executive with only bad personnel options in the crisis of 1864. The president's refusal to deal with the problems stemming from Bragg's quarrels with his chief subordinates and his general disinclination to involve himself in western matters came back to haunt him and the Confederacy in the summer of 1864. Nothing better illustrated the putrid mess Davis allowed to grow and fester in the western army than his two chief appointments in the December 1863–July 1864 period. Joseph E. Johnston, an officer whom the chief executive did not trust and in whom he had very little confidence, was the best option Davis had to succeed Bragg as commander of the army in December 1863. When Davis finally decided to sack Johnston the following July after his failure in North Georgia, his best option then was a young, not very competent, crippled general. When Davis had a competent commander with whom he could work, such as Lee, he performed fairly well; when he did not, the result was disaster. Unfortunately for Davis and the Secessionists, the Confederacy had only one Robert E. Lee.

To achieve a great military victory, goes an old saying, two conditions are necessary: a very good general in command on one side and a very bad general in charge on the other. Neither of those conditions existed in North Georgia in the spring and summer of 1864, and for that reason, there was no great military victory by either side. The campaign, however, resulted in a success of the greatest strategic magnitude for the Federal government and the national cause. Its political, psychological, and logistical results were immeasurable. It assured Lincoln's reelection, and in so doing it assured the eventual failure of the Southern bid for independence. Its result demoralized the Rebels and inspired the war-weary people of the North. In doing all those things, it made ultimate Federal victory, the abolition of slavery, and the end of the old national order inevitable.

Chickamauga Fever and Grant's Grand Strategy for 1864

In both his official report of the Union's 1864–65 operations and his postwar writings Ulysses S. Grant stressed his intention of using simultaneous advances on many fronts to freeze opposing troops in position and thus keep the Confederates from shifting units from secure areas to bolster their defenses at endangered points. Grant's imagination and fears greatly magnified the likelihood that the Secessionists would move troops from one of their major armies to the other. Only once—in September 1863—had the Rebels taken men from one of their two great armies and sent them directly to the other. Those reinforcements, rushed from the Army of Northern Virginia to North Georgia, played a crucial role in the great victory at Chickamauga. Despite the infrequency with which the Confederates moved troops between East and West, the Union high command was afflicted after September 1863 with what might be called "Chickamauga fever"—the fear that the Southerners would again execute such a maneuver. That fear lay behind Grant's 1864 grand strategy.

Historians have usually described Grant's general concept of simultaneous advances, praised his intent, and quoted his anecdote about Lincoln's remark when the general explained his plan. The president, who had long favored such a ploy, quickly caught the essence of the proposed scheme and compared it to his boyhood experiences in Illinois when, at butchering time, those not skinning an animal would hold the carcass while the skinner did his work. "If you can't skin, hold a leg." Having told this oft-told tale, the historians rush on to whatever subject is the central concern of their work. Rarely does anyone stop to ask how sound Grant's plan was or how well it succeeded.

Never before or since the spring and summer of 1864 did the Confederates shift troops about so freely, in such large numbers, and with such success as they did during those months. Some units from the Atlantic Coast defenses went north to Virginia to take part in the operations against Meade, Grant, and Butler. Other units from the Savannah area reinforced Johnston in North Georgia. Troops brought from Alabama and Mississippi provided Johnston and Hood with 25 to 30 percent of the men with whom they opposed Sherman in Georgia. Confederates from all over western Virginia concentrated at New Market to defeat Sigel, then many of them moved east to help Lee oppose Grant. Later, they shifted back to the west, where Early soon joined them with some twenty thousand men from Lee's army. In summary, to the extent that Grant's 1864 plan was intended to deny the Secessionists the advantage of moving troops about on their interior lines, it must be adjudged a total failure. That failure, in turn, goes a long way to explain why the Confederates had so much success on so many fields that spring and summer.

At least, some would say, Grant managed to prevent the transfer of reinforcements *between* the two principal Confederate armies. In fact, he did not. Assuming Rebel transportation equal to the task, Early's men could have been sent to Georgia rather than into the Shenandoah Valley. It was a Confederate policy decision (or possibly inadequate rail transportation) that kept Lee from sending troops to reinforce the Rebels in Georgia, not the pressure of Grant's assaults on the Confederates in Virginia. Indeed, on July 16 Grant himself expected Lee to send troops to Johnston while holding the Yankees in Virginia at bay with his reduced forces—and he so warned Sherman. That warning, in effect, constituted an admission on Grant's part that his plan had failed.[1]

We should also ask whether Grant's basic concept was even a good idea. If the Confederate government had sent, say, twenty thousand troops from Lee to Johnston, would the latter general have conducted his operations differently? Nothing in his record suggests that he would have. If we take what he wrote literally, he believed himself so heavily outnumbered that twenty thousand reinforcements would probably have made little if any difference in his campaign. Such a transfer, however, would have weakened Lee and in so doing would have benefited the Union cause beyond measure. Hood, of course, would have put those additional men to fighting, and their presence in his July and August battles might have made a real difference in the campaign although probably not in the outcome of the war. Given the poor conduct of tactical operations by Hood and his corps commanders, however, the presence of additional troops probably would not have altered even the results of the campaign. In all probability, the addition of more troops to the Army of Tennessee that summer might, at the most, have delayed the fall of Atlanta by a few weeks.

Had Rebel authorities taken troops from Johnston or Hood and sent them to Lee, the result almost certainly would have been an earlier end to the war. Even with twenty thousand more men, it seems unlikely that Lee could have accomplished much more than he did. At most, he might have held Grant in northern Virginia or pushed him back into that part of the state (depending on when the additional troops joined his ranks) and, perhaps, have crossed the Potomac for another Antietam- or Gettysburg-like raid. Lee thus would have repeated his successes of 1862 and 1863 without gaining Confederate independence. Meanwhile, Atlanta would have fallen much sooner than it did and Sherman would be marching across Georgia to the sea and northward through the Carolinas.

In summary, Grant's much-vaunted plan did not work, and had the Confederates *chosen* to do what Grant was most anxious to prevent them from doing, their action most probably would have redounded to the benefit of the Federal cause.

Numbers and Losses

Readers do not need much exposure to Civil War history to realize that numerical data concerning the strength of opposing armies can generate much dispute. The same is true for the casualties the armies suffered. Each general, it seems, tried to convince readers that his forces were outnumbered, but, even so, they managed to inflict very heavy casualties on the enemy—thanks, of course, to his superior ability as a commander.

Regulations governing the opposing armies from April to August 1864 required them periodically to submit strength reports ("strength returns"). These data are the "official" information we have as to how many men served under a particular general's command at a given time. Like all statistical data, however, they can be manipulated, and they should be used with great care. Fortunately, in most cases, it is not important to ascertain the exact numbers of the opposing forces or the casualties they suffered.

Returns from Sherman's armies from April to August 1864 show his strength as follows:

Apr. 30	May 31	June 30	July 31	Aug. 31
110,123	112,819	106,070	91,675	81,758

These numbers are called the "effective strength" of Sherman's forces, but as used in these returns that is an unofficial term. The context as well as the numbers themselves make it clear that they include officers. Thus the term as used with these data does not have the same meaning it does when used with Confederate strength returns (see below). For purposes of comparing the two forces, it is clear, these numbers should be called Sherman's "present for duty" strength.

Confederate "present for duty" strength returns show the following totals:

Apr. 30	June 10	June 30	July 31	Aug. 31
54,500	69,946	62,747	51,793	51,141

The Rebels reported their "effective strength" as follows:

Apr. 30	June 10	June 30	July 31	Aug. 31
43,887	60,564	54,085	44,495	43,467

In Confederate terminology an army's "effective strength" excluded all enlisted men not "present for duty, equipped" and all officers. Thus, any lieutenant, a private detailed for the day as orderly at regimental headquarters, or a cavalry sergeant whose horse had thrown a shoe would not be counted. Confederate "effective strength" in the Atlanta campaign ran at about 85 percent of the Rebels' "present for duty" strength. Confederate generals liked to use their "effective strength" in discussing their operations because that number made their forces seem smaller, thereby magnifying any successes they chanced to win and helping to explain any defeats they suffered.

In comparing opposing forces, we must be careful not to compare Sherman's "present for duty" strength with the Secessionists' "effective strength," as is often done. To get comparable figures, we must convert "effective strength" to "present for duty" strength or vice versa. To do so, multiply the total "effective strength" by 1.18, or the "present for duty" strength by 0.85 (ratios derived from Confederate strength returns above).

Confederate "present for duty" strength as a percentage of Sherman's "present for duty" strength (these numbers give us *by far* the best comparison of the opposing forces):

Apr. 30	May 10–31	June 30	July 31	Aug. 31
49.5%	62.0%	59.2%	56.5%	62.3%

Confederate "effective strength" as a percentage of Sherman's "effective strength" (former as reported by Johnston and Hood; latter determined by conversion formula above):

Apr. 30	May 31–June 10	June 30	July 31	Aug. 31
46.9%	63.2%	60.0%	57.1%	62.5%

(These Confederate data should be used with *extreme* care. For one thing, they are incomplete. They do not include the Georgia militia troops serving with the army in June, July, and August. For another, the August

31 numbers use Wheeler's cavalry strength as of August 1 because he submitted no later return.)

The most interesting of these numbers is that for August 31. The Rebels were then stronger relative to Sherman than they had been at any other time in the campaign. This unexpected result was owing to the drop in Sherman's strength in August (9,917 men) as some of his units completed their three-year term of service and went home for discharge.)[1]

The data we have on casualties in the campaign are also very imprecise and equally frustrating. Although many commanders on both sides reported their individual unit's casualties in this or that engagement or day's operations, meaningful overall figures for particular battles are difficult to find. In most cases they do not exist. Federal losses for May, June, July, and August (and September 1–5 for the Armies of the Tennessee and of the Ohio) were reported as follows:

	Killed		Wounded		Missing		Aggregate
	Officers	Enlisted	Officers	Enlisted	Officers	Enlisted	
Army of the Cumberland	261	2,748	780	14,676	46	1,729	20,240
Army of the Tennessee	91	1,357	365	6,628	77	1,796	10,314
Army of the Ohio	—	531	—	2,378	—	1,060	3,960
Grand Totals	352	4,636	1,145	23,628	123	4,585	34,514

The Army of the Cumberland reported losing 2,567 men from September 1–15, most of them in the battle of September 1 at Jonesboro.

Total reported losses in Sherman's army group for the campaign come to 37,081.[2]

Meaningful data on Confederate losses are very elusive. A. J. Foard, medical director of the Army of Tennessee, compiled a *partial* report of casualties while Johnston commanded the army (which many historians have accepted as a complete report of Johnston's losses):

	Killed	Wounded	Total
Hardee's Corps	558	3,468	4,026
Hood's Corps	526	3,441	3,967

Polk's (Loring's, Stewart's) Corps	274	1,705	1,979
Grand Totals	1,358	8,614	9,972

Assuming Foard's data are accurate as far as they go, they are notoriously incomplete. They do not include any losses for the period July 10 through 17 or any killed and wounded in one brigade of infantry (Brig. Gen. Robert C. Tyler's brigade, Bate's Division). Nor do they include the men lost as prisoners or any casualties in the Georgia militia or in either Wheeler's or Jackson's cavalry. Wheeler wrote on July 1 that his cavalry had lost one thousand men up to that time in the campaign.

For the period of Hood's command Foard put the Secessionists' losses at 1,756 killed and 10,267 wounded for a total loss of 12,023.

For the campaign, Foard listed Rebel casualties as 3,114 killed and 18,881 wounded. The total was 21,995.

To Foard's numbers we must add losses in the militia, the cavalry, the men taken prisoner, and the killed and wounded in the infantry and artillery during the last week of Johnston's command. The Yankees reported capturing 7,480 prisoners in the May through August period and 3,065 "prisoners and deserters" from September 1 to 20. It is unlikely that all those prisoners and deserters were from the Army of Tennessee. Probably some were from small Rebel commands in northern Alabama or East Tennessee.[3]

Reasonable estimates of losses in the Confederate cavalry and the Georgia militia plus those for men lost as prisoners would raise total Confederate casualties in the Atlanta campaign to about 35,000—roughly divided equally between the period of Johnston's command and that of Hood. Thus Rebel losses in the campaign (and probably for the tenures of Johnston and Hood separately) roughly equaled Union losses. In percentage terms, both Johnston and Hood lost a far greater part of their force than did Sherman.

The Yankees also reported that they apprehended 2,438 deserters in the May through August period (although, again, some were probably from commands other than the Army of Tennessee). Many other deserters from the Rebel ranks went home or into hiding rather than to the enemy.

Finally, both sides lost thousands of men either temporarily or permanently to sickness all during the campaign.[4]

Johnston's Railroad Strategy

As discussed in chapter 7, Johnston began, in late May, seriously to urge that Forrest's cavalry be sent from Mississippi to operate against Sherman's railroad line of supply. To be effective, as Johnston told Senator Hill on July 1, such a raid would have to break the railroad south of Dalton to cut the Yankees off from their advanced base. For the rest of his life Johnston believed passionately that such a ploy would have produced Sherman's defeat and vindicated his own conduct of the campaign. Since Davis refused to commit Forrest against Sherman's rail line, he—and certainly not Johnston—bore responsibility for the advance of the Yankees deep into Georgia, the loss of Atlanta, and eventual Confederate defeat. Ever since the war, Johnston's numerous disciples have reiterated this mantra with a conviction that puts to shame the faith of a monk who burns himself to death for a cause.

An evaluation of Johnston's proposed strategy requires answers to three separate but related questions. First, could the Southerners have cut the railroad between Dalton and Sherman's army group? Second, if so, which force—Forrest's horsemen from Mississippi or Wheeler's with Johnston's army in Georgia—was better situated to have done so? Third, had the rail line been severed, would the outcome of the campaign have been changed?

The answer to the first question is a clear "maybe" and necessitates a consideration of the second.

Could Forrest have wrecked Sherman's railroad as Johnston and his apologists have so confidently asserted? Could he even have reached the tracks? If Forrest were at, say, Tupelo, Mississippi, he would have had to have marched directly east 225 miles to reach the W&A in North Georgia. (This distance makes no allowance for *any* meanderings his column would have to make because of bends in the road, mountains, rivers, or other natural obstacles.) Such a march almost certainly could not have been concealed from Yankee scouts and spies in northern Mississippi and Alabama. Once the Federals spotted the marching column, they would know its destination and purpose. On such a march eastward Forrest's left flank would have been vulnerable to any Union force that might strike south from the Tennessee River valley against it.

Should Forrest make it across North Alabama, where should (or could) he reach the railroad? From Chattanooga to Dalton, Sherman had two rail lines (the W&A through Ringgold and Tunnel Hill and the route east to Cleveland, Tennessee, thence south to Dalton). Destroying only one of them would inconvenience Sherman but would not force him to give up his advance into Georgia. It, doubtless, was for that reason that Johnston specified attacking the rail line south of Dalton.

From Dalton to the Oostanaula, however, the looming height of Rocky Face Ridge shielded the railroad against a raid from the west. Should Forrest somehow reach the tracks east of the ridge, he ran a high risk of being penned there and cut off from Mississippi.

If Forrest approached Sherman's rail line to the south of Rocky Face Ridge, he would run into the fortified and garrisoned town of Rome. He could not storm the town (which had rail and telegraphic communication both to Sherman's army group and to Chattanooga). Besides, any assault on Rome risked a defeat or a pyrrhic victory that would delay him and cost the Rebels more than they could possibly gain. Forrest would have to bypass Rome, veering southeast up the left bank of the Etowah or northeast up the right bank of the Oostanaula.

Should Forrest choose the former course, he would have to cross the Coosa to reach the Etowah. His route would then take him dangerously close to the rear of Sherman's army group because of the railroad's bend to the east at Kingston, and he risked being trapped against the Etowah and the Coosa. Even should he reach the railroad in that area, he certainly could not linger because troops would pour northward from Sherman's force to drive him off.

If Forrest went up the Oostanaula and crossed that river at some ford, he probably could get to the railroad, but he would be in great danger of being trapped in the angle formed by the Etowah and the Oostanaula Rivers with the Rome garrison to the west, a division of Federal cavalry guarding the rail line itself, and additional troops arriving by rail from north and south to drive him off the tracks.

We must also remember that in the late May–early June period two divisions of XVII Corps infantry were moving up the Tennessee River and through northeastern Alabama and northwestern Georgia to join Sherman's main force. Had Forrest then been in North Georgia, those troops could probably have cut him off from Mississippi. In early July Rousseau's cavalry column, then beginning its raid into Alabama, would have posed a similar danger to Forrest's flanks, rear, or both.

In summary, it is about as certain as any such hypothetical thing can be that an effort to use Forrest against the W&A in North Georgia would, at the most, have resulted in only slight damage to the railroad and might well have led to the capture or dispersal of Forrest's raiding force. Such a Rebel disaster would have left northern Mississippi and Alabama virtually naked to Yankee raids from the Mississippi and Tennessee valleys and freed Sherman to bring thousands of rear area troops forward to reinforce his units in Johnston's front. In truth, Forrest's role as a potential threat to the Federal supply line may well have helped Johnston by compelling Sherman to divert to railroad protection scores of units that otherwise would have joined the Yankee armies in Johnston's front in Georgia or that would have been loosed on Central Alabama.

Could Wheeler have reached and wrecked the railroad from his position on the right flank of Johnston's army? When Davis commented on July 11 that it seemed more practicable for Rebel horsemen close to Sherman's rail line to cut it than for distant cavalry to attempt to do so, he raised a crucial question that Johnston and later historians never answered.

Three times in May, June, and July Sherman moved virtually all his force away from, to the west and south of, the railroad (the Dalton–Resaca operations, the Etowah–New Hope Church movement, and to flank Kennesaw Mountain). In all three cases those movements resulted in the bulk of his armies being deployed along a north-south line miles from the W&A. In all three cases the railroad to the north was exposed to a quick thrust by Wheeler's horsemen on Johnston's right. In not one of those cases did Johnston even make a serious attempt to strike at the rail line. Nor, as he retreated, did he undertake a systematic effort to damage the tracks.

Johnston's response to such observations would have been that he had so few men that he needed Wheeler to protect his right flank. In those three cases, however, so much of Sherman's army group was so far off to the south and west that the Federals were most unlikely to have threatened Johnston's right flank. Wheeler certainly would have had a much easier time getting to the railroad from the east than Forrest would have had approaching it from the west. In addition, had Wheeler threatened the tracks, say, twenty miles north of Sherman's position, the Yankee commander would have had to detach a sizable force to pursue him. The relative strength of the main bodies would not have changed or, if it did, it probably would have shifted in Johnston's favor. Besides, it was clear by late May that Wheeler's presence on Johnston's right flank did not in the least interfere with Sherman's customary flanking movements against the Rebel left.

Was Wheeler's force strong enough to have undertaken such a mission? The question of his strength has caused much confusion. Thomas Lawrence Connelly pointed out that on April 30 Wheeler reported 8,062 officers and men present for duty in his cavalry corps but only 2,419 of them were effective. Most of those classified as not effective were officers or men without horses. (See appendix 2 for an explanation of the term "effective" in Confederate strength returns.) Johnston's most recent biographer, Craig Symonds, took the 2,419 figure and erroneously assumed that it represented Wheeler's effective strength for the entire period of Johnston's command.

When the campaign opened, many cavalry mounts that had wintered in the river valleys miles south of Dalton (see chapter 3) returned to the army, and Wheeler's effective strength increased accordingly. For example, the two brigades of Brig. Gen. John H. Kelly's division numbered 1,545 effectives on May 5. They were not included in the April 30 total of 2,419 effectives. On June 10 Wheeler reported 7,700 effective cavalry; on June 30, 8,138; and on July 10, 7,618. (None of these numbers includes Jackson's cavalry division, which was not part of Wheeler's command.)

Connelly asserted, and Symonds agreed, that Wheeler often inflated his returns to enhance his own prestige. This seems unlikely for the 1864 numbers—Wheeler, after all, did get from somewhere 4,500 troopers for his August raid. Even if Wheeler did falsify his 1864 strength returns, Johnston accepted those numbers and sent them on to Richmond as part of his army's totals. The Confederate commander thus had nobody but himself to blame if Davis and Bragg studied his own reports and concluded from them that he had a very large mounted force.[1]

The big problem with Wheeler was not the numerical strength of his command but his utterly irresponsibility when entrusted with a major operation—as he demonstrated near Chattanooga in late 1863 and was to show again in August and September 1864. Johnston, of course, could not have known of the latter fiasco and may not have been aware of the former. If he knew of the former, he could have given Wheeler very strict orders as to how long he was to be away from the main army or he could have bombarded Richmond with demands for a competent commander for his cavalry—Wade Hampton, perhaps.

We must conclude that it is very unlikely that Wheeler, Forrest, or anybody else would have been able to damage the railroad sufficiently to force Sherman to abandon his campaign in Georgia. As McCook, Stoneman, Garrard, Kilpatrick, and Wheeler all demonstrated in 1864, cavalry, if faced with any real opposition, simply could not wreck a railroad.

Once the campaign opened, there were only two ways that the Rebel strategy of cutting the railroad *might* have worked. Either the Confederates would have had to wreck the rail line south of Dalton and *keep it out of operation* until Sherman exhausted the supplies with his army and whatever he could get from its immediate vicinity, or they would have had to cut the line anywhere, keep it cut, and hold Atlanta until at least late September.

It was most unlikely that raiding cavalry could have achieved the former objective, and had it done so, Sherman could simply have pulled back to the southern end of the operating line and hunkered down there until his repair crews had the railroad back in operation.

With regard to the latter possibility, we must ask if Johnston would have held Atlanta for another two or three months. Certainly he could not have done so had he been unwilling to abandon the passive defense he followed and undertake actively to fend Sherman off from his own railroads.

Had Hood kept possession of the city for another month, would a shortage of supplies have forced Sherman to abandon the campaign? We can never know. We do know, however, that by late August the rivers in Tennessee were rising and, in the words of Col. Langdon C. Easton, Sherman's chief quartermaster, "the crisis [of a possible supply shortage] was passed" on August 27.[2]

In summary, Davis, Bragg, and Senator Hill were correct. If the Rebels were to try to defeat Sherman by raids on his railroad, those raids would have had a far better chance of success if undertaken by the cavalry of Johnston's army. When Hill telegraphed Johnston that the general must do the work with his own force, he but pointed to the truth. He also indicated one of the great flaws in Johnston's conduct of operations in Georgia in 1864—the general's utter refusal to take any action that might involve the slightest degree of risk.

The important story of Rebel railroad strategy is what it tells us about the Confederate high command. All the high-ranking Secessionists involved in the matter—Davis, Bragg, Johnston, Hood, Lee, Forrest, and Wheeler—agreed that a cavalry raid against Sherman's rail line would have been a good response for the Secessionists to make. Despite this unanimity, the Rebels could never get their act together enough to implement a strategy that all of them favored. Can there be any greater indictment of Jefferson Davis's management of the Confederate war effort?

The Atlanta Campaign and the Election of 1864

Civil War historians have long been aware of the close and often causal connection between military events on the one hand and political developments on the other. As always, success on the battlefield helped those in political office; defeat hurt them. In 1992 Albert Castel presented the thesis that had Sherman not captured Atlanta, Lincoln probably could not have won reelection in November 1864 and the Southern states might have gained their independence. Military failure in Georgia, Castel concluded, would probably have cost the president seven states in which his margin of victory was slim (Connecticut, Illinois, Indiana, New Hampshire, New York, Oregon, and Pennsylvania). Without the 102 electoral votes of those states, Lincoln would have gone down to defeat at the polls. President McClellan and the Democrats might then have negotiated a cease-fire with the Confederacy. Such a development would have meant Confederate independence because Northern war-weariness would have made it impossible for the Federal government to resume hostilities. One can read Castel's thesis to mean that if the Rebels still held Atlanta at the end of September—perhaps even if they retained possession of the city until the middle of that month—Lincoln probably would have lost the election and the Confederacy become a sovereign nation.

In reaching this conclusion, Castel accepted Clement L. Vallandigham's June 1863 prophecy that if the war lasted until September 1864 the Northern people would elect a Democratic president who would make peace with the Secessionists. Castel also quotes and agrees with Lincoln's own August 23, 1864, "blind memorandum" in which the president wrote that "it seems exceedingly probable that this Administration will not be reelected."

Larry Daniel challenged Castel's thesis in 1998. The major weakness in Castel's argument, Daniel asserted, was that it left almost no room for error. Just as the Confederates had to win every military campaign in 1864, so McClellan had to carry every doubtful state. If Lincoln won even one of four key states on Castel's list (Illinois, Indiana, New York, or Pennsylvania), its electoral votes added to those of states that McClellan had no chance of carrying would have sufficed to keep the White House in Republican hands. It was highly unlikely, Daniel argued, that Lincoln would have lost his home state of Illinois under any possible circumstances. While the capture of Atlanta might have made Lincoln's reelection inevitable and enlarged his margin of victory, he almost certainly would have been reelected anyway. The Democrats, Daniel maintained, were so damaged by the fiasco of their convention that it was highly unlikely they could have won the election. Sherman's success in advancing the line of Union control south to the Chattahoochee River, Daniel believed, would have sufficed to keep enough voters in Lincoln's column to gain him at least one key state and, therefore, a second term.[1]

Such forays into counterfactual history can be instructive. They often help us get a better understanding of the past by forcing us to examine roads not taken and the reasons why they were not. Such exercises, however, lose validity as they become more and more complex. They must keep within the bounds of the possible. It helps if we limit them to possibilities that were probable.

To apply such counterfactual speculations to the Atlanta campaign and the 1864 election, we have to work our way successively through a maze of at least a dozen counterfactual scenarios. At each of those stops we must choose to continue through one of several possible alternatives, each of which, in turn, opens several other avenues for speculation about what might have been. We must, therefore, pile counterfactual speculation upon hypothetical situation atop theoretical results on fancied conclusions to arrive at imagined answers. Inevitably we end up with a very wobbly, jerry-built structure.

Consider:

Level One: The Confederates retain possession of Atlanta until, at least, well into September. I believe they would have had to have held the city through the presidential voting on November 8 or at least until a few days before the election for their success to have affected the political outcome.

Let's assume they were able to maintain possession of Atlanta until after Northern voters went to the polls. This assumption leads us to

Level Two: Hood must, therefore, have defeated or fended off Sherman's Jonesboro gambit. How did he do so? Did he get the Georgia Railroad back into operation and switch his supply line to the east? Did Hardee and Lee defeat Howard on August 31 and then join Hood and Stewart to smash the rest of Sherman's column on September 1? Did they merely push the Yankees back or send them reeling across the Chattahoochee (this latter a result that really would have hurt Lincoln)? Did Hood manage simply to extend and fortify his line from East Point on down the east bank of the Flint ahead of the advancing Federals? This last seems most likely, so let's assume that the Rebels just blocked Sherman's thrust at Jonesboro on August 30 as they had earlier blocked him at Utoy Creek. Thereafter the campaign settled back into its pattern of stalemate. Meanwhile,

Level Three: In early September McClellan wrote his letter accepting the Democratic nomination. Owing to Sherman's recent failure in Georgia, the Democratic peace plank appeared more and more viable. Could McClellan produce a masterful document fudging his Unionism a bit to retain the enthusiastic support of ultra-peace Democrats but not so much as to alienate moderate nationalists? If so, could he thereby keep the Democrats united behind his candidacy and enter the campaign in the strongest possible position? We must assume that he could and did so that we can move on to

Level Four: The Federals win the Third Battle of Winchester in Virginia on September 19. Was this victory sufficient to reelect Lincoln absent success at Atlanta? Let's assume it was not, so on to

Level Five: On September 21 Frémont did not terminate his candidacy and throw his support to Lincoln. How many Radical Republican votes would he pull away from the president? We can know only that any votes he received would have weakened Lincoln's chances for reelection. Meanwhile,

Level Six: The Federals win the Battle of Fisher's Hill in Virginia on September 21. See Level Four above, and then we can proceed to

Level Seven: With Sherman still bogged down before Hood's impregnable fortifications would the military commanders allow soldiers a furlough to go home to cast Republican ballots in those states that did not permit their soldiers to vote in the field? Let's assume the answer is no and ask,

Level Eight: Without the soldier vote would the Republicans have swept the crucial October elections in Indiana, Ohio, and Pennsylvania? If not, how would their failure affect the November balloting? Obviously, it would demoralize Republicans and inspirit Democrats. Meanwhile,

Level Nine: The Federals win the Battle of Cedar Creek in Virginia on October 19. See Level Four above, and then we can proceed to

Level Ten: McClellan defeats Lincoln on November 8. What impact would such a result have on soldier and civilian morale North and South? Some at the time speculated that a McClellan victory in the election would have lured the Rebel states back into the Union because a Mc-Clellan administration would not have been committed to the abolition of slavery. The opposite, in fact, was the case since McClellan pledged to respect the right of each state to determine its domestic institutions.[2] We must assume, however, that a McClellan victory inspired the Secessionists to continue their struggle for independence, so we, therefore, have to ask,

Level Eleven: What would the lame duck Lincoln do in the four months between the election in November 1864 and the end of his term on March 4, 1865? Would he order a massive military push in an all-out effort to win the war and present his successor with the fait accompli of a preserved Union? If so, would the renewed military effort succeed against the now optimistic Rebels? Would Confederate deserters return to the ranks now that they could see success looming in the near future? Would the reinforced Southern armies be able to defeat the last-gasp Lincoln military effort?[3] We must assume that any renewed Union military effort failed and ask,

Level Twelve: Would President McClellan honor his party's pledge to bring about a cease-fire or would he follow his own inclination and seek a victory that would preserve the Union? We can never know.

So many levels! So much complexity!

I believe both Castel and Daniel are correct—up to and from a point. (This solomonic conclusion reflects the fact that both are fine historians, great guys, and friends of mine.) In arguing that Lincoln had to have military success (or perceived success) in 1864 to win reelection, Castel was correct. I believe, however, that success came late on May 8 at Snake Creek Gap, not at Atlanta on September 2. Given the passive way Johnston was determined to conduct his campaign, loss of that gap meant that the Rebels could not—or at least really would not attempt to—halt Sherman's advance into Georgia.

So long as Johnston commanded the Secessionists, Sherman would have no difficulty maneuvering his way southward. Every step the Yankees took increased the impression that they were gaining success. By the time Davis replaced Johnston with Hood, it was too late for the Rebels.

Daniel was correct in thinking that occupation of the right bank of the Chattahoochee and all Northwest Georgia coupled with other Union successes of the late summer and early fall (Mobile Bay, Third Winchester, Fisher's Hill, Cedar Creek) would certainly have been enough to enable Lincoln to carry at least one of the four big doubtful states—most likely his home state of Illinois—and thereby win reelection. Absent a smashing Confederate military victory in Georgia after May 8, Lincoln's reelection was assured. With Lincoln in the White House for another four years, the Federal government would never have acquiesced in Southern independence unless the Rebel armies could force it to do so—something they manifestly were incapable of after mid-1863.

In asserting that the Confederacy could have won in 1864 by not losing, Castel was correct. Johnston's campaign, however, not the fall of Atlanta, was the first major defeat for the Secessionists that year, and gradually that fact would have become visible as more and more people came to realize the success Sherman had gained for the national cause by securing the area north of the Chattahoochee. Jefferson Davis seems at least to have sensed this fact at the time and to have realized that unless the Confederates could reverse the situation in Georgia, enough Northern voters would have agreed by November to give Lincoln victory in the election.

To achieve success in Georgia and thereby avoid defeat in 1864, the Rebels would have had to have defeated Sherman in North Georgia, to have blocked his advance into the heart of the state, or—failing either of those accomplishments—to have inflicted heavy casualties on his forces. Had the Yankees not penetrated deep into Georgia or had they lost fifty or sixty thousand men doing so (losses coming on top of Grant's massive casualties in Virginia), the election might well have gone to the Democrats, and Lincoln, the Confederacy's most dangerous enemy, would have been on his way out of office. What he would have done between his defeat in November 1864 and the inauguration of his successor in March 1865 cannot be known. What a McClellan administration might have led to is a political counterfactual question, not a military one.

Notes

I. PRESIDENTS AND GENERALS

1. Ulysses S. Grant, *Personal Memoirs of U. S. Grant*, 2 vols. (New York, 1885), 2:114–16, 121–23; William S. McFeely, *Grant: A Biography* (New York, 1981), pp. 152–55; Albert Castel, *Decision in the West: The Atlanta Campaign of 1864* (Lawrence KS, 1992), pp. 64–65 (hereafter cited as Castel, *Atlanta*); Don Lowry, *No Turning Back: The Beginning of the End of the Civil War, March–June 1864* (New York, 1992), pp. 15–21; Bruce Catton, *Never Call Retreat* (New York, 1965), pp. 295–99; Allan Nevins, *The War for the Union: The Organized War to Victory, 1864–1865* (New York, 1971), pp. 6–8; Howard K. Beale, ed., *Diary of Gideon Welles, Secretary of the Navy Under Lincoln and Johnson*, 3 vols. (New York, 1960), 1:538–39; United States War Department, *The War of the Rebellion: Official Records of the Union and Confederate Armies* (Washington, 1880–1901), series 1, vol. 32, pt. 1, p. 13. (hereafter cited as OR, with all references to volumes in series 1. Citations will be given as volume, OR, part, page; this citation would be 32 OR 1, 13.)

2. See Castel, *Atlanta*, pp. 7–12; James M. McPherson, *Battle Cry of Freedom: The Civil War Era* (New York, 1988), pp. 713–16; John C. Waugh, *Reelecting Lincoln: The Battle for the 1864 Presidency* (New York, 1997), pp. 91–93. For examples of conservative Northerners alarmed by the war's effect on American society, see Roy F. Nichols, *Franklin Pierce: Young Hickory of the Granite Hills* (Philadelphia, 1958), pp. 519–23; and Bryon C. Andreasen, "Proscribed Preachers, New Churches: Civil Wars in the Illinois Protestant Churches during the Civil War," *Civil War History* 44 (1998): 197–211 (journal cited hereafter as CWH). See also Grant's comments in 38 OR 1, 12. As will be seen, I question Grant's evaluation of his 1864 operations.

3. For background on the Davis-Johnston relationship, see Richard M. Mc-Murry, " 'The *Enemy* at Richmond': Joseph E. Johnston and the Confederate Government," CWH 27 (1981): 5–31, and "Ole Joe in Virginia: Joseph E. Johnston's 1861–1862 Period of Command in the East," in Steven E. Woodworth, ed., *Leadership and Command in the Civil War* (Campbell CA, 1995), pp. 1–27; and Joseph

T. Glatthaar, "'I Cannot Direct Both Parts of My Command at Once': Davis, Johnston, and Confederate Failure in the West," in his *Partners in Command: The Relationships Between Leaders in the Civil War* (New York, 1994), pp. 94–133. Other works that differ to a greater or lesser degree are Gilbert E. Govan and James W. Livingood, *A Different Valor: The Story of General Joseph E. Johnston, C.S.A.* (Indianapolis IN, 1956); Craig L. Symonds, *Joseph E. Johnston: A Civil War Biography* (New York, 1992); and Steven Newton, *Joseph E. Johnston and the Defense of Richmond* (Lawrence KS, 1998).

4. My views of Davis have been shaped by the sources cited in my articles listed in note 3 above and by William C. Davis, *Jefferson Davis: The Man and His Hour, a Biography* (New York, 1991).

5. On the Davis-Lee relationship, see Davis, *Davis*, and his "Davis and Lee: Partnership for Success," in his *The Cause Lost: Myths and Realities of the Confederacy* (Lawrence KS, 1996), pp. 35–50; Steven E. Woodworth, *Davis and Lee at War* (Lawrence KS, 1995), and his "Davis, Lee and the Generals: Wisdom or Weakness?" paper presented to Blue & Gray Education Society, San Antonio, Feb. 1, 1997; and Charles P. Roland, *Reflections on Lee: A Historian's Assessment* (Mechanicsburg PA, 1995).

6. See my articles cited in note 3 above; Johnston's wartime letters to his wife (especially those of Jan. 15, Mar. 5, Apr. 23, May 12, 1862, and July 12, 1863) in McLane-Fisher Papers, Maryland Historical Society, Baltimore; 38 OR 5, 988; and 51 OR 1, 597.

2. GRAND STRATEGY FOR 1864

1. On Grant's grand plan for 1864, see his *Memoirs*, 2:116–40; 32 OR 2, 100–101, 411–13; 32 OR 3, 245–46; 38 OR 1,1–6.

2. Grant, *Memoirs*, 2:116. See Richard M. McMurry, *Two Great Rebel Armies: An Essay in Confederate Military History* (Chapel Hill NC, 1989), for reasons why the Federal government should have accepted a stalemate in Virginia and concentrated its efforts on winning the war in the West—which, after all, was what it wound up doing but only after tens of thousands of needless casualites.

3. See Castel, *Atlanta*, pp. 67, 85–87; Joseph T. Glatthaar, "'If I Got in a Tight Place You Would Come—if Alive': Grant, Sherman, and Union Success," in *Partners in Command*, pp. 134–61; John E. Marszalek, *Sherman: A Soldier's Passion for Order* (New York, 1993); Francis F. McKinney, *Education in Violence: The Life of General George H. Thomas and the History of the Army of the Cumberland* (Detroit MI, 1961), pp. 3, 12, 15, 138, 201–3, 272, 274, 281, 310–12, 495; 32 OR 2, 383–443 (several Grant letters); and 32 OR 3, 18.

4. See Gary W. Gallagher, *The Confederate War* (Cambridge MA, 1997), pp. 5–11, 27–40, 44–45, 50–52, 56–59, 72–77; and Josiah Gorgas *The Journals of Josiah Gorgas, 1857–1878*, ed. Sarah Woolfolk Wiggins (Tuscaloosa AL, 1995), p. 102.

5. This fruitless correspondence is in 31 OR 2 and 3, 32 OR 2 and 3, and 52 OR 2. For examples, see 52 OR 2, 634–35, 642–44. See also Thomas Lawrence Connelly, *Autumn of Glory: The Army of Tennessee, 1862–1865* (Baton Rouge LA, 1971), chap. 11; Symonds, *Johnston*, chap. 17; Steven E. Woodworth, *Jefferson Davis and His Generals: The Failure of Confederate Command in the West* (Lawrence KS, 1990), pp. 272–74; and Davis, *Davis*, pp. 546–49. For examples of reports of Federal troops going to Virginia, see 52 OR 2, 645–46, 649, 650, 664; *Savannah Morning News*, Dec. 21, 1863, reprinting reports from the *Rome (GA) Southerner*, n.d., via the *Marietta (GA) Confederacy*, n.d. For a good example of Rebel authorities misunderstanding the situation in Georgia, see Gorgas, *Journal*, p. 107. See also 31 OR 3, 873–74; 32 OR 2, 510–11; 32 OR 3, 295.

3. PREPARATIONS FOR THE FIELD

1. Destruction of one or more railroad tunnels between Nashville and Sherman's army would have put a real crimp in the Yankee supply line, especially had it been done before the beginning of the campaign. (The only tunnel south of Chattanooga was at Tunnel Hill, and an alternate route via Cleveland, Tennessee, offered a bypass should that be blocked.) Destruction of a tunnel, however, is a major engineering feat, necessitating extensive drilling into the surrounding rock. Given the hand-powered tools and the relatively weak blasting powder used in the 1860s (dynamite had not yet been invented), raiding Confederate cavalry simply could not "destroy" a railroad tunnel. Rebel engineers, given sufficient time and labor, could have done so, but that option was not available to the Southerners once the campaign got under way. Even today such an undertaking is so complex as to be impracticable in most cases with conventional explosives. Many thanks to Paul Chiles for calling this matter to my attention. (See appendix 3.)

2. On supplies for the Federals, see Grant, *Memoirs*, 2:46–48; William T. Sherman, *Memoirs of General William T. Sherman, by Himself* (Bloomington IN, 1957), 2:8–12, 31, 398–99; 32 OR 3, 149; 38 OR 1, 62; 38 OR 3, 90; 38 OR 4, 4, 20, 81, 154–55, 167–68, 258–59, 265, 274, 275, 289, 294–95, 387, 418–20, 640; 38 OR 5, 13; 52 OR 2, 661. General studies are Arm E. Mruck, "The Role of Railroads in the Atlanta Campaign," CWH 7 (1961): 264–71; James J. Cooke, "Feeding Sherman's Army: Union Logistics in the Campaign for Atlanta," in *The Campaign for Atlanta and Sherman's March to the Sea*, ed. Theodore P. Savas and David A. Woodbury (Campbell CA, 1994), pp. 97–114; and James G. Bogle, "The Western & Atlantic Railroad in the Campaign for Atlanta," *Campaign for Atlanta*, pp. 313–40.

3. Symonds, *Johnston*, pp. 256–57; 52 OR 2, 585–86, 593, 596, 598, 601, 602, 603, 607–8, 614–17, 619, 621–23; R. M. T. Simmons to _____, Apr. 28, 1864, extracts from letters of . . . , Alabama Department of Archives and History, Montgomery; Charles T. Jones Jr., "Five Confederates," *Alabama Historical Quarterly* 24 (1962): 191.

4. This might better be called the Grant-Sherman clique with Halleck (formerly their commander) tagging along as the other two rose in prominence.

5. See 31 OR 2, 339–45; 38 OR 1, 89–117; M. A. DeWolfe Howe, ed., *Home Letters of General Sherman* (New York, 1909), p. 303; Walter H. Hebert, *Fighting Joe Hooker* (Indianapolis IN, 1944), pp. 41, 271, 273, 278–79, 291; and Marszalek, *Sherman*, pp. 277–79.

6. Detailed citations to sources on the Federal armies' organization are in Richard M. McMurry, "The Atlanta Campaign, December 1863-July 1864" (Ph.D. dissertation, Emory University, 1967), pp. 8–25. See also Castel, *Atlanta*, pp. 79–89; Jacob D. Cox, *Atlanta* (New York, 1882), p. 4; John M. Schofield, *Forty-Six Years in the Army* (New York, 1897), pp. 122–24, and comments on Sherman's *Memoirs* and Cox's *Atlanta*, Box 95, Schofield Papers, Library of Congress; 38 OR 1, 66; 32 OR 3, 503–4; 38 OR 3, 474–75; 38 OR 4, 120; 38 OR 5, 120, 521.

7. Confederate brigades, divisions, and corps were officially designated by their commanders' last name. Thus "Hindman's Corps" (but not "Thomas C. Hindman's corps") is a proper noun and should be capitalized accordingly. In the Union army such units were numbered. "Hooker's corps" is not a proper noun and should not be capitalized.

8. On Confederate organization, see McMurry, "Atlanta Campaign," pp. 32–41; 32 OR 2, 560, 698, 808; 52 OR 2, 624, 633, 642, 646–47. For the often misunderstood circumstances surrounding Hood's appointment, see Richard M. McMurry, *John Bell Hood and the War for Southern Independence* (Lexington KY, 1982), pp. 85–89.

9. On the condition of the Rebel army, see McMurry, "Atlanta Campaign," pp. 62–70; Symonds, *Johnston*, pp. 249–68; and Larry J. Daniel, *Soldiering in the Army of Tennessee: A Portrait of Life in a Confederate Army* (Chapel Hill NC, 1991), esp. pp. 137–40.

10. Woodworth, *Davis and Generals*, p. 263, and "Davis, Lee, and the Generals." On the sorry situation in the high command of the Army of Tennessee, see Thomas Lawrence Connelly, *Army of the Heartland: The Army of Tennessee, 1861–1862* (Baton Rouge LA, 1967), and *Autumn of Glory*, pp. 283–89, 313–24, 365–66.

11. 31 OR 2, 339–45; Hebert, *Hooker*, pp. 41, 271, 273, 278–79, 291.

4. THE BEST LAID PLANS

1. Joseph E. Johnston, *Narrative of Military Operations Directed during the Late War between the States* (Bloomington IN, 1959), pp. 264–90; Robert M. Hughes, ed., "Some War Letters of General Joseph E. Johnston," *Military Service Institution of the United States Journal* 50 (1913): 319; Connelly, *Autumn of Glory*, p. 330; 32 OR 2, 640, 644; 38 OR 4, 216; 52 OR 2, 640.

2. Johnston, *Narrative*, pp. 277–78, 570, and "Opposing Sherman's Advance to Atlanta," in *Battles and Leaders of the Civil War*, ed. Robert Underwood Johnson

and Clarence Clough Buel (New York, 1956), 4:262 (collection cited as B&L; all citations to Volume 4); 32 OR 2, 698; 32 OR 3, 11 12; 52 OR 2, 596.

3. 38 OR 4, 71–72, 91, 99, 665. Although W. C. P. Breckinridge ("The Opening of the Atlanta Campaign," B&L, p. 278) claimed that Snake Creek Gap was "well known" to the Confederates, the earliest reference to it I have seen in Rebel records is an entry in the diary of Lt. Thomas B. Mackall for May 8, 1864, in the library at William and Mary (all references to this document are to the version known as "A"—see the bibliographical essay). If Johnston knew of the gap, his failure to defend it is even more serious than if he were ignorant of its existence.

4. Sherman, *Memoirs*, 2:26; 32 OR 3, 245–46; Marszalek, *Sherman*, pp. xvi, 249; Castel, *Atlanta*, p. 19, and "The Atlanta Campaign and the Presidential Election of 1864: How the South Almost Won by Not Losing," in his *Winning and Losing in the Civil War: Essays and Stories* (Columbia SC, 1996), p. 20.

5. William T. Sherman, "The Grand Strategy of the Last Year of the War," B&L, p. 252; 32 OR 2, 313; 32 OR 3, 63, 163–65, 312–14; 38 OR 1, 60; 38 OR 5, 266.

6. Sherman, *Memoirs*, 2:27–28; 32 OR 3, 409; 38 OR 1, 59.

5. TO THE OOSTANAULA

1. Sherman, *Memoirs*, 2:25; Oliver Otis Howard, "The Struggle for Atlanta," B&L, p. 296; 32 OR 2, 489; 32 OR 3, 275–76, 420, 422, 437, 443, 455, 459, 465–66, 479–80, 485, 510, 514; 38 OR 4, 39–40.

2. Connelly, *Autumn of Glory*, p. 309; Johnston, *Narrative*, p. 317; Mackall, Diary, May 5, 1864.

3. 32 OR 3, 792; 38 OR 3, 760–61; 38 OR 4, 654–63, 668–70; 52 OR 2, 666, 671–672; Johnston, *Narrative*, pp. 304–8.

4. 38 OR 4, 660–64, 673–75; Mackall, Diary, May 5–7, 1864.

5. 38 OR 1, 63, 292, 519–20, 593–94, 683–84; 38 OR 2, 203, 216–17; 38 OR 3, 30, 90, 614; 38 OR 4, 65, 70, 77, 79, 84, 85, 90, 100, 673, 677–79, 683. I have not provided detailed citations for the battles. See the relevant sections of Castel, *Atlanta;* McMurry, "Atlanta Campaign"; and Errol McGregor Clauss, "The Atlanta Campaign, 18 July–2 September 1864" (Ph.D. dissertation, Emory University, 1965). William R. Scaife's *The Campaign for Atlanta* (Atlanta, 1985) contains many useful maps. Its text, however, is very weak and should be used with extreme care.

6. 32 OR 3, 527; 38 OR 3, 16–17, 30–31, 90, 376–78, 488–89; 38 OR 4, 47, 87, 88, 96, 104–6, 682–84; Grenville M. Dodge, *Personal Recollections of . . . General William T. Sherman* (Council Bluffs IA, 1914), pp. 207–11.

7. Johnston, *Narrative*, pp. 316–17, and "Opposing Sherman's Advance," pp. 263–67; Howard, "Struggle for Atlanta," p. 299; Connelly, *Autumn of Glory*, pp. 315–16; Mackall, Diary, May 8–12, 1864; 38 OR 3, 829; 38 OR 4, 92, 114, 123–24, 126–27, 148, 160, 684, 686, 687, 689, 692, 698.

8. Mackall, Diary, May 13–15, 1864; 38 OR 3, 31–32, 64, 91–94; 38 OR 4, 111–12, 158, 175, 184, 195–97, 711, 714–16.

9. 38 OR 4, 111 (see also p. 173).

6. ON TO THE ETOWAH

1. Johnston, *Narrative*, pp. 319–20, 352–53; Connelly, *Autumn of Glory*, p. 367; 38 OR 3, 704; John M. Palmer to wife, May 20, 1864, Palmer Papers, Illinois Historical Society, Springfield.

2. Connelly, *Autumn of Glory*, pp. 343–44; 38 OR 1, 65, 142, 191, 857; 38 OR 2, 511; 38 OR 3, 33, 94, 704–11; 38 OR 4, 173, 198–99, 201–5, 210, 211, 217–19, 222–23, 225–27, 234–35, 729–30, 750; 52 OR 1, 555.

3. 38 OR 1, 9.

4. Johnston, *Narrative*, p. 320; 38 OR 1, 142; 38 OR 2, 511; 38 OR 3, 615–16; 38 OR 4, 242–44.

5. Johnston, *Narrative*, pp. 320–24; John Bell Hood, *Advance and Retreat: Personal Experiences in the United States and Confederate States Armies* (Bloomington IN, 1959), pp. 99, 100–116; Mackall, Diary, May 19, 1864; John Michael Priest, ed., *John T. McMahon's Diary of the 136th New York, 1861–1864* (Shippensburg PA, 1993), p. 95; 38 OR 1, 65, 142, 191–92, 522; 38 OR 2, 381, 450, 752; 38 OR 3, 634–35, 983; 38 OR 4, 250, 257–58, 260, 728, 732; 52 OR 2, 672.

6. 38 OR 4, 298, 728; James R. Robinson to "Friend Hunt," May 21, 1864, Robinson Papers, Ohio Historical Society, Columbus; Johnston to wife, May 23, 1864, McLane-Fisher Papers.

7. INTO THE HELL HOLE

1. Mackall, Diary, May 24, 1864; 38 OR 1, 60; 38 OR 2, 511–12; 38 OR 3, 33–34, 616, 705, 990; 38 OR 4, 248, 271–72, 274, 288, 296, 388–89, 737, 742; Account of staff ride from Dennis Kelly, then historian at Kennesaw Mountain National Battlefield Park, who accompanied the officers and related the incident (date unknown). Connelly (*Autumn of Glory*, pp. 353–54), believed that poor roads would have made such a strategy impracticable. I doubt that Connelly ever went over the ground himself.

2. Charles W. Wills, *Army Life of an Illinois Soldier* (Carbondale IL, 1996), pp. 245–46; Sherman, *Memoirs*, 2:44; 38 OR 1, 66; 38 OR 2, 29–30, 41, 46, 60–61, 122–24, 207, 279; B. L. Ridley, "The Battle of New Hope Church," *Confederate Veteran* 5 (1897): 459–60, and comments, p. 534; Henry Stone, "The Atlanta Campaign," Military Historical Society of Massachusetts *Papers* 8 (1910): 409; Milo M. Quaife, ed., *From the Cannon's Mouth: The Civil War Letters of General Alpheus S. Williams* (Detroit MI, 1959), p. 312.

3. 38 OR 1, 144, 193–95, 377, 387, 402, 600, 631; 38 OR 2, 623; 38 OR 3, 34, 379, 726; Entry for May 27, 1864, in diary of Oliver C. Hascall, Indiana Historical Society, Indianapolis.

4. Hood's attempted attack is often misdated to the night of May 28–29. See Mackall, Diary, May 28, 1864; Johnston, *Narrative*, pp. 332–34, and "Opposing Sherman's Advance," p. 270; Hood, *Advance and Retreat*, pp. 120–22, 335.

5. 38 OR 1, 60–61, 66, 195; 38 OR 2, 242, 265, 680–81; 38 OR 3, 96–97, 363; Florence Marie Ankeny, comp. and ed., *Kiss Joey for Me* (Santa Ana CA, 1974), pp. 218, 220 (letters of Henry G. Ankeny, Fourth Iowa Infantry).

6. 38 OR 1, 59, 66, 148, 631; 38 OR 2, 16, 383, 512; 38 OR 3, 65, 616–17; 38 OR 4, 379, 387–88; 52 OR 2, 674; Wills, *Army Life*, p. 253; William Bircher, *A Drummer Boy's Diary: Comprising Four Years of Service with the Second Regiment Minnesota Veteran Volunteers 1861 to 1865* (St. Paul MN, 1889), pp. 116–17; Oliver Otis Howard, *Autobiography of Oliver Otis Howard, Major General, United States Army*, 2 vols. (New York, 1908), 1:560; John Y. Foster, *New Jersey and the Rebellion* (Newark NJ, 1868), p. 630.

7. McMurry, "Atlanta Campaign," pp. 282–98; Connelly, *Autumn of Glory*, pp. 355–56; 38 OR 2, 93; 38 OR 4, 115.

8. Johnston to wife, May 16, 1864, McLane-Fisher Papers; Robert D. Little, "General Hardee and the Atlanta Campaign," *Georgia Historical Quarterly* 29 (1945): 1–22 (journal cited hereafter as GHQ).

9. Mackall, Diary, May 30, 1864; 38 OR 4, 387, 752–53; 52 OR 2, 675; Craig L. Symonds, "Joseph E. Johnston and the Atlanta Campaign," unpublished paper generously made available to the author by Symonds.

10. Johnston's May 1864 letters to his wife in McLane-Fisher Papers; 38 OR 4, 535, 586, 656, 749, 769, 770, 775; 38 OR 5, 27, 63–64, 71–72; Symonds, "Johnston and Atlanta Campaign."

8. ON THE KENNESAW LINE

1. 38 OR 1, 67; 38 OR 3, 33, 35; 38 OR 4, 435, 572–73.

2. 38 OR 4, 413–14, 424; John M. Palmer Jr. to mother, June 8, 1864, Palmer Papers.

3. 38 OR 1, 67, 149–50, 196–97, 223, 243; 38 OR 2, 126–29, 513; 38 OR 3, 35; 38 OR 4, 445–46, 481, 519; Johnston, *Narrative*, pp. 337–38; *Memphis Daily Appeal*, June 23, 29, 1864.

4. McMurry, "Atlanta Campaign," pp. 195–204; Mackall, Diary, June 22, 1864; 38 OR 2, 41–42, 49; 38 OR 4, 544.

5. Sherman, *Memoirs*, 2:57–58; Hebert, *Hooker*, pp. 280–81; 38 OR 1, 68; 38 OR 4, 557–61; 38 OR 5, 793, 857.

6. 38 OR 4, 492–93, 588–89, 591–92, 596, 607; 38 OR 5, 91–92, 123.

7. McMurry, "Atlanta Campaign," pp. 213–21; 38 OR 3, 36, 99, 178–79; 38 OR 4, 607.

8. McMurry, "Atlanta Campaign," pp. 221–25; 38 OR 4, 597–98, 602–7, 616–19, 620.

9. Johnston, *Narrative*, pp. 344–45; Mackall, Diary, July 1, 2, 1864; 38 OR 1, 69; 38 OR 2, 514–15, 615; 38 OR 3, 100, 617; 38 OR 4, 611–22; 38 OR 5, 8, 29, 860; Gustavus W. Smith, "The Georgia Militia about Atlanta," B&L, 332; Samuel Merrill, *The Seventieth Indiana Volunteer Infantry in the War of the Rebellion* (Indianapolis IN, 1900), p. 131.

9. ACROSS THE CHATTAHOOCHEE

1. Johnston, *Narrative*, p. 345; Smith, "Georgia Militia," pp. 332–33; Howard, *Autobiography*, 1:599, 601–2; 38 OR 1, 69, 129, 154–55, 200, 424, 515; 38 OR 2, 356, 515; 38 OR 3, 18–19, 37, 209, 617; 38 OR 5, 29–31, 45–46, 50, 54.

2. Sherman, *Memoirs*, 2:71, and "Grand Strategy," p. 253; 38 OR 1, 130, 155; 38 OR 2, 515–16, 683–85, 721, 735, 760; 38 OR 5, 42, 48–49, 60–61, 78–79, 86, 91–92; B. F. Thompson, *History of the 112th Regiment of Illinois Volunteer Infantry in the Great War of the Rebellion* (Toulon IL, 1885), pp. 224–25.

3. 38 OR 1, 70; 38 OR 2, 747, 760–61; 38 OR 3, 38, 65, 382–83; 38 OR 5, 68, 73, 76, 99, 100, 109; B. F. Magee, *History of the 72d Indiana Volunteer Infantry* (Lafayette IN, 1882), pp. 334–35; Joseph G. Vale, *Minty and the Cavalry: A History of the Cavalry Campaigns in the Western Armies* (Harrisburg PA, 1886), pp. 322–23; W. R. Carter, *History of the First Regiment of Volunteer Cavalry* (Knoxville TN, 1902), pp. 169–73; and the sources cited in note 2 above. See also Connelly, *Autumn of Glory*, p. 398.

4. Johnston, *Narrative*, pp. 347–48, 357–58, 572–73; 38 OR 3, 618, 871; 39 OR 4, 785–87; 52 OR 2, 681, 687–88. The delay in Stewart's promotion may have stemmed from a desire on Davis's part to find some other officer to fill the vacancy. By mid-1864, however, the Confederacy was running short of generals competent even for corps command. In fact, it had never had many. See Sam Davis Elliott, *Soldier of Tennessee: General Alexander P. Stewart and the Civil War in the West* (Baton Rouge, 1999), pp. 191–93.

5. David Evans, *Sherman's Horsemen: Union Cavalry Operations in the Atlanta Campaign* (Bloomington IN, 1996), chaps. 2, 3, and 6–9; 38 OR 1, 70; 38 OR 2, 904–9, 912–13; 38 OR 4, 582; 38 OR 5, 16–17, 146.

6. 38 OR 1, 71, 156; 38 OR 3, 38, 100; 38 OR 5, 65–66, 108, 123–25, 134, 142, 147, 149–50, 158, 164–65.

10. ON OTHER FIELDS

1. See comments in James M. McPherson, *Ordeal by Fire: The Civil War and Reconstruction* (New York, 1982), pp. 406–8, 424–29; David Donald, ed., *Inside Lincoln's Cabinet: The Civil War Diaries of Salmon P. Chase* (New York, 1954), pp. 231–32, 236–37; Larry E. Nelson, *Bullets, Ballots, and Rhetoric: Confederate Policy for the United States Presidential Contest of 1864* (University AL, 1980).

2. William C. Davis, "The Turning Point That Wasn't: The Confederates and the Election of 1864," in his *Cause Lost*, pp. 132–34; Nelson, *Bullets*, pp. 16–17.

For an example of a Confederate following the price of gold, see Gorgas, *Journals,* p. 113.

3. Nelson, *Bullets,* esp. pp. xii, 17, 75–84.

11. HOOD TAKES COMMAND

1. Ankeny, *Kiss Joey,* p. 224; Richard M. McMurry, "Confederate Morale in the Atlanta Campaign of 1864," GHQ 54 (1970): 226–43; Daniel, *Soldiering,* pp. 140–46; 38 OR 4, 233, 725, 729–30.

2. Jefferson Davis, *The Rise and Fall of the Confederate Government,* 2 vols. (New York, 1881), 2:472–74; Gorgas, *Journals,* pp. 109, 111, 119, 120; Edward Younger, ed., *Inside the Confederate Government: The Diary of Robert Garlick Hill Kean* (New York, 1957), pp. 151, 154.

3. Castel, *Atlanta,* pp. 302–3; Johnston to wife, June 26, 1864, McLane-Fisher Papers; Mackall, Diary, June 24, 1864; 38 OR 4, 795–96; Alvy T. King, *Louis T. Wigfall: Southern Fire-Eater* (Baton Rouge LA, 1970), pp. 196–98.

4. 38 OR 4, 770; 38 OR 5, 858, 868–69; 52 OR 2, 680–81, 693–95, 704–7. Johnston later denied that he had had such a conversation with Hill ("Opposing Sherman's Advance," p. 277). The important point, however, is that Hill told Davis that Johnston had made the statement.

5. 38 OR 5, 874–76; 52 OR 2, 619–20, 678–79; Mackall, Diary, July 7, 1864; Davis, *Rise and Fall,* 2:472–74.

6. Davis, *Rise and Fall,* 2:472–74; Gorgas, *Journals,* p. 121; 38 OR 1, 24; 38 OR 5, 875, 879; 52 OR 2, 693–95, 704–7.

7. Johnston, *Narrative,* p. 364; 38 OR 5, 867, 875–76, 878, 881; 52 OR 2, 692, 707.

8. 38 OR 5, 879–80; 39 OR 2, 712–14; 52 OR 2, 692.

9. Johnston, *Narrative,* p. 358; 38 OR 5, 882, 883.

10. Mackall, Diary, July 17, 1864; 38 OR 5, 885, 887.

12. THE REBELS STRIKE BACK

1. 38 OR 1, 71; 38 OR 3, 101; 38 OR 5, 169, 170, 176–77, 210–11, 876.

2. See Connelly, *Autumn of Glory,* pp. 421–23, 432; James W. Raab, *W. W. Loring: Florida's Forgotten General* (Manhattan KS, 1996), p. 160; Mackall, Diary, July 24, 1864; 38 OR 5, 892, 907, 910, 924–25, 930, 934, 948, 956, 987–88. Hood put his "effective strength" on July 18 at 49,012, which would have made his more significant "present for duty" strength about 58,000. See appendix 2.

3. See 38 OR 5, 867.

4. 38 OR 5, 183, 186, 196.

5. See Connelly, *Autumn of Glory,* pp. 440–42.

6. Connelly, *Autumn of Glory,* pp. 439–41; Castel, *Atlanta,* pp. 369–71; 38 OR 2, 33; 38 OR 5, 185, 894.

7. 38 OR 2, 50; 38 OR 3, 38; 38 OR 5, 185, 194, 196–206, 211, 894–96; Raab, *Loring*, p. 166; Castel, *Atlanta*, pp. 369–78.

8. 38 OR 5, 897.

9. Evans, *Sherman's Horsemen*, pp. 89–90; 38 OR 1, 72–73; 38 OR 3, 20, 39, 101; 38 OR 5, 179, 181, 209, 219, 893, 894, 895, 898–900.

10. Connelly, *Autumn of Glory*, pp. 444–46; 38 OR 5, 900.

11. Connelly, *Autumn of Glory*, pp. 444, 448; 38 OR 2, 35; 38 OR 3, 24–29, 102–3; 38 OR 5, 241, 271–74, 522–23.

12. 38 OR 3, 40–42, 104–5; 38 OR 5, 282–83, 912–14, 916–19.

13. Evans, *Sherman's Horsemen*, chaps. 12–19; Byron H. Matthews, *The Mc-Cook-Stoneman Raid* (Philadelphia, 1976); *Staunton* (VA) *Vindicator*, Sept. 16, 1864, quoting *Macon Christian Index*, n.d.; 38 OR 5, 264, 409–10, 913–14, 927–30, 933–34, 936–37, 940.

14. McMurry, *Hood*, pp. 149–51; and Stephen Davis, "A Reappraisal of the Generalship of John Bell Hood in the Battles for Atlanta," in *Campaign for Atlanta*, pp. 49–95.

15. McMurry, "Confederate Morale"; 38 OR 5, 930.

13. BATTLE FOR THE MACON & WESTERN

1. Ankeny, *Kiss Joey*, p. 234; 38 OR 5, 517.

2. Castel, *Atlanta*, pp. 455–60, and "Union Fizzle at Atlanta: The Battle of Utoy Creek," *Civil War Times Illustrated* 16, no. 10 (Feb. 1978): 26–31; 38 OR 5, 352–85 (various letters and telegrams), 446, 667, 947, 950.

3. Howard, "Struggle for Atlanta," p. 320; Richard Harwell and Philip N. Racine, eds., *The Fiery Trail: A Union Officer's Account of Sherman's Last Campaigns* (Knoxville TN, 1993), p. 18 (Maj. Thomas O. Osborn, chief of artillery, Army of the Tennessee); 38 OR 3, 87, 211; 38 OR 5, 342, 344, 350, 392, 400, 413, 447, 448, 450, 580, 609; 52 OR 1, 698–700.

4. Harwell and Racine, eds., *Fiery Trail*, pp. 17–18; 38 OR 5, 412–19, 434, 448–49, 452–54, 546; Stephen Davis, " 'A Very Barbarous Mode of Carrying on War': Sherman's Artillery Bombardment of Atlanta, July 20–August 24, 1864," GHQ 79 (1995): 57–90.

5. Connelly, *Autumn of Glory*, pp. 434–37; 38 OR 3, 632; 38 OR 5, 505–7, 940, 944, 946, 953–54, 957, 967, 990, 993, 997, 1029, 1031.

6. 38 OR 1, 79–80; 38 OR 5, 320–21, 326, 457, 459, 490, 493–94, 497, 499–500, 511, 524, 530–32, 538, 541, 547–51, 555, 639, 981–82.

7. Stephen W. Sears, *George B. McClellan: The Young Napoleon* (New York, 1988), pp. 384–86; Irving Katz, *August Belmont: A Political Biography* (New York, 1968), pp. 123–33; Waugh, *Reelecting Lincoln*, pp. 278–92; Howard, *Autobiography*, 2:32.

8. Harwell and Racine, *Fiery Trail*, pp. 19–20; McMurry, "Confederate Mo-

rale" pp. 236–38; 38 OR 3, 42–45, 87–88, 108–10; 38 OR 5, 106–7, 688–89, 695–97, 708, 985, 990, 993, 997.

9. Harwell and Racine, *Fiery Trail*, p. 21; 38 OR 3, 45–46, 88, 109–10; 38 OR 5, 717–21, 726, 1001, 1003, 1005–7.

10. Castel, *Atlanta*, pp. 522–24; 38 OR 5, 1007–8, 1011.

11. 38 OR 1, 81–82, 136–37, 166; 38 OR 3, 46; 38 OR 5, 746, 747, 750–51, 754–55, 760.

12. Castel, *Atlanta*, pp. 527–29; 38 OR 2, 20, 35, 633; 38 OR 3, 46, 694–95; 38 OR 5, 763–65, 768, 771, 774, 1016.

13. Harwell and Racine, *Fiery Trail*, pp. 15, 22; Sherman, *Memoirs*, 2:108; 38 OR 1, 81–83; 38 OR 2, 20; 38 PR 3, 46, 695; 38 OR 5, 765–66, 771, 774, 777, 789, 792, 794, 801, 1015, 1017, 1020.

14. "LET OLD ABE SETTLE IT"

1. Castel, *Atlanta*, pp. 543–44; Roy P. Basler, ed., *The Collected Works of Abraham Lincoln*, 9 vols. (New Brunswick, 1953), 7:533–34; Waugh, *Reelecting Lincoln*, p. 297; Harwell and Racine, *Fiery Trail*, p. 18; 38 OR 1, 86–87, 89; 38 OR 5, 854.

2. Waugh, *Reelecting Lincoln*, pp. 276–361; Katz, *Belmont*, pp. 121–49; Sears, *McClellan*, pp. 373–380; David E. Long, *The Jewel of Liberty: Abraham Lincoln's Re-Election and the End of Slavery* (Mechanicsburg PA, 1994); Harold M. Hyman, "The Election of 1864," in *History of American Presidential Elections, 1788–1968*, ed. Arthur M. Schlesinger Jr. and Fred L. Israel, 4 vols. (New York, 1971), 2:1155–79.

3. 38 OR 3, 777.

4. See Connelly, *Autumn of Glory*, pp. 361–73, and Glatthaar, *Partners in Command*, p. 116, Detailed citations for my evaluation of Johnston are in my articles cited in note 3, chapter 1, and in "A Policy So Disastrous: Joseph E. Johnston's Atlanta Campaign," in *Campaign for Atlanta*, pp. 223–248, and "The Atlanta Campaign of 1864: A New Look," CWH 22 (1976): 5–15.

5. See 52 OR 2, 641, 647.

6. See McMurry, *Hood*, esp. pp. 149–51; and Davis, "Reappraisal of Hood"; Connelly, *Autumn of Glory*, p. 442; 38 OR 5, 1004.

APPENDIX 1

1. 38 OR 1, 1–2; 38 OR 5, 149–51; Grant, *Memoirs*, 2:127–28, 142–43; Castel, *Atlanta*, pp. 322–23.

APPENDIX 2

1. 38 OR 1, 115–17; 38 OR 3, 675–83; 38 OR 4, 601–2.

2. 38 OR 1, 85.

3. 38 OR 1, 85; 38 OR 3, 686–87; Johnston, *Narrative*, pp. 576–78; Wheeler to Braxton Bragg, July 1, 1864, Bragg Papers, Western Reserve Historical Society, Cleveland; McMurry, "Policy So Disastrous," pp. 237–38.

4. See 38 OR 1, 119, 184; and James O. Breeden, "A Medical History of the Later Stages of the Atlanta Campaign," *Journal of Southern History* 35 (1969): 31–59.

APPENDIX 3

1. See 32 OR 3, 866; 38 OR 1, 158; 38 OR 3, 676–79; 38 OR 4, 542, 665; 38 OR 5, 65–66, 878, 963; Connelly, *Autumn of Glory*, pp. 384–90, 435–37; Symonds, *Johnston*, p. 311; Aplin Kelly to mother, May 22, 1864, Kelly Letters, Georgia Historical Society, Savannah.

2. 38 OR 5, 350; 52 OR 1, 698–700.

APPENDIX 4

1. Castel, *Atlanta*, pp. 8, 478–79, and "Atlanta Campaign and Election of 1864"; Daniel, "The South Almost Won by Not Losing: A Rebuttal," *North & South*, No. 3 (Feb. 1998): 44–51.

2. See Sears, *McClellan*, pp. 376–77.

3. Davis, "Turning Point," esp. pp. 140–44. Davis speculates that had Lincoln lost the election he might have transferred major portions of Sherman's force to Virginia to reinforce Grant for an all-out effort to win the war before McClellan took office. Such a ploy would, in fact, have repeated the Federals' grand strategic error of March 1864 and enhanced Rebel chances for independence. It would have been far better for the Unionists to have sent reinforcements from Grant to Sherman in an effort to achieve such a success. If nothing else, the Yankees would have had better weather for a winter campaign. In fact, of course, Sherman, Thomas, and the western Yankees were able to accomplish such a feat without help from Union forces in Virginia. By March 4, 1865 (when McClellan would have been inaugurated), the Confederate army in the West had been destroyed and Sherman and his force were in North Carolina having devastated Georgia and South Carolina. Only bad weather and orders from Grant kept them from marching into Virginia.

Bibliographical Essay

Despite its great importance, the Atlanta campaign remained for a century in the obscurity that long characterized historians' treatment of Civil War military operations outside Virginia. Not until publication of Albert Castel's *Decision in the West: The Atlanta Campaign of 1864* (Lawrence KS, 1992) did we have an adequate overall account of that year's crucial events in North Georgia. Before the appearance of Castel's work, the best published general treatment of the struggle was Jacob D. Cox's *Atlanta*, an 1882 volume in the Scribner's, Campaigns of the Civil War series. Two dissertations, both written at Emory University under the supervision of Bell I. Wiley, covered the operations with all the authority and expertise of graduate students: Richard M. McMurry, "The Atlanta Campaign, December 23, 1863, to July 18, 1864" (1967) and Erroll McGregor Clauss, "The Atlanta Campaign, 18 July–2 September 1864" (1965).

The starting point for all serious study of the campaign (and of all other Civil War military operations) is the United States War Department's great compilation *The War of the Rebellion: Official Records of the Union and Confederate Armies* (Washington DC, 1880–1901)—the oft-cited OR of these pages—and its *Supplement* (now being published). Material on the Atlanta operations is in volumes 31, 32, 38, 39, 51, and 52 (all in series 1) of the OR and in volume 7 of the *Supplement*. (Scattered relevant documents can be found in volumes in the other three series of the OR.)

Unpublished letters and diaries are crucial for a study of the campaign. Serious students would do well to consult those in depositories in states of the Mississippi Valley whence came most of the troops on both sides of the great struggle for North Georgia. A special word should be said about the most important such Confederate document, the pocket diary of Lt. Thomas B. Mackall in the library at the College of William and Mary. That little document is the key that unlocks much of the Confederate side of the campaign during Johnston's tenure as commander. Unfortunately, it does not lend itself to separate publication, but for its fascinating history see Richard M. McMurry, "The Mackall Journal and Its Antecedents," *Civil War History* 20 (1974): 311–28.

All three commanding generals left memoirs of their military service. Those self-serving publications should be used with great caution, especially when dealing with controversial matters. The same care should be exercised when using the postwar writings of lower-ranking officers and enlisted personnel, especially those penned by Confederates. To some extent the modern biographies of the generals can offset those weaknesses. See John E. Marszalek, *Sherman: A Soldier's Passion for Order* (New York, 1993); Craig L. Symonds, *Joseph E. Johnston: A Civil War Biography* (New York, 1992); and Richard M. McMurry, *John Bell Hood and the War for Southern Independence* (Lexington KY, 1982).

Space constraints will permit only a few other listings. Thomas Lawrence Connelly's *Autumn of Glory: The Army of Tennessee 1862–1865* (Baton Rouge LA, 1971), filled a long-standing void in the scholarship of the war in the West. Unfortunately, we have no similar studies on the Union armies, but Larry Daniel is presently hard at work on a volume covering the Army of the Cumberland that will be a welcome addition to the literature on the struggle for the West. Daniel's *Soldiering in the Army of Tennessee: A Portrait of Life in a Confederate Army* (Chapel Hill NC, 1991) introduces us to the men who fought in the West for the Rebel cause. There is no exactly comparable volume on the Yankees who followed Sherman, but see Joseph T. Glatthaar, *The March to the Sea and Beyond: Sherman's Troops in the Savannah and Carolinas Campaigns* (New York, 1985).

For other works see the bibliographies in Castel's *Atlanta*; those in the dissertations listed in the first paragraph above; and Stephen Davis and Richard M. McMurry, "A Reader's Guide to the Atlanta Campaign," *Atlanta Historical Journal* 28 (Fall 1984): 99–111.

Index